SCHOLARS
ON PARADE

Alma Mater at Columbia University. This famous statue, with crown of laurel, open arms, scepter and open book, symbolizes wisdom. It is the work of Daniel Chester French. COURTESY COLUMBIA UNIVERSITY.

SCHOLARS ON PARADE

Colleges, Universities, Costumes and Degrees

❧⚜☙

DAVID A. LOCKMILLER

The Macmillan Company
Collier-Macmillan Ltd., London

DEDICATED TO

THE COLLEGES AND UNIVERSITIES

WHICH WELCOMED ME AS A STUDENT

Emory University
Cumberland Law School (Samford University)
University of North Carolina
University of Chicago
University of Paris
Oxford University

AND

TO THOSE WHICH PROVIDED
OPPORTUNITIES FOR TEACHING,
RESEARCH AND ADMINISTRATION

North Carolina State University
Emory University
Meredith College
North Carolina College at Durham
University of Chattanooga
Ohio Wesleyan University

AND

TO THOSE GENEROUSLY CONFERRING
SPECIAL HONORS UPON ME

Cumberland University
Emory University
University of Chattanooga
Tennessee Wesleyan College
The American University

Contents

APPENDICES

Preface

ALTHOUGH HIGHER EDUCATION in America is basic to our social and economic order, it is not well understood by laymen. Academic costumes, emblems and degrees are even more obscure, and for some they possess an esoteric aura.

This study is an outline of the history of colleges and universities in the United States from colonial days to the present. It contains definitions of a university, gives essential European and British origins and emphasizes academic degrees, costumes and public occasions. It is concerned with inherited curricula and traditions and contrasting growth and change to meet the needs of a dynamic society.

Specialists in the history of higher education will encounter little that is new in this work. Along with citizens generally, however, many administrators and professors are not students of history. It is the author's hope, therefore, that this study will meet a need on the campus and be of service to candidates for degrees, parents of graduates and the general public.

The subject is so vast in space, time and varieties of institutions that one can do little more than introduce the numerous facets in a single volume. Certainly those who bestow and receive academic degrees and who march in colorful processions can take pride in the record of scholars over past centuries. With a knowledge of the history of higher education, also understood and appreciated by the public, they can more effectively interpret the present and plan for a future that will require vastly more education for more people.

Since the manuscript of this book was completed and the preface first written, disturbances on college and university campuses from Brandeis and Columbia to Stanford and San Francisco State and in centers of learning around the world have greatly disturbed serious scholars and thoughtful persons in all walks of life. Intellectual ferment, critical inquiry, dissent, and proposals for change should be welcomed and defended, but "sit-ins," riots, arson, threats against the lives of college officials and visitors, and the destruction of property are not to be condoned. "Power groups" encourage the authoritarian, and scholars should be the first to speak out against violence. No educational institution can function properly as long as some students and professors ignore the rights of others and demonstrate a preference for anarchy over education.

Considerable time will be required to evaluate the fruits of the present academic revolution at home and abroad. The quality of undergraduate instruction, one cause of much unrest, will surely receive greater attention. The concept of campus autonomy has received a serious setback. Faculties, having won a large measure of control from administrators and trustees during recent decades, may find their appointments, promotions, course offerings, research projects, and academic freedom strongly influenced and partially controlled by student activists. To the extent that this happens, higher education will be changed and institutions will have turned full cycle to some of the chaos besetting the early Italian universities.

In seeking information for this work, I visited numerous historic centers of learning abroad including Bologna, Paris, Heidelberg,

Uppsala, Oxford and Cambridge. My travels in the United States extended from Cambridge, Massachusetts, to Berkeley, California; and from New Orleans, Louisiana, to Minneapolis, Minnesota. General and special references are included in the bibliography, and the appendices supplement the narrative. The publisher has generously included numerous old and modern illustrations, and it is believed that these will enliven the text and make it more meaningful.

In writing this book, I have had the cooperation and assistance of numerous libraries and museums, institutions of higher learning, publishers, manufacturers of academic costumes and individuals. To all mentioned here and to any inadvertently omitted, I am most grateful. Any errors of interpretation or fact are my own.

I want to acknowledge the valued assistance of and thank the following libraries, archives and museums: Archives of the Académie, Paris; Berlin State Library; Bibliothèque Nationale, Paris; Bodleian Library, Oxford; Central Public Library of Washington; Convento S. Maria Novella, Florence; Folger Shakespeare Library, Washington, D.C.; Helsinki University Library; Historical Museum of the Reformation, Geneva; Innsbruck University Archives; Cologne State Museum; Library of the American Council on Education, Library of the Association of American Colleges, Library of Congress, Library of the State University of Groningen, Library of the University of Coimbra, Library of the University of Paris at the Sorbonne, New York Public Library, Royal Library of Copenhagen, University of Bologna Library and the University of Vienna Archives.

The help of the following colleges and universities in supplying information and illustrations is acknowledged with appreciation: The American University, Brigham Young University, College of William and Mary, Columbia University, Cornell University, Emory University, Georgetown University, Harvard University, Heidelberg University, Jagellonian University, The Johns Hopkins University, Joliet Junior College, Knox College, Mount Holyoke

College, Oberlin College, Rutgers—The State University, Stanford University, Transylvania College, Tulane University, Tuskegee Institute, United States Air Force Academy, United States Military Academy, United States Naval Academy, University of California, University of Chicago, University of Geneva, University of Georgia, University of Granada, University of Groningen, University of Illinois, University of Michigan, University of Munich, University of North Carolina, University of Notre Dame, University of the Pacific, University of Pennsylvania, University of Salamanca, University of Siena, University of Virginia, Uppsala University, Virginia Military Institute, Washington and Jefferson College, Wesleyan College and Westminster College, Missouri.

The following agencies, associations, publishers and academic costume companies provided information or generously gave permission to quote from published works or to reproduce illustrations: *Changing Times;* Culver Pictures, Inc.; Herman Bohlaus Nachf. of Vienna; Historia Photo; The Macmillan Company; Newspaper Enterprise Association; Photographic Giraudon; Pistoia Ministero del Tourismo; Charles C. Thomas, Publisher; Press Office, Roger-Viollet, The White House; Bentley & Simon, Inc., New York; Collegiate Cap and Gown Co., Champaign, Illinois; Cotrell and Leonard, Inc., Albany, New York; E. R. Moore Company, Chicago; National Academic Cap and Gown Company, Philadelphia, and C. E. Ward Company, New London, Ohio.

Individuals in the United States and abroad who helped with information and illustrations include: Günther Albrecht, W. Bickel, Miss Patricia J. Black, José Mª Stampa Braun, Mrs. Shirley M. Brigham, L. Buzás, G. Calmette, Leo M. Corbaci, Andre Corboz, Noel Duerden, Miss Audrey Evans, L. H. Foster, Franz Gall, Edmund J. Gleazer, Jr., Kurt Graff, Henrik Grönroos, A. J. Hardin, Jens Boesen Helle, Börje Holmberg, William Holmes, Joe B. Humphreys, Franz Huter, Ray Karsted, W. P. Kellam, Hal V. Kelly, William J. Kilkenny, W. R. H. Koops, Axel Axelsson Liljencrantz, M. I. Marelu, Henry R. Martin, Edward McCrady, Evelyn Montgomery, Stanislaw Mossakowski, Frau

Dr. L. Mugdan, Joseph A. O'Rourke, Boyd Crumrine Patterson, César Pegado, Otto Peters, Robert Quick, Walter E. Reeves, John Reynolds, The Rev. P. Paolo M. Ricozzi, George K. Schweitzer, Warren B. Smith, W. Earl Strickland, Mrs. Mary E. Turner, Dan White and D. R. Venables.

I am most grateful to the following for reading all or parts of the manuscript and for helpful criticisms and suggestions: The Rev. Lowrie J. Daly, S.J., Frank G. Dickey, William A. Fowler, Gilbert Govan, John O. Gross, Ross H. McLean, William K. Selden, Robert L. Taylor, Henry Q. Wellman, Mrs. Carlotta L. Wildhack and F. L. Wormald. Mrs. Nada Rode generously assisted with translations, and I thank Mrs. Ruth McVeagh, Mrs. Norma Fowler and Mrs. Shirley Brigham for typing the final copy of the manuscript.

To my wife, Alma Russell Lockmiller, who typed the original copy, read proof and helped with the index, and Robert Markel, Executive Editor of The Macmillan Company and his able staff, I am indebted for counsel and help that enabled me to complete a fascinating and enjoyable assignment.

DAVID A. LOCKMILLER

Washington, D.C.

August 1, 1968

CHAPTER I

❦

Advancement by Degrees

HIGHER EDUCATION IN the United States is primarily concerned with serious intellectual endeavor, but it also offers entertainment for students and the public, carries on research for industry and government and is big business. It is a mosaic of differing institutions, goals, standards and attitudes. It is an essential part of the nation's cultural and economic history. It is diverse, complex and subject to rapid change. Many of its facets are well known, but others are obscure even to members of the academic fraternity. This is particularly true of the history, meaning and variety of academic degrees, costumes and emblems.

During each June commencement season in the fifty states, District of Columbia, Puerto Rico and the outlying parts of the United States, some 2,500 institutions of higher learning—junior colleges, technical institutes, academies, colleges, and universities —confer approximately 2,600 different types of earned and honorary degrees on some 900,000 happy recipients. Because of the various types and numbers, it has been said that students truly "advance by degrees."

This phenomenon is a result of the boom in education, and it

I

will undoubtedly continue for many years to come. A generation ago the goal was a high school diploma for everyone. Now the states, led by New York, Florida and California, plan to provide college degrees for all residents intellectually qualified to earn them. Currently there are some 6,900,000 men and women in institutions of higher learning in the United States, and it is estimated that about 9,500,000 students will be seeking higher courses or degrees by 1975. Most colleges and universities will have to double in size and possibly a thousand new ones will need to be established to accommodate the increased numbers seeking higher education. If we may judge from the past, this will mean additional varieties as well as numbers of degrees.

Most of the present degrees with their abbreviations are listed in Appendix I. With several hundred bachelor and master titles and some seventy-five varieties of earned doctorates plus an equal number of honorary doctorates, there is just reason for confusion. We are concerned here with legitimate degrees as opposed to spurious titles still prevalent in many quarters. Furthermore, new degrees are being created from year to year despite occasional pleas for redirection and a limitation on their variety.

For the principal degrees there are black hoods adorned with carefully patterned colors representing the academic subject field and institution. Gowns are traditionally black, but the trend is to solid colors such as Harvard Crimson or Yale Blue to indicate more clearly the college or university that conferred the degree. Caps or mortarboards frequently display colored tassels indicating subject fields. The total effect is like a rainbow, and the pageantry of graduation exercises, inaugurals and anniversary convocations pleases and mystifies hundreds of thousands year after year.

There is nothing quite like the charged atmosphere of a small college town or a great public or private university campus on commencement day. The hundreds or thousands of graduates from campus to campus are excited with success and farewells, parents and friends move about in reflected glory, and the deans and professors are suitably nonchalant.

Color guard at commencement, College of William and Mary.
COURTESY COLLEGE OF WILLIAM AND MARY.

Commencement is usually preceded by class functions, alumni reunions, and the baccalaureate sermon, although the last is being discontinued in many places. On the appointed day, firmly fixed on the academic calendar, well in advance of the opening of the exercises, music is heard, color guards take position, and the chief marshal and his assistants form the line of scholars according to strict protocol. For this occasion *An Academic Costume Code and An Academic Ceremony Guide* of the American Council on Education is the chief and best authority in the field.

The ceremonies, formerly held for the most part in college chapels, churches and auditoriums, now generally take place on the campus green or in athletic stadiums or gymnasiums. Most commencements, and other formal academic occasions, begin and end with an academic procession. In most cases the president or chancellor and guest speaker, usually preceded by the chief mar-shal or mace-bearer, are followed by trustees, administrative officers, and members of the party that will be seated on the platform. These in turn are followed by the faculty or faculties of the several colleges in order of rank and seniority, and then come the candidates for degrees with those for advanced degrees in the lead. Occasionally a civil dignitary may head the procession. Sometimes the various groups march in reverse order, the pro-spective graduates taking position along the route and facing the center line of march as a mark of respect while the other groups and the platform party proceed to their assigned places. The entire convocation is an outgrowth of religious services of medi-eval times, and it is conducted with dignity.

College or university arms or the institution's seal are frequently displayed during public convocations. The seal contains the name of the institution, date of founding and its official motto, often in Latin but sometimes in Greek, Hebrew or English. Mottoes range from words such as *Veritas* and *Faciemus* to *Lex et Libertas* and *Esse Quam Videri*. Often seals picture religious symbols, ancient lamps or historic buildings; or they closely resemble the seal of the state in which the school is located.

The institution's banner or flag may also be displayed on the platform, and frequently it is carried in the academic procession subordinate to the national flag and accompanied by color guards. The banner in the authorized color or colors usually includes the arms or seal of the institution. The official rules of heraldry are not always followed, but American academic emblems are usually attractive and in good taste.

Ceremonies vary and the speaker may be witty or dull, but the climax is the conferring of degrees. With the advent of large classes, candidates for degrees usually wear their hoods during the procession, but in many cases hoods and diplomas for doctoral candidates are presented individually when the degree is conferred. In many large institutions it is customary for hoods to be dispensed with by those receiving the bachelor's degree. Earned degrees are usually conferred first and in ascending order.

Many colleges and universities delight in conferring honorary degrees with individual citations upon distinguished alumni, prominent men and women in public life and "benefactors of mankind." The commencement speaker often receives a degree, and past and prospective donors who appreciate the merits of higher learning are not overlooked. The recipients of honors are members of the platform party. They are usually escorted by senior members of the faculty and even though the gown may be rented or borrowed, the hood with its bright velvet and institutional colors becomes a prized keepsake.

Caps or mortarboards are an essential part of academic dress. They are worn during formal processions and degree ceremonies. It is customary for the men to remove their caps during prayer and the playing of the National Anthem or the *Alma Mater*. Usually they are removed in unison during the baccalaureate sermon or commencement address. Although there is no formal

Commencement at Tuskegee Institute. An honorary LL.D. is conferred on Dr. Charles H. Wesley (left) of Washington, D.C., by President L. H. Foster.   COURTESY TUSKEGEE INSTITUTE.

Commencement at Mount Holyoke.

rule for the position of the tassel, general practice calls for degree candidates to wear it on the right front before receiving degrees and to shift it to the left front immediately after the degrees are conferred.

Most of the early universities of Europe were creations of the Pope, and degrees were conferred by his representative and by virtue of his authority. In Spain and Portugal the universities were essentially royal creations. In the United States public and private colleges and universities, excepting those chartered by Congress, exercise their rights and privileges under the laws of the states or commonwealth in which they are located. Degrees, therefore, are conferred in accordance with the institution's charter and the laws of a particular state and with the approval of the board of trustees or regents. It is customary for the faculty or faculties to recommend candidates to the board for approval, certifying through the registrar and dean that they have satisfactorily met all requirements for a particular degree.

Before 1900, many degrees were written or printed in Latin and presidents or chancellors conferred them in Latin. There is no one form of conferral, but most chief officers say something similar to the following: "Acting under the authority of the state and by virtue of the powers vested in me as president, I confer upon these students, who have been recommended by the faculty and approved by the board, the degree of bachelor of arts (or other titles) with all of its rights, privileges and responsibilities."

Presidents and chancellors of many institutions wear distinctive gowns and caps to indicate their rank. In some cases special officers wear beefeater hats. These are usually made of velvet in one of the school's colors. A list of the colors of leading institutions conferring doctorates appears in Appendix II, and the colors of the academic fields are explained in Chapter X. Generally, the American system of academic dress is simple—and far more logical and uniform than the degrees.

At a few institutions members of the senior class wear plain black gowns during the year or semester prior to graduation. Most wear class rings and some affect blazers with fraternity or college arms. In former years prospective graduates wore distinctive hats and sported canes during the spring of their final term. Certainly the gowns are not used, as they once were, for warmth in unheated buildings and hoods are not required for tonsured heads.

The current use of gowns by clergymen, judges and members of religious orders shares a common history with those worn by the teaching profession. Members of church orders usually wear their customary habits when participating in educational ceremonies. The same rule applies to military personnel and persons in special attire required by a civil office.

Many of the roots of American higher education, including academic dress, go back a thousand years to the Middle Ages and its branches extend to all areas of life. Higher education in the United States embraces two-year colleges, institutes of technology, government academies and four-year private and public colleges and universities with branches, off-campus centers and extension divisions. Some institutions are church related or controlled, others are private or secular, and many are public with a mixture of municipal, state and federal support. Some privately controlled institutions receive state tax funds. Names, too, are confusing because some colleges are universities and several of the latter represent as yet the unfulfilled dreams of their founders.

To trace the history of higher education, convocations, degrees and costumes one must know something of Bologna, Paris, Oxford and other medieval centers of learning. From them and the colonial colleges of this country, beginning with Harvard in 1636, the record follows an old but changing pattern through the American Revolution and the Civil War periods into the present era. In this story, we shall find answers to the questions: whence came our colleges and universities with their degrees and costumes, what is their meaning, and by what authority are they conferred and worn? We shall see all types of institutions and educational programs in the building of America, and we shall gain a better understanding of the role of higher education in this revolutionary era.

CHAPTER II

⌬

What Is a University?

HISTORIANS FREQUENTLY REFER to the university as one of the greatest achievements and noblest legacies of the Middle Ages. It has survived wars, political revolutions and social change. If the light went out in one place, it was quickly lighted in another.

The university is an attempt to help mankind realize an ideal way of life. It is a place to think and assay great thoughts, a refuge for men thinking. It is a citadel of those who believe in the imperative of the intellectual pursuit of truth. It grew like a great Gothic cathedral. Leaders of different countries and different generations have attempted to define a university, but in reality each generation must arrive at its own definition because time brings changes in man and his institutions.

In attempting to define a university we shall resort to leaders of various periods at home and abroad. Each provides a key to a very complex institution. It may relate to the university, its purposes or to university men. For instance, Johann Comenius (1592–1670) advocated a pansophical institution where universal education and knowledge would be available to men of all nations. He desired a universal language, coeducation and a centralized pooling of learning. John Milton (1608–1674) expressed an ideal of education when he wrote, "I call therefore a compleat and generous education that which fits a man to perform justly, skillfully and magnanimously all the offices both private and publick of Peace and War." He did not envisage narrow practical training, but it is important to remember that universities came into being to meet vocational needs—medicine, law, theology, and teaching.

The famous Dr. Samuel Johnson (1709–1784) presented a modern definition without historical foundation when he said, "A university is a school where all the arts and faculties are taught and studied." His words were echoed years later by Ezra Cornell (1807–1874) when he said, "I would found an institution where any person can find instruction in any subject."

Thomas Jefferson (1743–1826), author of the Declaration of Independence and father of the University of Virginia, was one of the most enlightened men of his time. After a life of public service and letters, he led the campaign for a university, designed the buildings, served as the first rector, planned the curriculum,

Mr. Jefferson's university—Virginia. COURTESY UNIVERSITY OF VIRGINIA.

selected the first professors and wrote one of the textbooks. He envisaged the university as the capstone of the state's educational system with instruction to be given on the graduate level in eight schools: ancient and modern languages, mathematics, natural philosophy, natural history, moral philosophy, anatomy and medicine, law and engineering. This program was very advanced for 1819, and much of it was not realized until the end of the century.

Following the vision of Mr. Jefferson, the faculties and administration of the University of Virginia today give the following definition of the purposes of the institution. "A university is a community of scholars having as its central purpose the enrichment of the human mind by stimulating and sustaining a spirit of free inquiry directed to an understanding of the nature of the universe and man's role in it. This central purpose is served by activities designed (a) to quicken, discipline and enlarge the intellectual capacities of the members of the university; and (b) to record, preserve and disseminate the results of intellectual inquiry."

Thomas Carlyle (1795–1881), a strong advocate of self-instruction, said, "All that mankind has done, thought, gained or been is lying as in magic preservation in the pages of books." He continued, "The true University of these days is a Collection of Books." Benjamin Disraeli (1804–1881), British prime minister, who was largely self-educated, expressed the true spirit of higher education when, in a speech to the House of Commons, he said, "A university should be a place of light, of liberty, and of learning."

Cardinal Newman (1801–1890) in "The Idea of a University" advocated the education of the intellect to reason well in all matters to enable it "to reach out toward truth, and to grasp it." The true end of a university he said, ". . . is not learning or acquirement, but rather, is thought or reason exercised upon knowledge." Newman believed in self-education and contended that one must be possessed of knowledge and not by it. Foreseeing the evils of mass education, he wrote, "A University is . . . an *alma mater,* knowing her children one by one, not a foundry or a mint, or a treadmill."

Emerson (1803–1882), in his famed Phi Beta Kappa address, "The American Scholar," expressed the ideal in similar words. He conceived of a college as teaching the elements creatively; to him a scholar was "man thinking." He emphasized the power of reason to see truth beyond sense experience. Men should love books but not become bookworms. They should know the best thoughts of others from time past and proceed beyond to original sources and thought. The scholar must be "an university of knowledge," educated by nature, books and action, and have the duty of service, to be the "eye and heart" of mankind.

Largely as a result of the Civil War, the classical concept of collegiate or university education was broadened by the adoption of the Morrill Act by Congress in 1862. Among other things this law provided funds from the sale of public lands for the "endowment, support and maintenance of at least one college [in each state], where the leading object shall be, without excluding other scientific and classic studies, and including military tactics, to teach such branches of learning as are related to agriculture and the mechanic arts . . . in order to promote the liberal and practical education of the industrial classes in the several pursuits and professions of life." Education of the industrial classes was not entirely new, but this idea backed by the funds and prestige of the federal government ushered in a new type of university, one that was to contribute mightily to the building of the country during the next century.

Modern graduate education in American universities leading to the doctorate is based more on German than British antecedents. The famous University of Berlin, founded by Wilhelm von Humboldt in 1810, was widely known for its scholarly faculty and scientific investigations. Citizens of the United States studied at Berlin and others went there to observe and talk with its professors. When The Johns Hopkins University was established in Baltimore in 1875, under the leadership of President Daniel C. Gilman (1831–1908), the idea of graduate education in the liberal arts and sciences in the manner of German research took root and rapidly spread to other institutions. This was our first great graduate school and marks the beginning of the modern American university as distinguished from a college. Shortly thereafter, Harvard College, Yale College, Columbia College, Princeton College and other centers of learning were reorganized to include graduate schools with Ph.D. programs and their names changed to universities.

The ideal of service was carried by William Rainey Harper (1856–1906) from Yale and the Methodist Assembly at Chautauqua, New York, to the new University of Chicago. While president there he declared, "The motto of the universities of modern times should be 'Service for mankind, wherever mankind is.' " He helped to popularize extension and correspondence instruction, and a protégé of his, Charles R. Van Hise (1857–1918), did much while president of the University of Wisconsin to establish the concept of the entire state as the campus of the university. The ideal of service through education, training, research and extension has characterized America's land-grant colleges and state universities.

The concept that a university should be involved in the world was generally advocated by Charles W. Eliot (1834–1926) of Harvard and President Gilman of Johns Hopkins. They would have agreed that a university is "a community that thinks," but they knew that matters worth thinking about had consequences in the world of affairs. This understanding was shared by John Dewey (1859–1952) and Alfred North Whitehead (1861–1947), the latter insisting that "celibacy does not suit a university. It must mate itself with action."

Woodrow Wilson (1856–1924), one of the best known university men of his time, had definite ideas about the ideal university for the United States. He knew the strengths and weaknesses of the British, French and German institutions, and he conceded that America had no university ideal of its own. He questioned the need for one, contending that learning was cosmopolitan and must be free. He said, "There is a truth of spirit as well as a truth of fact. A university should be an agent of the State for the transmission of its best traditions. Every man sent out from a university should be a man of his nation, as well as a man of his time." He wrote, "A university should put a man in possession of the materials for a systematic criticism of life, and it has the duty to implant a sense of duty." It is, according to Wilson, learning plus "a spirit of service which will give a college place in the annals of the nation."

The late Pandit Jawaharlal Nehru (1889–1964) of India expressed his own philosophy of higher education, gained in England and the arena of world politics, when he said, "A University stands for humanism, for tolerance, for reason, for the adventure of ideas and for the search of truth. It stands for the onward march of the human race toward ever higher objectives. If the universities discharge their duties adequately, then it is well for the nation and the world."

Sir Richard Livingstone of Oxford, known to many in the United States through his writings and lectures here, caught the spirit of contemporary higher education when he referred to "restless human intelligence within" struggling with the changing circumstances of life without, "modifying them to meet new conditions, developing new activities, introducing new subjects." He observed that changes not foreseen would result from investigations and that philosophy and religion as well as science should be elements in any university education. He felt that a university should make clear that the intellectual and spiritual disorder of our time is not new and a university should provide the Platos to clear our minds and provide a working hypothesis by which to live, a definite philosophy of life.

The eminent British historian Arnold J. Toynbee, also well known to Americans, stated the case in a different vein when he observed that society and knowledge are now dynamic and that formal education, including postgraduate and professional studies, is not enough. "Education," he states, "should be life-long self-education." The initiative should be transferred from instructors early in life and continued beyond retirement to assure constructive activities and prevent the hardening of the mental arteries.

In 1967, William C. Friday, president of the University of North Carolina, characterized this oldest state university as follows: "The University is a major source for creative ideas, and within its faculties are men and women who devotedly seek the new knowledge that will improve man's understanding of his world, his relationship one to another, and his lot as an individual citizen. The University is also an instrument of national purpose. It is indeed an institution of regional, national and international distinction, and it is involved in the world community in a meaningful way."

Recently a great deal has been said and written, not about the university but about the multiversity, a conglomerate merger. This institution, according to Robert M. Hutchins, is one responsive to pressure groups in the country. It is operated to meet the more immediate needs of society, "training, information, and service." It will do for us anything society will pay for and it "exists to flatter the spirit of the age." According to Dr. Hutchins, the multiversities will fail; certainly they will not become the great universities of the future, which will be world universities. Emphasis on low-level needs characterizes the multiversity, and this is not ". . . merely a non-university, a pseudo-university; it is anti-university." The multiversity may be a means of becoming powerful and prosperous, but this is not the true role of a university in building a better and nobler civilization.

In addition to the term multiversity, the United States has given birth to what is sometimes called the megaversity. This is largely a post-sputnik conglomerate and it may include a multiversity, several state universities, colleges, branch campuses, research institutes, experiment stations and special purpose agencies scattered throughout the state. Sheer bigness at various units has created problems from the parking lot to loss of identity with IBM cards, but the trend continues. A few institutions have had to shorten class periods from 50 to 45 minutes to permit students to reach other buildings across sprawling campuses. Some large institutions have twenty-story dormitories which provide space for 1,800 students, more than were in most colleges and universities a few years ago.

Debate over the size, nature and purposes of the modern American university will probably continue for many years, particularly over its role in the area of public service. At one extreme there are those who deem public service an inappropriate function of the university on the ground that it is incompatible with the basic responsibilities of teaching and research. They would keep the university free from odd jobs, "involvements" and pressures for changing services. At the other pole is the view that the university has an inescapable responsibility to be a "protagonist," a shaper of society. Those holding the latter view claim that the days of the academic cloister are past and that the university must in its own defense respond to the legitimate demands of society. Actually, universities have long since entered the public arena and generally to the advantage of society. Future debates should properly relate to what kind of service for what ends and to what extent and under what conditions. There has been too much haphazard growth and service-station approach in this area, and universities need to define a workable philosophy of public service that will protect them and meet reasonable social needs.

Today the university is an integral part of the everyday world and it finds itself in the middle of highly controversial issues. Of no other institution is so much expected and no other agency has a greater responsibility or opportunity for involvement. It must be free to analyze, act, and to publish its findings, but in doing so it must know its goals and establish priorities as related to human and material resources. The university is the chief but by no means the only source of new knowledge and methods. In its role as teacher, researcher, and critic it must make clear that it relies on reason, fair play and persuasion, as opposed to force, and that it is truly dedicated to the long-term welfare of mankind.

As a trustee of the past and present, it must ever be alert to change so that it may intelligently and effectively guide those on the campus and citizens at large.

The picture would not be complete, however, without mention of Headline University—"Old Moo" and "Urban Complex"— where things really happen. Here one finds the demonstrating students, striking professors and emphasis upon all the freedoms. From football, marching bands and fraternity rush to midwinter informals and the rites of spring in Bermuda or Florida, all is modern and on the "go-go." Administrators lobby and chase grants, teachers not protesting are busy with committee work or away learning about research, students debate the sins of their elders, military service, CIA involvements, and the merits of LSD, and the organized alumni in teams of "Orange" and "Purple" struggle to help finance *alma mater*. But real scholars know that much of this is but a modern version of problems and activities dating from the Middle Ages and that other features of the Moo-U-Complex, anarchy and nihilism, constitute real threats to the university as a center of learning.

In our time the university is deemed essential in the preservation and transmission of knowledge. As an intellectual community it is the most sophisticated agency we have for advancing knowledge through research and scholarship. It is an arm of church, state, business and industry. It is an instrument and expression of our highest purposes. It may no longer emphasize religion and character or know its students "one by one" but hopefully it is the home of "man thinking." Regardless of its evolution, lack of precise definition, fields of study and training and varied sources of support and control, it is important. It was not really created, rather it evolved over the centuries as an expression of the spiritual, intellectual and social energies of free men.

Higher education in Colonial America and in the United States was represented by small colleges on the Oxford-Cambridge pattern until well after the Civil War. It is a general term that customarily includes all programs of instruction taken after the completion of high school or secondary training. It embraces colleges and universities and other institutions regardless of the lax use of title or the degrees conferred.

A person who has long understood that one of our leading universities is located in Cambridge, Massachusetts, is confused when he learns that the corporate legal titles of the controlling bodies of this institution are The President and Fellows, and the Board of Overseers, of Harvard College. He is further perplexed to learn that the phrase, Regents of the University of the State of New York, does not refer to a university but that it is the corporate title of the state's Department of Education. This department in turn is concerned with but entirely separate from the several units of the State University of New York, which is not the same as New York University. Puzzlement grows as we contemplate Boston University and Boston College, both universities. Also there are numerous cooperative groupings of autonomous institutions, and educator and layman alike must now reckon with consortia such as the Committee on Institutional Cooperation of the Big Ten Universities and the University of Chicago, and the Associated Colleges of the Midwest.

The United States Office of Education includes in the university category those ". . . institutions in which there is considerable stress on graduate instruction, which confer advanced degrees in a variety of liberal arts fields, and which have at least two professional schools that are not exclusively technological." Colleges, including many junior colleges, emphasize programs of general undergraduate education, usually liberal but including many vocational courses. All this reflects the complexity of American education, which is directly related to but vastly changed from European origins.

Initially a *universitas* meant any organized body of individuals or a corporation. In time the term was applied to a *universitas scholarium* or a *universitas magistrorum*—a guild of students or of teachers without trustees and administrative officers. The *universitas* was not a campus or a group of buildings in which classes were conducted; rather it was a fraternity of scholars. The place of study was called a *studium* and if the institutions there gave instruction in the superior faculties and received students from several countries, it was known as a *studium generale*. *Studia generalia* were generally lesser institutions which arose through secession and existed without papal or imperial charters. The term university, meaning a lawful community of teachers and scholars in a definite location, did not stand alone until the latter part of the fourteenth century. The term as originally used did not include the concept of universality.

In the Middle Ages the university was an institution of higher learning recognized by the Pope or emperor or by the king of Spain as such. It was a place where students or teachers or both were joined in guilds to pursue standard fields of study in philosophy, law, medicine, and theology. Music was occasionally included and law was often divided into civil and canon. The medieval university was created and maintained for a definite purpose; it did not cultivate the arts for their own sake.

The term doctor, which characterizes the staffs of universities ancient and modern, is derived from the Latin word *docere,* to teach, and it originally meant a person who teaches. It was known in Biblical times as the title of a teacher or learned person because in Luke 2:46, it is written that Christ when he was twelve years old went to Jerusalem with his parents and when he was apparently lost amidst the passover crowds for three days ". . . they found him in the temple, sitting in the midst of the doctors, both hearing them and asking them questions." The title of doctor was applied by the Romans to those who gave learned lectures in public places, and it was used by the early church for instructors in the cathedral schools. Those who taught catechism and basic subjects were *doctores audientium* and the most scholarly theologians and philosophers were *doctores ecclesiae.* This term was also applied to learned teachers of law and medicine.

The terms doctor, master and professor were synonymous

throughout the early Middle Ages. The title of doctor was some-times used as a sobriquet. Duns Scotus was called the "Subtle Doctor," William of Ockham the "Invincible Doctor," Roger Bacon the "Wonderful Doctor" and Thomas Aquinas the "Angelic Doctor." Those who received their degrees in course were *doctores rite promoti,* and they had to prepare a thesis in Latin and defend it in public. Those who received the degree *honoris causa* from popes or emperors were known as *doctores bullati.*

Although ancient Athens, Alexandria and Rome had various academies and lyceums for debate and literary improvement, the university is definitely an outgrowth of the medieval period. Fol-lowing the barbarian invasions of the fifth and sixth centuries and amid the ferment of the Crusades, learning was kept alive and advanced by monasteries and cathedral schools such as those at Monte Cassino and York. Schools for the more advanced studies evolved slowly, chiefly in metropolitan and trade centers, and they were of uneven quality. From humble and rather informal beginnings the university came to full flower during the era of the Renaissance.

The eleventh and twelfth centuries marked a general revival of learning. Instruction was needed in fields that did not fall within the ecclesiastical mold. The University of Salerno, often called the first of all universities in Christendom, was not a true univer-sity; rather, it was a school of medicine, well established by the middle of the eleventh century. The study of medicine was fol-lowed by a revival of the study of Greek dialectic and Roman law. Latin translations were made of the writings of Aristotle. In time Christian theology was related to Aristotelian philosophy, and the development of scholasticism followed.

To meet the demands of the new learning, some teachers were drafted by eager students and others set themselves up to provide instruction. Students were more attracted by famous teachers than by the name of the school. The learned person who headed a group of students in a particular discipline was called a master or doctor.

To teach at a cathedral or palace school, one needed approval from the head of the institution, usually a chancellor. This took the form of a license to teach, *licentia docendi* or *ius ubique docendi,* which was awarded on evidence that the prospective teacher was thoroughly grounded in the subject he proposed to teach, and of sound faith and good repute. In theory a master teacher or doctor belonged to a guild; generally, but not always, he could carry on his profession at any existing Christian university or at one established in the future. Many early scholars taught without formal institutional controls, but with the establishment of the office of chancellor or rector we have the beginning of university administration as distinguished from teaching and research.

In England and northern Europe, cathedral schools were fore-runners of universities; in the south, especially in Italy, teachers and students gathered into the growing trade centers. They came from all parts of Christendom and pursued curricula in Latin. Often a center of learning enjoyed a long and successful existence before receiving official recognition as a *studium generale* by papal bull.

In addition to the use of a common language and being international, the early European universities possessed many similar characteristics and a common philosophical spirit, a concept of the university world as an academic republic where students were free citizens. Be it Bologna in Italy, Paris in France, or Oxford in England, the courses of study were standard, instruction and examinations followed a uniform pattern, and they all, at least nominally until the Reformation, shared a common church. These like features, including origin, control, purposes, and philosophy, were generally known, and they distinguish universities of old from their variegated successors in the United States.

Legacies of academic dress and degrees have also withstood many changes. The dress evolved from gowns worn by common folk and the clergy. It was utilitarian, worn daily and subject to special regulations. The original teaching license became the prototype of our numerous degrees.

Universities, then as now, were centers of conflict, internally and between town and gown. Perhaps the permanent characteristic of a university is the perpetual war between tradition and the needs and desires of a dynamic social order. This conflict became dominant when men learned that they could shape their own destinies and even change society through education. A university must embody an ideal and have sufficient stability to sustain it. At the same time it must be flexible enough to be relevant to the society that makes it possible. As John W. Gardner has so aptly stated, it must develop qualities of "self-renewal."

In many ways modern universities resemble business conglomerates. They publish and sell books, operate computer centers, conduct industrial and military research, manage recreation parks, host conventions, sell produce, manage clinics, control patents, sponsor athletic contests, offer radio-TV programs, operate art galleries, theaters, and museums, and advise government agencies. Many institutions profit from the sale of spin-offs from research and noneducational items. Numerous professors, trustees, and administrators serve on corporate boards, and an increasing number of teachers collect royalties and fees from textbooks and lectures, serve as consultants, and double as tour conductors. Some of these activities are helpful and relate to classroom theory, but others raise unanswered questions, usually avoided, concerning the purpose of the university.

Most colleges and universities today are adrift in a world that has rejected traditional authority. They exist in an open society free from the dominion of churches and monarchs but with vague goals. The transition from the old order of community and authority to a measure of stability in an atomic age will be difficult because new purposes and guide posts will have to be agreed upon as teachers and administrators seek to know and discharge their duties amid the pressures and problems of daily life.

At the very time institutions of higher learning are striving for identity, they are called upon to perform new tasks—tasks that in times past usually fell to the church or government. They must preserve and advance knowledge, perform numerous public services and essay the role of critic. As was noted at a recent annual meeting of the American Council on Education in Washington, these new demands raise questions such as: whose goals for American higher education; what standards for the operation of colleges and universities; which federal research projects and may they be classified under contract; what kind and how much public service; and, as critic, must the university remain objective or may it champion causes? All these questions, along with others relating to personal and academic freedom, finance, authority, athletics and institutional citizenship (all generally subject to state and national laws), concern present-day scholars as they ponder loyalty to campus, professional disciplines and off-campus employment at home and abroad.

There is no one or final answer to the question: What is a university? There are many answers, and others will be advanced with the passing years. Colleges and universities are agencies of the society that they helped to produce, and they are the best hope mankind has of finding answers to perplexing problems and known and unknown opportunities. If the university does not discover, interpret and help apply new knowledge, some other agency will have to be created to perform this essential task. The record of higher education since the establishment of the University of Bologna in the eleventh century offers hope that true scholars will find and chart the course and that the university which shelters them will truly be a lighthouse for the world.

John Masefield (1878–1967), late Poet Laureate of England, was a man of the sea and a laborer before he turned to writing. He saw the university from afar and eloquently described it in the following lines:

There are
few earthly things
more beautiful
than a
University.

In these days of
broken frontiers
and collapsing values,
where the dams are down and
the floods are making misery,
when every future
looks somewhat grim and
every ancient foothold
has become
something of a quagmire,
wherever a University stands,
it stands and shines;
wherever it exists,
the free minds of men,
urged on to
full and fair inquiry,
may still bring
wisdom into human affairs.

CHAPTER III

❧❧❧

Early European
Universities

THE FORERUNNER OF modern institutions of higher learning was established at Salerno in southern Italy in the ninth century. Under Constantine the African, famed as a teacher of medicine, the medical school's influence spread throughout Europe. This institution, drawing upon Greek, Arabic and Jewish knowledge, became a model for later colleges; in 1231 it was designated as the only authorized school of medicine in the kingdom of Naples by Frederick II. The works of Galen, Hippocrates and Avicenna were avidly studied. Surgery was usually considered apart from medicine.

Bologna in northern Italy is the oldest university in Europe. Begun in the latter part of the eleventh century (1088) with a revival of the study of civil law, it continues to flourish today. The fame of Irnerius as a teacher of the Justinian Code and the writing of a textbook by Gratian on canon law led to the establishment of a *universitas scholarium,* actually two schools of law. These schools or guilds of students operated the university in the manner of other corporations of the day and elected their own rector. Subsequently Bologna became a *studium generale* by authority of a papal bull.

During its early years the University of Bologna had no fixed residence, the professors lecturing in their homes or in rented halls or donated public buildings. They were dependent on their *collecta* or student fees for their income. The students, many mature men from foreign countries, were organized into "nations," and through these they controlled fees, class hours, absences and the like. They also sought to protect their members from the exploitation of townsmen, particularly in the prices charged for food and lodging.

One nation was for students beyond the Alps, and the other for students from the Italian states and neighboring islands. Students who were citizens of Bologna required less protection, and they were not allowed membership in the nations. Each nation was headed by a protector. As we shall observe later, the nations here differed from those in Paris, the latter being composed of masters. Frequently, however, a master in one discipline was a student in another.

Bologna prospered: during the twelfth to fifteenth centuries, it is estimated that 3,000 to 5,000 students thronged the town annually. Among those later achieving lasting fame were Dante, Cino da Pistoia, Petrarch and Savonarola. The renown of the center was such that coins used the legend *Bononia docet,* Bologna teaches.

In addition to law, Bologna offered the first courses in human anatomy. It even had a few women professors, some like Novella d'Andrea, reported to be so attractive that they lectured behind a veil to avoid distracting students. It was at Bologna that Petrarch (1304-1374) met the celebrated Laura whose withheld charms are alleged to have made him the great poet of his age. Savonarola (1452-1498), who entered a monastery at the age of twenty-three, voiced an opinion on academic life with a modern ring. "To be considered a man here you must fill your mouth with . . .

blasphemies. . . . If you study philosophy and the good arts, you are considered a dreamer; if you live chastely and modestly, a fool; if you are pious, a hypocrite; and if you believe in God, an imbecile."

Shortly after arrival students were hazed, treated as "rats" or other animals, but after a period of time during which they learned to respect their elders, they were freed from indignities amid considerable horseplay. That students had to be hearty is indicated by the fact that they fought duels and were sometimes robbed en route to the university. If they got into trouble, they were usually tried before the rector. As early as 1158, the Emperor Frederick I of the Holy Roman Empire issued a decree providing that scholars could be tried by their masters or bishop rather than by local magistrates.

There were occasional church holidays, but vacations were restricted to one month a year. The daily schedule was full and rigorous. Students usually rose at four, attended a lecture at five, went to Mass at six and then had breakfast. Lectures and formal debates were held before the noon meal, then came recitations, lectures and disputations. Following the evening meal at six there were more repetitions and most students were usually glad to be in bed by nine o'clock.

Many students rebelled against such routine and the cloistered life. There were innumerable rules, punishments and fines for going over the city wall at night, attacking the city gates, over-indulging at the tavern, playing chess or dice, fencing, attacking servants or molesting citizens of the town and the like. Students could not keep dogs or birds, wear masks, and were not encouraged to engage in games and sports. They were required to speak Latin in the halls and to be dressed properly. They were warned against women, minstrels, jesters and other instruments of the Devil. Poaching was a serious offense but very popular. Musical instruments were discouraged, but in later years some of the German universities permitted "music at reasonable hours if it was musical." Visitors to Heidelberg today may see the old university jail with autographs of student offenders still on the walls, some of whom later achieved distinction.

Degree programs at Bologna and other institutions varied because of different historical origins, yet the unity of medieval society produced generally common subject fields and methods of instruction. Often students studied at one or more universities and took their degrees at another to save on graduation expenses. The three grades common to all were scholar, bachelor and master or doctor. The time required for the latter degree ranged from six to twenty years depending on the field of study, on the university conferring the degree and on the abilities and diligence of the student. Generally, academic standards were high, but there were occasional charges of bribery and laxity.

Students in Italy were often older than their northern counterparts, but regardless of place or age, they had to be fluent in Latin, then the international language. They studied the seven liberal arts, a program deemed befitting free men. The threefold *trivium* included grammar, logic and rhetoric, the last consisting largely of a study of Aristotle. Upon completing these subjects, the student became a bachelor and was admitted to the fourfold *quadrivium* consisting of music, arithmetic, geometry and astronomy. The *quadrivium* required four years and qualified a student to teach and to proceed to the degree of master or doctor.

Upon passing the baccalaureate examinations, the successful candidate put on a *cappa* or hooded gown and took a seat among the bachelors. It was a great day and an expensive one, since he had to buy food and drink for distinguished guests and fellow students. To qualify for a doctorate in civil or common law, theology or medicine, an additional period of study of eight or more years was required.

By the fourteenth century the term doctor was being recognized as a higher mark of distinction than master or professor. All students had clerical status, but many who became lawyers, physicians and priests took the higher degree. Those who followed teaching or became clerics found the title a distinct advantage in academic work. The doctorate, then as now, became a "union card" with recognized immunities and privileges. The latter originally included the *ius ubique docendi,* the right to teach everywhere, protection in travel including shelter at churches or universities and, in many cases, exemption from taxes.

Before the advent of the printing press, books and manuscripts were few, expensive, and closely guarded. It required six to eight months for a skilled scribe to copy a book, and ancient, chained tomes may be seen in a few European university libraries today.

Instruction was chiefly by means of lectures, and learned professors had to perform acceptably or they lost both students and fees. They spoke from a high lectern and the students sat on benches or piles of straw. Student notes on lectures were most important. Some notes were scribbled on wax tablets, but those written in ink on parchment were handed down from generation to generation. Recitation was primarily through oral disputation.

Like its descendant, the intercollegiate debate, the medieval disputation tended to become a contest in mental gymnastics and sophistry. Lectures from antiquated sources and endless quibblings checked efforts to discover new truth. Liberal theologians, experimental scientists and humanistic classicists found it difficult to improve the curriculum or educational methods. In many cases they were forced to work and teach outside of university halls. Examinations included disputation, and doctoral candidates had to defend their dissertations in private and finally in public against faculty members and sometimes outside critics.

The private examination was the real test of competence, the public testing being ceremony or commencement. The candidate upon passing the former became a *licentiate* and proceeded shortly thereafter with the ceremonies that would make him a master or doctor. As a preparation for the final public ceremony the candidate in *cappati,* full academic dress, rode about the city preceded by mace-bearers and university officials. They announced the time and place of the event and invited public officials and friends to attend.

Doctors of civil law at Bologna wore scarlet robes trimmed with ermine as if they were nobles. In time, however, scarlet was adopted by many universities for canon law or theology. Actually, there was no uniformity of faculty colors during the medieval period, and among European universities today logical symbolism is lacking.

Notwithstanding the absence of a color code, degrees and commencements were fairly uniform. At the final exercises, the candidate gave an address and defended his thesis. Thereupon the archdeacon (chancellor) complimented the graduate and presented his license by the authority of the Pope. The candidate was invested with the marks of his office and presented with a book and the master's blessing. The candidate next sat upon the *cathedra* or magisterial chair and a special *biretta* was placed on his head and he was presented with a gold ring. The ceremony was concluded with a benediction and the kiss of peace.

Following the Commencement, there was usually a triumphal parade through the city preceded by trumpeters and pipers, in honor of the new doctor. This was costly to him, as was the custom of giving robes, money payments and assorted gifts of gloves, caps and candy to the various doctors and officials. The prior of the college usually received a ring. Gifts were later governed by statutes. At Bologna one poor student received his degree free each year. After the gifts there came the banquet for friends and colleagues. Wealthy students occasionally staged tournaments, and in Spain the new doctor sometimes staged a bullfight.

Universities were sponsored by wealthy princes and church leaders. Various popes established universities and officially recognized the existence of others. By the time of the Renaissance some seventy universities existed in Europe. Some developing centers of learning, such as Modena (1175), Vicenza (1204), and Padua (1222), originated in migrations of students from Bologna.

Envoys from rival cities sought to bribe away discontented students and teachers, and the situation became so serious that professors were punished or fined if they entered into a conspiracy to move the university. To assure the community's economic stability, teachers had to take an oath not to move to another institution during an agreed period, usually two years. Rectors also had to give security that they would not depart before the end of the term. Wars and changes of dynasties also led professors to change positions. Cino da Pistoia (1270–1356), a graduate of Bologna and famed as a poet and jurist, taught at Treviso, Siena, Florence and Perugia in succession.

Occasionally universities were suppressed by political or religious authorities, and often they suffered from war and pestilence, but their survival rate was most remarkable as attested in the Reformation period. In addition to Bologna and institutions mentioned above, posterity is indebted to the following Italian universities: Naples (1224), Siena (1246), Rome (1303), Perugia (1308), Pisa (1343), Florence (1349), Treviso (1318), Turin (1405) and Catania (1444).

The Italian universities generally were modeled on Bologna. They emphasized the study of civil and canon law, with medicine following in popularity. Aside from Rome, the study of theology centered in Paris. In Italy the universities tended to be municipal in character and by the fifteenth century they were housed in buildings provided by the cities or their rents were paid by cities or local patrons.

It appears that dress was regulated at all institutions but few specific codes have survived. The rector at Padua was required to wear a silk, hooded robe for his installation. Doctors of law and medicine tended to wear the same type of costume after 1500. At Pisa the rector's dress consisted of brocaded silk interlaced with gold. Clerical dress and the tonsure were required at Pavia. Florence prescribed plain black cloth for the gowns of doctors and the cloaks of bachelors, but the rector was distinguished by a special headdress. These and other variations may be noted on the sculptured tombs of prominent doctor-citizens in Florence, Bologna and nearby cities.

In France and on the Iberian peninsula, university development was similar to that in Italy. Paris became to theological and philosophical learning what Bologna was to law, and it greatly influenced Oxford and Cambridge. Curricula, instruction, control, degrees and costumes tended to follow a common pattern. Some universities won renown in particular fields, attracted students from afar, and prospered. Others struggled along, envious of their affluent sisters, and some were forced to close because of war, outside pressures and general lack of support.

In Portugal, the University of Coimbra was founded in Lisbon in 1290, was moved back and forth to Coimbra twice, and was permanently reestablished in the latter city in 1537. The present University of Lisbon was founded in 1911, but traces its history back to the university established in Lisbon in 1290. Visitors to the ancient Roman city of Coimbra today will see several thousand students wearing black suits and flowing black capes reminiscent of earlier times.

Spain proudly boasts of the following early universities: Salamanca (1227), Valladolid (1250), Seville (1254), Barcelona (1450), Zaragosa (1474), Palma (1483), Madrid (1509), Granada (1531) and Oviedo (1604). Of these Salamanca is perhaps the best known. Its schools of canon and civil law were widely and favorably known, and Columbus lectured there following his discoveries in America. This ancient Spanish institution was the first to give instruction and degrees in music. The universities of Spain were essentially national or royal creations. They served as models for the National University of San Marcos (1551) in Peru and the National Autonomous University of Mexico (1551).

France rivaled Italy in intellectual and cultural activities and her status advanced when the papacy flourished at Avignon. Before the University of Paris (1160) is discussed, the following centers of learning should be noted: Montpellier (1220), Toulouse (1229), Orléans (1235), Grenoble (1339), Aix-Marseilles (1409), Poitiers (1431), Caen (1432), Bordeaux (1441), Nantes (1460), Besançon (1485). Of these institutions the University of Montpellier was most renowned because of its excellence in medicine. The University of Toulouse, the first founded by papal charter, was established to oppose the Albigensian heresy.

Among the universities of France as well as those of Spain and Portugal there was no uniformity of dress or color for the faculties. In 1321, graduates at Coimbra were directed to wear tunics reaching to their heels, and undergraduates were to wear them well above the knees. From portraits it appears that doctors of canon law at Salamanca wore crimson skull-caps that covered most of the ears. At Valladolid students wore short, pleated cassocks and Castilian caps. Doctors and masters were forbidden to lecture at Toulouse or take part in public ceremonies unless wearing a proper *cappa*.

Students at Montpellier wore long, full black tunics without hoods, and as late as 1711 a Doctor of Medicine was described as wearing white boots and gilt spurs at public ceremony. At most French universities the bachelors and *licentiates* were not allowed to wear *birettas*. Statutes of Caen prescribed violet *cappas* and round bonnets for doctors of medicine. At Paris, dress varied from college to college in the early days. Faculty colors included black for theology, violet for medicine, scarlet for law and blue for philosophy. Fur trim was popular and bonnets became fashionable.

The rise of the University of Paris may be illustrated in the career of Peter Abélard, a young Breton, who went to Paris because of the fame of William of Champeaux. Abélard's brilliant mind soon tired of lectures, and he openly challenged Champeaux and other teachers. When called upon to prove his case, he started classes of his own and students attended them in large numbers. He was driven out by jealous professors, taught elsewhere, studied theology, and eventually returned to Paris. At that time there was no university organization and students might set themselves up as teachers. Abélard's lectures were so popular that he soon had a large following

Most students today know of this great teacher because of his famous love affair with Héloïse. Although he exempted the Bible from criticism, his success, tactlessness and unorthodox views invited the opposition of conservative theologians headed by St. Bernard. Abélard was tried for heresy and forced to retire from teaching. His career exemplifies the drawing power of schools in Paris, the unorganized structure of education and the virtues and evils of specialization in theology and logic—scholasticism.

Students from all regions, rivalries of teachers and church pressures hastened the development of university organizations at Paris. The university, growing out of schools attached to the cathedral on the Île de la Cité during the twelfth century, was presided over by a chancellor who conferred licenses to teach. It was confirmed by Philip II in 1200, and by a bull of Pope Innocent III in 1215.

Paris rapidly became the great school where theology was studied in the rational spirit, and the decisions of its doctors on the abstruse questions of the Middle Ages were virtually final. Thomas Aquinas (1225–1294) studied and lectured here and possibly more than any other person he brought about the wedding of faith and reason. The Papacy had not yet defined the doctrine of infallibility, and, being supported by Paris, it discouraged the creation of faculties of theology elsewhere. The dialectic of Paris became the "science of sciences" and it would be difficult to overestimate the influence of the university on other European and English institutions.

The reconciliation of the doctrines of the Catholic Church with the philosophy of Aristotle is beautifully illustrated in a famous fourteenth century fresco in Santa Maria Novella in Florence entitled "The Triumph of St. Thomas." The painting, attributed to Andrea di Bonaiuto, places the medieval Dominican "Angelic Doctor" in the center of an allegory of human and spiritual activities. Atop his head are the three theological virtues, Faith,

Hope and Charity, and the four cardinal virtues, Temperance, Prudence, Fortitude and Justice. The book of wisdom in his hand displays the passage, "I prayed, and understanding was given me." Seated level with the throne are ten saints of the Old and New Testaments. At his feet are three heretics defeated by Christian knowledge. Below the throne are fourteen stalls with seven women on each side. These represent the seven religious arts under the influence of the Holy Spirit and the seven liberal arts under the influence of the planets. The fourteen men at the bottom represent historical personages, leaders of church, state and the several fields of scholarship. The fresco, with its many additional details, united all learning within the framework of Christianity.

Paris had faculties of theology, law, medicine and arts. The latter embraced four nations of teachers and students. The French nation included the French, Spaniards, Italians and Greeks. The Picard nation was composed of persons from the Northeast and the Low Countries. The Norman nation included those from Normandy, and the English nation embraced all teachers and students from the British Isles, English provinces in France and those from Germany. Estimates of enrollments vary, but there were probably 5,000 to 7,000 students at the University of Paris during most of the medieval period.

By the fourteenth century the University of Paris encompassed forty colleges, the best known being the Sorbonne. This college was a residence hall for students of theology. Each faculty was headed by a dean and each nation by a proctor. The collective head of the university was the rector, who was also the elected head of the faculty of arts. The faculties or schools of theology, law and medicine were professional or graduate schools, the faculty of arts and its nations being comparable to undergraduate colleges. With few variations, curricula, instruction and degrees followed the pattern previously discussed. Academic gowns were the order of the day.

The statutes of the University of Paris prior to the Revolution

College of Sorbonne, Paris, 1550.   COURTESY BIBLIOTHEQUE NATIONALE.

of 1789–1804 prescribed the following costumes: Master of arts, black robe with a small *chaperon* or cape without fur; bachelors in medicine, law and theology, black robe with a *chaperon* of ermine; doctors in arts, medicine and law, red robe with hood or *chaperon* lined with ermine; and doctor of theology, black or violet robe with hood or *chaperon* lined with ermine. The rector wore a violet robe with a silk violet waistband adorned with a gold tassel. A fur pocket was suspended from the robe, and all was adorned with a round cloak lined with ermine. All doctors' hats were square-shaped.

Most universities followed a common rule of precedence for faculties and degrees. A statute of the University of Vienna in the late fourteenth century directed the following order for processions. The banner of the university was to be carried first, then came the bachelors of arts, medicine, law and theology. These were followed by masters of arts, and then the doctors of medicine, law and theology. Nobles walked with the doctors, and bachelors accompanied their scholars. Masters of arts and doctors also walked with their licentiates. The status of noblemen, scholars and commoners was generally recognized at all institutions.

Although the predominant influence on American higher education stemmed from Bologna, Paris, Oxford and Cambridge, the influence of universities in central and northern Europe was considerable, because scholars traveled widely and, particularly after the invention of movable type, their works were read by other scholars. The listing that follows does not include all the European institutions of learning; it is limited chiefly to those established before 1600.

Prague or Charles University is the oldest in central Europe. It was founded in 1348 by King Charles IV who had studied at Paris. It is reported to have had some 3,000 students. Cracow in Poland dates from 1364. It was organized on the Bologna pattern and held in high repute as an institution of humanistic and astronomical studies. Vienna, the leading university of Austria, was established by Duke Rudolph IV in 1365. Heidelberg, the oldest university in Germany, dates from 1386. Cologne on the Rhine, long a center of learning, claims university status from 1388. It was not created by a prince but by the public spirit of a great commercial municipality.

Others in the central European group with dates of founding are: Erfurt (1392), Leipzig (1409), Rostock (1419), Freiburg (1455), Basel (1460), Munich (1472), Mainz (1476), Tübingen (1476), and Wittenberg (1502). There are no precise figures, but enrollments at these institutions ranged from 225 at Heidelberg to about 500 at Leipzig.

Louvain, long the pride of Belgium, dates from 1425. It was a federation of several colleges, and for a time this university rivaled Paris in its number of students and its reputation for excellence. Erasmus said, "No one could graduate from Louvain without knowledge, manners and age." Leyden (1575), Groningen (1614) and Utrecht (1634) were established in Holland after the provinces won their fight for national freedom under William the Silent. Leyden was known for its distinguished and well-paid professors. It frequently offered shelter to those of liberal thought, and it will be recalled that the Pilgrim Fathers resided in that city for a time before sailing for America. Copenhagen (1473), Uppsala (1477), Helsinki (1640) and Lund (1668) represent north Europe; the first two received charters from Pope Sextus IV and were modeled on Cologne.

The Reformation rocked Europe for many decades particularly during the sixteenth century. Several Catholic universities in Protestant areas became Protestant in doctrine and control. Several Protestant institutions were founded, the first being Marburg in 1527. Others of distinction were Königsberg (1544), Jena (1558), Geneva (1559) and Helmstedt (1575). For many years it was generally impossible for Protestants to enter Catholic universities or for Catholics to enroll at old or new institutions under Protestant control. Protestant gains were partially countered by the Society of Jesus which was founded by Ignatius Loyola in 1534. The Jesuits, excepting the period from 1773 to 1814 when the order was suspended in most countries, were able leaders of Catholic missionary and educational activities.

In a very real sense the revival of learning and the universities sparked the Reformation. In like manner universities helped to expand and perpetuate its results. With the development of Nationalism many institutions of learning were closed and the international nature of others was changed. Scholars, however, continued to think and dream of an ideal international center of learning.

One notable proposal of the seventeenth century was that of Bengt Skytte (1614–1683) of Sweden for an international university and research center. Sponsored by Friedrich Wilhelm of Brandenburg the "Universitas Brandenburica gentium, scientiarum et artium" was to be a center for teaching and research wherein scholars of all nations and faiths could carry on their work in full freedom. It was to be located at Sophopolis and consist of lecture rooms, libraries, laboratories, a museum, a botanic garden and a printing press. It was to be a sanctuary in time of war and a beacon of truth for all mankind at a time when war and religious persecutions were a way of life. The university never came into being, and after 300 years the ideal of Skytte remains to challenge those who envisage a universal university.

The German universities developed characteristics that differed considerably from those of France. The rector might be chosen from any faculty, nations existed as a division of the whole university and they were of less importance, and the teachers were endowed. This latter feature led to a permanent faculty that gradually removed the unendowed masters from any real academic power. In the German institutions, colleges were designed primarily to supply teachers and most teaching was in the hands of the university. Subjects to be lectured on were carefully distributed among the professors. The old colleges came to have little existence independent of the universities, and by the sixteenth century the bachelor of arts degree had disappeared and the master of arts was incorporated in the new doctor of philosophy degree.

The new German and Swiss universities and most of the older ones, probably as a result of the Reformation, did not use the traditional academic gowns and hoods. Later full black robes were worn by many professors on ceremonial occasions, the graduates wearing formal civilian attire. More recently some of the European universities have revived ancient styles of dress during commencements, but the practice is by no means universal. Uppsala scholars do not wear gowns of Swedish origin, and public degree ceremonies are restricted to the doctors who wear top hats with their golden faculty symbols. The only remnant of academic regalia at Copenhagen is the golden chain worn by the rector. The University of Geneva reintroduced black gowns and velvet bonnets on the occasion of its Four Hundredth Anniversary in 1959.

The French universities were closed during the Revolution and

Rector of the University of Geneva, Théodore de Bèze (1519–1605).
COURTESY HISTORICAL MUSEUM OF THE REFORMATION, GENEVA.

greatly changed when reopened by Napoleon. The costume code decreed in 1809 is essentially for professors and it includes the cape, scarf and square hats. Violet is the color for the rector and administrative officials. The professors wear black robes but the cloaks vary in color according to the faculty: black for theology, red for law, crimson for medicine, purplish red for science, and orange for philosophy. Other European universities follow distinctive and nonuniform patterns of dress. The hood color of Berlin is purple, of Heidelberg red and of Prague red and white. Professors at the University of Leyden wear black gowns and black berets. The rector of Munich wears a regular faculty gown with a gold chain of office. At the University of Vienna the rector and deans wear full black mantles over which they place brocaded capes bordered with ermine. The capes are of various colors, representing the various schools, and all officials wear gold chains of office.

At Helsinki the ceremony for conferring degrees and the three-day celebration follow ancient customs. Invitations are issued in Latin, friends prepare the laurel wreaths worn by the candidates and the senior professor or Promoter confers the degrees in the Great Festival Hall. Members of the faculty and candidates for degrees wear formal civilian dress. The undergraduates are given certificates of their final examinations. The masters receive a wreath of laurel, a ring with the symbolic lyre and laurel, and a certificate in Latin. The doctors are presented with a Latin diploma and the traditional top hat and sword. The doctoral awards are based on oral and written examinations and a public defense of the thesis. The commencement exercises include a religious service, grand ball and boat excursion.

Most persons in the United States holding degrees from German universities wear traditional black gowns and mortarboards. They use hoods of their appropriate degree lined with the colors of their institution, and they place upon the lining the German tri-colored chevron of black, white and red. In similar manner, graduates of Swiss universities residing in the United States use

Degree Day, University of Helsinki. A laurel wreath is placed on the head of a graduate receiving a master's degree.

the black hood appropriate to their degree. It is lined with the colors of their university and the national white cross is laid thereon. There are other variations from different universities and countries, but generally an effort is made to comply with the American Academic Costume Code.

The academic costume of Paris is a black gown over which a colored scarf is worn. The wide part of the scarf hangs a short way down the back and the narrow part reaches below the waist. The scarves of doctors have three rows of ermine at each end, the licentiates or masters have two, and the bachelors have one.

Lecture in law, University of Uppsala, early 19th century. Students in center are Crown Prince Charles (later Charles XV of Sweden) and his brother Prince Gustav; others also in top hats are their attendants.   COURTESY UNIVERSITY OF UPPSALA.

Each French university has a distinctive color. Graduates of Paris living in the United States often use a black hood of American design appropriate for their degree, with crimson and gold lining and a chevron of red, white and blue.

Some universities in Europe, such as Uppsala and Lund, have the popular custom of awarding jubilee doctorates to doctors who have held their degrees for fifty years. This ceremony takes place at the same time as that of the other conferments. The returning graduates receive a most cordial welcome, and there are various ceremonial details including special music.

There are also anniversaries for those who have worn their doctoral wedding rings for twenty-five, fifty or sixty years. The gold band represents a marriage of the individual with philosophy; the custom is rooted in religious tradition, probably derived from the jubilee mentioned in the Bible, Lev. 25:9–15. The term golden or silver wedding for academic occasions is current in Holland and Germany as well as in Scandinavia.

Much more could be said about early European universities and their life and customs. University life during the Renaissance and Reformation, which moulded them and was shaped by them, is a fascinating and formidable story that cannot be included here. The fine arts—music, painting, drama, and architecture—flourished in many areas and became part of our cultural heritage, but the main route of scholarship led to the British universities, especially Oxford and Cambridge. Just as Bologna and Paris were models for later schools in Europe, the colleges of the universities on the Isis and Cam were archetypes of the early colleges in America.

CHAPTER IV

Early British Universities

No EXACT DATE can be given for the establishment of a university at Oxford, but it is generally thought that it began with the exodus of English students who were excluded from the University of Paris in 1167. They were undoubtedly attracted by the presence of small church schools in the area, and by 1190, a *studium generale* had been fully developed.

Cambridge was a center of learning because of the monasteries there. Some writers state that the university there originated in 1200 or earlier, and others contend that it began in 1209 following disturbances at Oxford, which led to a migration of scholars. Both institutions were modeled on Paris and became *universitates magistrorum*. Oxford's right to confer advanced degrees was confirmed by Pope Innocent IV in 1254, and Cambridge was formally recognized as a *studium generale* by Pope John XXII in 1318.

Oxford came under the supervision of the Bishop of Lincoln, and Cambridge was within the Diocese of Ely. The bishops relied largely on deputies called chancellors. Both institutions grew along common lines and had similar problems, Oxford being larger, stronger and generally more advanced during the first three centuries.

45

Both universities had frequent conflicts with the towns where they were located, but having the church and crown on their side they gradually gained supremacy over the municipal governments. The two institutions also had troubles growing out of the rivalries of monastic orders, mendicants and others having been admitted to degrees in England before this privilege was granted in other countries. In the early centuries the monasteries at Oxford and Cambridge were far stronger and more important than the struggling colleges and hostels of the universities.

As one considers the early history and development of the two ancient and famous universities of England, their rivalry should be kept in mind. Which came first, which served the church and nation best, and why was Oxford later called "Tory" and Cambridge "Whig"? After the Reformation, why did Oxford generally espouse the Anglican Church and Cambridge tend toward Puritanism? There is no one answer, but as the late Professor Frederic Maitland of Cambridge once wryly remarked, "The oldest of all interuniversity sports was a lying match."

There were two nations at Oxford, the *Boreales* or northern students, who came from England north of the River Trent and from Scotland, and the *Australes,* who came from south of the Trent plus any Latins, Welsh or Irish who were enrolled. There was frequent warfare between the sectional groups. Each nation elected two proctors annually, and these enforced the regulations enacted by the congregation of masters and collected the fees.

There were also northern and southern groups or nations at Cambridge, which elected rectors instead of proctors, but they were never as strong or as well organized as those at the rival university. At both institutions the office of chancellor, under strong leaders and far removed from the bishop, gradually came to represent the corporate university with its affiliated colleges.

Colleges or foundations existed at both universities from their early history. Up until 1500, they were primarily for graduate students, the undergraduates living in halls and hostels about the town. Cambridge has Peterhouse (1284), University Hall—later

Clare College (1326), Pembroke (1347), Gonville—later Gonville and Caius (1326), Trinity Hall (1350), Corpus Christi (1352), King's (1441), Queen's (1448), St. Catherine's (1473), Jesus (1496), Christ's (1505), St. John's (1511), Magdalene (1542), Trinity (1546), Emmanuel (1584), and Sidney Sussex (1596). Subsequently, additional colleges were founded for men, and in the late nineteenth century colleges were established for women.

The older colleges at Oxford are University (1249), Balliol (1263), Merton (1264), Exeter (1314), Oriel (1326), Queen's (1340), New College (1379), Lincoln (1427), All Souls (1437), Magdalen (1458), Brasenose (1509), Corpus Christi (1517), Christ Church (1525), Trinity (1554), St. John's (1555), Jesus (1571), Wadham (1610), and Pembroke (1624). There are more recent foundations for men, and several in the late nineteenth and twentieth centuries for women.

The founding dates of English colleges, like their successors in the United States, do not always tell the entire story. By tradition University and Balliol are older than Merton; but the claim of the latter, despite whatever hostels, halls or embryonic colleges existed earlier, merits special attention. Walter de Merton, Chancellor of England and subsequently Bishop of Rochester, drew up in the 1260's statutes for a corporate body that became Merton College. This provided the model for all Oxford and Cambridge colleges and, by derivation, for all the liberal arts colleges in the modern world.

Since its establishment, Oxford has had many distinguished alumni and teachers. Among them, for the most part before American independence, were Robert Grosseteste, Roger Bacon, Duns Scotus, William of Ockham, John Wycliffe, Thomas Wolsey, Archbishop Laud, Thomas Hobbes, John Locke, John Wesley and William Blackstone. Some of the influential men of Cambridge were Robert Barnes, William Tyndale, Ralph Cudworth, Archbishop Cranmer, Francis Bacon, Edward Coke, William Harvey,

John Milton, Samuel Pepys, Isaac Newton, Thomas B. Macaulay, Alfred Tennyson, W. M. Thackeray and John Harvard.

Two of the above graduates, John Harvard (1607–1638) and John Wesley (1703–1791), were very influential in the development of American education. Harvard was a graduate of Emmanuel College, a foundation established in 1584 by Sir Walter Mildmay, Chancellor of the Exchequer under Queen Elizabeth I. Its chapel was designed by Christopher Wren and contains a memorial to Harvard. John Wesley, famous as the founder of Methodism in the eighteenth century, was a graduate of Lincoln College, Oxford. It was founded in 1427 by Richard Fleming, Bishop of Lincoln, and was intended to be a center for students of theology.

Both Oxford and Cambridge benefited from the New Learning of Erasmus, Dean Colet, Thomas Linacre and Thomas More. By their time scholasticism was in decline, but their leadership hastened its death by a royal injunction in 1535. Undoubtedly both universities would like to claim William Shakespeare (1564–1616), probably the best known of all Englishmen, but there is no evidence that he attended college. It would be impossible to say what higher education, the United States and the world owe to the men of intellect and letters of Oxford and Cambridge. Certainly, there is a continuing fellowship in the field of learning.

Until about the fifteenth century, the colleges at Oxford and Cambridge had no buildings of their own but rented lecture rooms in halls and churches. The principal teachers before the Reformation were members of various monastic orders—Benedictines, Franciscans and Dominicans. Colleges of each center of learning were independent self-governing bodies with their own property and income. They were and are distinct from the sheltering universities but also parts of them. Both institutions over the years became famous for their beautiful buildings, quadrangles and library collections.

The universities suffered during the Reformation, particularly from the dissolution of the monasteries. A law of 1553 required all students seeking degrees to subscribe to the Anglican Articles of Religion, and these tests were not abolished until 1871. Oxford and Cambridge were reincorporated under Queen Elizabeth I by an act of Parliament in 1571. Under the new statutes all students had to be members of colleges, and the government of each university was largely in the hands of the several colleges.

Both institutions lost enrollment during the Civil War. Oxford was the headquarters of the king, and Cambridge was occupied by the Parliamentary Army. A contemporary student, probably of the occupied Christ Church at Oxford, wrote: "I did attend the armed troops of Mars, instead of books I Sword, Horse, Pistols bought, and on the field I for degrees then fought."

From early times there was intermittent warfare between students and townsmen at both schools. At Oxford on St. Scholastica's Day, February 10, 1354, hostile camps engaged in battle, and so many were killed—some sixty scholars—that 1354 became known as the Year of the Great Slaughter. At Cambridge in 1381, a mob broke into a college and "took all their charters, evidences, privileges, and plate to the value of four score pounds." Crowds threatened the chancellor with fire and sword and burned the university's charters in the marketplace. Both institutions early gained special controls over the towns, and although these were often challenged, they were not surrendered until late in the nineteenth century.

Forbidden to engage in athletics, the students often fought among themselves. All too often they spent their energies in "profanity, tippling, and venery; taverns and brothels throve on their patronage." Flogging was introduced into the universities in the fourteenth century, but this did not abate all problems.

Many of the students were subsidized fellows or scholars; a goodly number were from noble or wealthy families, but many were poor. It was after the Tudor period that social prestige and wealth came to be associated with the universities. University officials attempted to control rents and the high cost of food. For those living in the halls with wooden shutters instead of glass windows, life was dull and difficult. Students often lacked proper clothing and fuel for winter weather, and it was the exceptional clerk who owned his own candle. Tea, coffee and tobacco were unknown in that era.

The curricula of the English universities followed those of Paris. Law, however, was studied at the Inns of Court in London. Classes began at dawn and continued until evening. Instruction was provided by lectures and debates. There were occasional plays in churches and theaters; but according to an early statute, if students attended them they should "observe propriety and stay only a short while." Comedies were not acted by students in their halls and colleges until the latter part of the fifteenth century. The model student, like Chaucer's Clerk of Oxenford, spent his days studying in the college and the libraries and "amused himself little or not at all."

After the expulsion of John Wycliffe (1324–1384) from Oxford for heresy, academic freedom was rigorously curtailed by the church. Cambridge profited from Oxford's troubles and the revolt of the Lollards. Conservatives sent their sons to the younger university, and by the end of the fifteenth century the enrollment of the rivals was about equal.

Three universities were founded in Scotland in the fifteenth century. St. Andrews was established by Bishop Henry Wardlaw in 1412 and confirmed by Pope Benedict XIII of Avignon the following year. It was partially a product of the Great Schism and was based on the Bologna system. This institution was located in an ancient Celtic center, later famed for golf as well as learning. John Knox (1505–1572) was active there in the stormy days of the university.

The University of Glasgow owes its origin to Bishop William Turnbull, who obtained a papal bull from Pope Nicholas V in 1450 for a *studium generale*. It also followed the Bologna pattern and it received some municipal support. The student of history will associate the names of Adam Smith, James Watt, James Boswell and Lord Kelvin with this northern institution.

"The *Academical Habits* of the several *Degrees* and *Offices* in the University of *Cambridge 1748*"

A graduate of Glasgow, William Elphinstone (1431–1514) founded the third Scottish university at Aberdeen, long noted for its scholarship, Gothic architecture and the red gowns of its students. Elphinstone became Bishop of Aberdeen, and in 1494 he obtained approval from Pope Alexander VI for the establishment of the University of Aberdeen. At the time, a Scottish law required all barons and freeholders to send their sons to school until they had mastered Latin and then to a university for three years. The law was largely a dead letter, but it indicated an appreciation of education.

The University of Edinburgh was founded in 1583 under the authority of a royal charter. It was sponsored by the Town

Council, and its college of theology became well known to Presbyterians in America. Edinburgh was one of the first coeducational universities in Great Britain.

The Scottish universities long suffered for want of endowments. In curricula, instruction and dress they followed the medieval system. Here, as in Germany, however, there was a gradual fusion of college and university systems. The first degree in the Scottish universities is the three-year M.A. The Reformation changed religious policies but the conservative, classical outlook generally prevailed. Even today the universities of Scotland regard themselves as the best training ground for the ministry, medicine and law. Once every third year the undergraduate nations elect rectors.

The University of Dublin, better known as Trinity College, was established by royal charter in 1591. It was sponsored by Oxford and Cambridge men living in Ireland. This institution has many famous alumni, including Jonathan Swift, Oliver Goldsmith, and Edmund Burke, and along with those in Scotland its influence was felt in America. Although the Republic of Ireland is now independent, this college belongs in our outline of early British universities.

If a medieval student could rise from the dead and talk with a present-day student, he would have considerable difficulty, aside from language, in making himself understood. The former would know virtually everything about his narrow curriculum, and the modern one who had majored in this and minored in that and specialized in the other would probably disclaim responsibility for matters beyond his course. It is doubtful if the "integrated" surveys of history, culture and philosophy, and the new experiments with curricula would solve the problem. The modern student is better informed than his scholastic brother, but he would have to confess that he had only touched the edge of the circle of liberal scholarship. The student of old had the scholastic mill but not the grain; the modern student has an abundant harvest of expanding knowledge but is he as well equipped to grind it fine? All this is to ask, when is a person or an age modern and which philosophy of education is best?

Whatever the course of study or method, students must take examinations and receive degrees. During the general period under consideration, these, with few variations, followed the pattern of Bologna and Paris. The degrees were bachelor, master or doctor, there being no Ph.D. in the modern sense; and the gowns, *chaperons* or hoods, and *biretta* or caps were appropriate thereto. Colors were gradually adopted for the professional disciplines, and the inception or commencement contained many features used today.

The academic dress of the masters or doctors, as distinguished from gowns usually worn by clerks and others, is specified early in the history of Oxford. Ordinances were passed prescribing proper attire and to prohibit showy secular garb such as puffed sleeves, ostentatious fur, and shoes and hose in colors other than black. Furthermore, the shoes were not to be pointed or embroidered.

Bachelors generally wore the sleeved *cappa* or gown and a hood, the latter of rabbit fur or wool. The distinctive item of dress for masters was the black sleeveless *cappa,* reaching to the heels with a border and miniver hood of white fur. The white tie and collar generally prevailed for clerks. The chancellor and other dignitaries wore special robes of office ranging in color from black to scarlet, or the costumes appropriate to their degrees. The *biretta* in time came to be replaced by a square cap with a tuft or tassel, and the *pileum* or round cap was worn by regent masters. The round velvet bonnet frequently seen today belongs to a later period. In 1564, a poem entitled "The Ballad of the Caps" was published, which humorously referred to the varieties: "Any cap, whate'er it bee,/ Is still the sign of some degree."

The Chancellor's Book at Oxford contains a regent's ordinance of 1358 on gowns. It decreed that "a tailor when he cuts and measures the material . . . shall dispose and measure the fabric in such a way as to give the masters and beadles their robes not as short and reduced garments but as full length robes as they were wont to wear in times past." The penalty for violating the ordinance was punishment in prison. About a century later, in deference to the weather, it was decreed that silk hoods could be used instead of fur ones from Easter to All Saints' Day. Tailors making caps for the sons of noblemen often attached gold tassels to add distinction.

Robert de Eglesfield, patron of Queen's College, Oxford, gave directions to the fellows on their livery. Doctors were to wear purple cloaks with fur trim, and the M.A.'s were directed to dress in unadorned cloaks of color "to suit the dignity of their position and to be like the blood of the Lord." Some of the Cambridge colleges still prescribe gowns of special cut for their under-graduates. At Oxford in former times, candidates for the M.A. degree had to swear that they owned dress appropriate for this degree and that they would wear it on proper occasions.

Oxford was also strict in specifying material and the proper color for the hoods of each faculty. This is happily commemorated at Queen's College in a custom dating from its foundation in 1340. On January first at the Gaudy dinner, each guest is given a needle with silk thread of the color of his faculty and is requested to take the symbols and be thrifty. The mending of gown and hood was often the lot of those who lacked pence to pay the tailor.

From almost the beginning of the university, the chancellor of Oxford wore a long loose *supertunica*. The gold-brocaded, black robe often pictured was a development of the Elizabethan period. The chancellor of Cambridge wore the dress of his degree until the early seventeenth century, when a gown similar to that worn by the Lord Chancellor was adopted. This was a black-brocaded, wing-sleeved robe with gold braid and a train. The vice-chancellors usually wore the dress of their degrees. The round velvet bonnet for secular doctors appeared during the sixteenth century. In the seventeenth century, doctors of divinity wore boots and the masters wore loose breeches and shoes. At this time the inceptors wore boots if in divinity and shoes if in other disciplines. In 1588, it was decreed that all bachelors of civil law should give gloves to the vice-chancellor on their presentation, and this custom continued all the late seventeenth century.

Following the Civil War, dress in the British universities was both lax and confusing. Many wore dress who did not have the right; apparently, they wanted to be accepted as gentlemen commoners. As noted earlier, noblemen were accorded special privileges and this included their academic costumes. Special dress was ordered for the servitors, but this rule was increasingly difficult to enforce. In 1770, commoners at Oxford were ordered to wear square cloth caps with silk tassels.

There were wide variations of academic dress at the Scottish universities and at Trinity College, Dublin. St. Andrews tended to follow Paris, the M.A. gown being of full black cloth lined with red silk. Glasgow looked to Bologna, and its M.A. costume was black silk lined with heather red silk. At Aberdeen the faculties of canon law and medicine generally adopted the costumes and colors of Paris, but the faculty of civil law followed Orléans. The M.A. gown was of black silk lined with white silk. Edinburgh at first had no gowns, but later red ones were authorized for the undergraduates. The principals of this civic university generally wore Geneva gowns. The M.A. gown was of simple design, black silk lined with white silk. The vice chancellor of Trinity and most of the professors followed the lead of Cambridge. The B.A. gown was of black silk edged with white fur.

During the sixteenth century, and possibly earlier at British universities and at some institutions on the continent, it was customary for the faculty to name two opponents on the occasion of a doctor's disputation. Sometimes a candidate could select a friend to serve as an opponent, and in time this person became a jester who was expected to relieve the seriousness of the occasion. At Oxford the third opponent was called a "Terrae Filius" or "Merry Andrew," and at Cambridge he was known as the "Tripos Jester" or "Bachelor of the Stoole." In time their ridiculous and often insulting speeches tended to lessen the dignity and importance of the public examination, and the custom of the third opponent or jester was abolished in the eighteenth century.

At Oxford, and the same is generally true for Cambridge, the wearing of prescribed academic dress is compulsory at formal ceremonies, at lectures, examinations, and generally when in the presence of university officials. Mortarboards are worn with full dress by men when outside, and soft caps without tassels are worn at all times by women. At Oxford, the university marshal wears a black gown with silver badge and a soft black bonnet. He carries a silver-mounted, ebony staff. The beadles wear plain black gowns and soft black bonnets. They carry staves or maces and assist the chancellor and vice-chancellor on formal occasions. The university verger wears a black gown with black bonnet. He assists with all formal ceremonies and carries a silver staff in academic processions.

Over the years encaenia or commencement at Oxford provided much of the same kind of excitement that thousands know in our twentieth century. On the appointed morning the bell of St. Mary's Church rang from nine until ten, and the parties assembled in their robes and regalia for the march to the Sheldonian Theater. Once assembled and with the preliminaries finished, the registrar announced that the candidates had been duly approved by their colleges and by him. Each candidate swore "to observe the statutes, privileges, customs and liberties" of the university, and they then advanced toward the vice-chancellor, who was seated on a raised dais and attended by two proctors. The candidates stepped forward individually and knelt with palms pressed together as supplicants. The vice-chancellor pressed the candidate's hands between his and spoke the words conferring the degree.

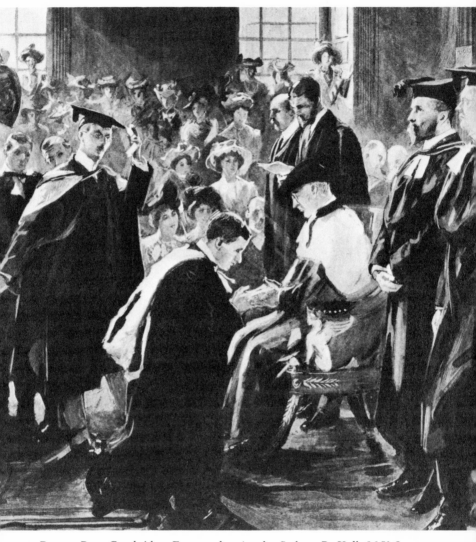

Degree Day, Cambridge. From a drawing by Sydney P. Hall, M.V.O.
COURTESY NEW YORK PUBLIC LIBRARY.

Today's graduation ritual has many features of former years but the entire process has been accelerated. The ceremony is applied to groups rather than to individuals. By 1900, Bologna and Padua used the ring; Scandinavian universities used the ring and a crown of laurel, and the universities of Scotland used the cap. The words of conferral were similar, generally in Latin. Some of the older Catholic universities such as Rome, Coimbra, Granada, and Louvain adhere more strictly to ancient traditions going back nine hundred years to Bologna.

Time has brought many changes to British universities, but their system of academic dress is not as simple or logical as the one generally followed in the United States. For the B.A. degree, Oxford and Cambridge use black silk gowns. The M.A. hoods differ; Oxford has crimson silk lining and Cambridge uses white. Doctors of Divinity at Oxford wear square caps and full scarlet robes with black velvet facings and sleeves. Doctors of music wear velvet bonnets with robes of cream silk, the sleeves and facings being of pink silk. Aberdeen and St. Andrews use purple hoods lined with white silk for the divinity degree. The D.D. at Edinburgh is different from the others mentioned in that it calls for a hood of black cloth lined with purple silk.

There is even greater confusion because some British institutions use the same hood for different degrees. At Oxford, a scarlet cloth with a crimson silk lining is used for the doctor of medicine and doctor of civil law degrees. At Cambridge the hood of scarlet cloth with lining of pink silk may represent the doctor of medicine, doctor of divinity or the doctor of laws degrees. The caps for the M.D. and D.C.L. full dress are black velvet bonnets, but square caps are worn with convocation dress. Equal confusion exists with other degrees, and one must have rather intimate knowledge to determine the subject field and institution represented.

Occasionally laxity prevailed in connection with persons seeking degrees. Complaints were not always substantiated, but from time to time universities took measures to check on examiners and students. Noble and wealthy persons generally enjoyed special privileges in the Middle Ages, and this included the "pass degrees." The *ius natalium,* which excused a year's residence and the general examination for the sons of nobles, was not abolished at Cambridge until 1884.

The Ph.D. degree was offered in Scotland and on the continent as a cultural, nonprofessional degree during the nineteenth century, but it was not conferred at Oxford and Cambridge until after World War I. It became popular with those planning to enter the teaching profession, particularly in the United States.

The universities of the medieval and early modern period were centers of liberal learning, and they trained the professional classes. They were the custodians of knowledge and the clearinghouses of ideas. They made many mistakes. They were dogmatic, disputatious and lacking in experimental methods. In defense it would be argued that they had to contend with war, ignorance, astrology and quackery as well as with theology.

The medieval and early modern period was the age of the inquisition and of witchcraft. Even the best minds were convinced of the importance of magic, alchemy and astrology. Granted that these led to the advancement of science, the methods were faulty and had to be corrected and many mischievous results had to be overturned. The age had queer notions of the shape of the earth, and it was more concerned with the power of God than with the nature of the universe. Facts were usually selected and interpreted according to theological systems rather than empirically. Notwithstanding the blind spots and mistakes of princes, clerics and scholars, it gave us continuity and made clear that learning, teaching and research are really one.

The universities of medieval Europe and Great Britain, which have been described in summary fashion, were great human institutions. They were bulwarks in man's quest for freedom and a better, nobler life. In a world dominated by force, they became instruments of persuasion. All too often they failed, but they kept on trying. Considering the nature of men and the times, they served church and state well. Most of all they gave us an opportunity to avoid their mistakes and to build on their wisdom. University men were among the first settlers in New England, and, as will be seen, the new environment and new times brought many changes while retaining much of a great heritage.

CHAPTER V

❦

Higher Education in Colonial America

FROM THE FOUNDING of Harvard College at New Towne, Massachusetts, in 1636, to 1776, when the constitution of North Carolina provided for a state university, higher education in the colonies was the monopoly of church groups. This was in keeping with British tradition, and the majority of the early graduates entered the ministry. Colonial leaders deemed it unnecessary to spend limited public funds in competition with flourishing church colleges. During the Revolutionary Era the climate began to change but for one hundred and fifty years religion and education were inseparable.

Great credit is due the church and the liberal arts colleges for the rise and development of the United States. As the early settlers moved westward they established houses of worship, schools and colleges. By 1776, there were nine colleges along the Atlantic seaboard; within seventy-five years after the signing of the Declaration of Independence, Methodists had established California Wesleyan University, which became the University of the

Pacific. Two years later, in 1853, Presbyterians and Congregationalists founded Contra Costa Academy, which is today the University of California at Berkeley.

The prototype of today's liberal arts college closely resembled the individual colleges of Oxford and Cambridge. Colonial institutions in the order of their founding were: Harvard College (1636), William and Mary College (1693), Yale College (1701), College of New Jersey (Princeton) (1746), King's College (Columbia) (1754), College of Philadelphia (Pennsylvania) (1755), Rhode Island College (Brown) (1764), Queen's College (Rutgers) (1766), and Dartmouth College (1769).

These institutions were far more than theological seminaries, and generally there was no practice of excluding persons who were not members of the denomination controlling the college. The curriculum was designed for professional men (theological students being most numerous), and it included Greek, Latin, Hebrew, logic, rhetoric, history and mathematics. There was little or no training in the applied sciences, modern social studies or modern languages. In fact, the studies failed to represent adequately knowledge that the world possessed by the middle of the seventeenth century. Most of the early colleges offered preparatory courses, but there were no "pass degrees" for gentlemen.

The presidents of the early colleges were clergymen and most of the professors were ordained ministers. Initially some presidents taught every subject listed in the catalogue and preached every Sunday. Caps and gowns were not in general use, but scholars were careful of their dress. Even in a fluid society college men were generally set apart, and the atmosphere of the classroom and campus was far more authoritarian and formal than today. Life for most was hard, and the Puritan outlook generally prevailed in theory if not always in fact.

Within sixteen years after the Pilgrim Fathers landed at Plymouth, the Great and General Court of Massachusetts Bay passed on October 28, 1636, an act for the establishment of a "Colledge or Schoale" to be opened in New Towne, shortly thereafter named Cambridge. The purpose of the institution was "to advance Learning and perpetuate it to posterity. . . ." The initial appropriation for the project was £400. The founding of a college so soon after settlement was a truly remarkable accomplishment.

Although Harvard was the first college in what became the United States, it was preceded by institutions in Hispanic America and French Canada. In 1551, the Emperor Charles V established the National University of San Marcos in Lima, Peru, and the National Autonomous University of Mexico by royal decrees; both were later confirmed by papal bulls. In 1635, priests of Quebec founded the Collège des Jesuites, one of the predecessors of Laval University (1852).

The early demand for higher education in Massachusetts is more readily understood when it is recalled that the early population of the bay area included some seventy graduates of Cambridge and thirty from Oxford. Among the former was the Reverend John Harvard, M.A., of Emmanuel College. This young man was greatly interested in the new educational venture, but he had the misfortune to die on September 14, 1638, a year after his arrival in Massachusetts. By will he left his library of 320 volumes and half of his estate, totaling some £380, to the new college. In recognition of these liberal gifts the General Court, on March 13, 1639, voted that "the Colledge agreed upon formerly to bee built at Cambridge shal bee called Harvard Colledge." In 1650, a charter was granted by the General Court of the Massachusetts Bay Colony for the college which is still in effect, the institution previously being administered by the General Court. Massachusetts at that time was a theocracy.

Harvard was essential for New England, being far more than a bit of the old country in America. The Puritans were a people with a mission. They intended to set the world straight, and if they could not do this in England, they were determined to make the new world safe from the evils of the old. This required zeal and a lettered people with pure religion. The quest for the ideal,

"The First Lecture"

even in a frontier environment, was stormy, but it was pushed against the flesh and the Devil, including witchcraft, with considerable success.

Nathaniel Eaton (1609–1674) was the first master of the new college, and his wife provided room and board for three or four students. Numerous complaints of beatings and poor food forced the resignation of the Eatons before the end of the second year and the college closed. It was reopened in the fall of 1640 under the Reverend Henry Dunster, president and sole member of the faculty. Dunster, a thirty-three-year-old graduate of Cambridge, organized a sound program and the college prospered, but when he refused to allow his youngest child to be baptized he found that the religious tolerance granted to students did not apply to the president. He resigned in 1654 and was succeeded by another Cambridge graduate, Charles Chauncy.

During most of its first century, Harvard's teaching staff consisted of the president and three to five tutors. It was customary for the tutors in turn to take charge of a freshman class and

"The Arrival of the Puritan Profs"

conduct it through all subjects for four years. The curriculum closely followed that of Cambridge and it was the same for all students. The time required for the B.A. degree was soon increased from three to four years. After taking the first degree a student could follow his profession for three years and then submit a thesis for the M.A. degree. The first professional school, medicine, dates from 1782, but the Ph.D. was not offered until the late nineteenth century.

Some of the early rules at Harvard and other schools required students to read the Holy Scriptures daily, attend church with regularity, avoid profane language, and have manners befitting

" '1769' Declares for Homespun and Free Trade"

gentlemen. Fines were levied for lying, tumultuous noises, skating, firing a gun or pistol in buildings or on the campus, and numerous other offenses. Attendance at chapel was compulsory, and the use of tobacco and strong drink was generally forbidden. A great deal of faculty time was consumed with hearing and disposing of cases of discipline.

"The College Toga"

The records of most colonial colleges are strangely silent on the matter of dress. Clothing was homemade and limited in variety, and students and tutors made do with what they had. That some type of gown was worn at Harvard daily rather than as commencement dress appears from the following regulation of 1655: "No Scholler shall goe out of his Chamber without Coate, Gowne or Cloake, and every one, every where shall weare modest and

"*Ye Faculty Vetoes ye Smokinge*"

sober habit. . . ." Regulations also applied to the length of one's hair, but styles varied, barbers were scarce and the authorities usually acquiesced in nonenforcement.

Harvard gradually escaped from Congregational control, but throughout the eighteenth century the college required that each professor be a Protestant Christian. After 1760, Anglican students could attend Christ Church instead of the Congregational Meetinghouse. Enrollments were never large, the graduating class of 1776 numbering forty. About half of the graduates entered the ministry during the college's first century. In 1851, the legislature repealed the requirement for the election of ministers to the Board of Overseers.

The role of Harvard in the building of the nation is well known. Distinguished alumni during the Revolutionary Era included John Adams, Samuel Adams, John Hancock, James Otis, Josiah Quincy, James Bowdoin and Increase Sumner. Many Harvard men served the American cause with distinction, and when Boston was occupied by British troops the Massachusetts House of Representatives met in the Harvard Chapel. The sentiment of most of the students is indicated by the fact that the senior class of 1768 voted to wear gowns made of American cloth at commencement.

Indian troubles and political and economic upheavals retarded the development of higher education in Virginia. As early as 1619 large sums were collected by the Church of England to establish a college at Henrico, near the present site of Richmond, for the

Indians. George Thorpe was sent to the colony as "Superintendent," but he and some three hundred other settlers were massacred
by the Indians in 1622. Bacon's Rebellion and Civil War in
England retarded plans but the idea did not die. In 1693, through
the efforts of the Reverend Dr. James Blair, a native of Scotland,
King William and Queen Mary granted a charter for the establishment of a college to be located near Yorktown. The purpose of
this institution, named William and Mary College in honor of
their majesties, was to assure ". . . that the Church of Virginia
may be furnished with a seminary of ministers of the Gospel, and
that the youth may be piously educated in good letters and manners, and that the Christian faith may be propagated amongst the
Western Indians to the glory of Almighty God." The officers and
professors of the college were required to be Anglicans.

A unique feature of this royal charter called for the election
of a chancellor every seven years. The Bishops of London, with
one exception, held the more or less honorary title until George
Washington was elected chancellor in 1788. The charter also gave
the college 20,000 acres of land and the proceeds of a tax on
tobacco. It is the only American college to have a coat of arms
from the College of Heralds in London. The father of the college,
James Blair, served as president for fifty years.

The College of William and Mary at Williamsburg, now a state
institution, has provided the nation with many eminent graduates.
Among these were Thomas Jefferson, James Monroe, George
Wythe, Peyton Randolph and John Marshall. The original college
building, now restored, was designed by Sir Christopher Wren,
and it is the oldest college hall in the United States. The Phi Beta
Kappa scholastic society was organized in Williamsburg on De-
cember 5, 1776.

William and Mary trained many able ministers and it had a
preparatory Department for Indians. It also pioneered in the study
of common law. William Blackstone (1723–1780) lectured on
this subject at Oxford in the 1750's, and he rescued the common
law from Norman French and Latin in his famous *Commentaries*.

In 1779, Thomas Jefferson, then governor of Virginia, named the venerable George Wythe, a judge in the Court of Chancery, professor of law at William and Mary. This was the first common-law professorship in America and the second in the world after the Vinerian Chair at Oxford. One of Wythe's first students was John Marshall, later Chief Justice of the United States.

College life in Virginia reflected classical education in that students were required to compose verses in Latin, but Cavalier influences stood in contrast to Puritan rules. One regulation forbade the sale of wine or spirituous liquors to be consumed at any time or place other than at ordinary meals, but another proviso made sure that this would be adequate by stating that "No liquor shall be furnished or used at table except beer, cider, toddy, or spirits and water."

At various times during the Revolution, the buildings of William and Mary were occupied by British, French and American troops, and the college was forced to close for the duration of the war. Although the enrollment was generally less than a hundred and opinions were divided, there was no lack of patriotism; three professors and thirty students joined the American cause when independence from Britain was declared.

Yale College, originally chartered as the Collegiate School, was founded at Branford in 1701 by ten Connecticut clergymen. The idea of a college originated with an Oxford alumnus, the Reverend John Davenport. For a few years it was located in Saybrook, but in 1716 it was moved to New Haven and in 1718, it became known as Yale College in honor of Elihu Yale (1648–1721), an English East India merchant and generous benefactor. In 1745, a new charter legalized the name Yale College, and this was used for the entire institution until it became Yale University in 1887.

It is reputed that the Reverend Cotton Mather of Harvard was ill-humored with the Cambridge institution for its failure to support sound religious principles and that he urged Mr. Yale to make a substantial gift to the college in Connecticut. Apparently the

Yale College, 1830.

determining factor was Mather's unauthorized statement that it would "wear the name of Yale College."

The act of the General Court authorizing the new college called for an institution wherein "youth may be instructed in the Arts and Sciences who through the blessing of Almighty God may be fitted for Publick employment both in Church & Civil State." The classical curriculum of the era was adopted, and the Bachelor of Arts degree was first conferred in 1703. Protestant clerical attire prevailed over academic dress. The college prospered and soon attracted students from the South and West.

The first rector or president of Yale was a graduate of Harvard, and he and some eleven successors until 1899 were ministers of the Congregational Church. The college received gifts of money and books from religious groups in England and occasional support from the Connecticut Legislature, including proceeds from a tax on rum. To avoid lapses of faith, such as occurred with President Timothy Cutler, who embraced the Church of England, the trustees required all officers to give "satisfaction of the soundness of their faith." In 1748, all professors and students at Yale had to subscribe to the Westminster Confession of Faith.

Student life at the college reflected theocratic control. Morning prayer was held at six o'clock. Evening prayer followed dinner, and all were supposed to be in bed by "nine of ye clock." Students were not permitted to enter taverns or inns unless accompanied by their parents. Organized sports were unknown, and minds were occupied by the requirement of turning English into Greek and translating parts of the Bible from Latin or English into Greek. When about the campus or town, students removed their hats when passing or in the presence of college officials or tutors. Fines were collected from those who were tardy, absent from church or caught with cards or dice.

Stern discipline produced able and stern men. Among those attending Yale during the colonial period were Jonathan Edwards, Eleazar Wheelock, Eli Whitney, Noah Webster, Timothy Dwight, Ezra Stiles, who served as president of his *alma mater,* and a large number of men who served as presidents of new colleges established shortly after the Revolution. One of the best known sons of Yale was the schoolteacher Nathan Hale. While serving the American cause as an intelligence agent, he was captured and hanged by the British. His final words, "I only regret that I have but one life to lose for my country," challenge us today.

Six colleges were established during the three decades preceding the Revolution. This reflects population growth and increased activity on the part of church groups. The College of New Jersey, subsequently Princeton, was organized in 1746 by Scottish Presbyterians as a result of the religious revival later known as the "Great Awakening."

The New Lights or revivalists were unpopular at Harvard and Yale, but they won thousands of converts and found it necessary to establish a college to educate ministers and others to be "ornaments of the State as well as the Church." The Awakening deplored the religion of faith and form of the cities and of the established colleges. It spoke for people, generally rural, who had experienced earth-shaking, soul-shattering religious experiences.

The College of New Jersey was first located in Elizabeth. Instruction was started in 1746, and the first bachelor's degree was conferred a year later. The college was subsequently moved to Newark and finally located in Princeton in 1756. It was popularly known as Nassau Hall in the early days and the present name of Princeton University was not adopted until 1896. The college was firmly under control of the Presbyterians and they were predominant in the student body, but it should be noted that the original charter provided that there should be "free and equal liberty and advantage of education" for all, notwithstanding different sentiments on religion.

Early leaders in the history of Princeton were the Reverend Jonathan Dickinson, a Yale graduate who was the first president; the Reverend Aaron Burr, father of the Aaron Burr who was later associated with Thomas Jefferson and Alexander Hamilton; the Reverend William Tennant, a graduate of the University of Edinburgh who was an able fund raiser; and the Reverend Dr. John Witherspoon, who became president in 1768, advanced the college, became a signer of the Declaration of Independence, and helped to effect a reunion of the Old Light and New Light Presbyterians.

Princeton concentrated on the liberal arts. Graduate and professional programs were not available until after the Civil War. The pomp and circumstance of public occasions were moderated by Calvinistic simplicity. Student life closely paralleled that at Harvard and Yale. Alumni of the College of New Jersey included James Madison, Henry and Charles Lee of Virginia, Aaron Burr Jr., numerous Presbyterian ministers, six members of the Con-

Princeton College, 1836 (Nassau Hall in center).

tinental Congress and several future college presidents and political leaders.

The fifth colonial college was established in New York in 1754 under a royal charter and named King's College in honor of George II. By an act of the New York Legislature in 1784, the property of the college was vested with the Regents of the University of the State of New York and named Columbia College. In 1787, all property and franchises were vested in the trustees of Columbia College in the City of New York.

The Reverend Dr. Samuel Johnson, a graduate of Yale and a missionary for the Society for the Propagation of the Gospel, was elected as the first president. He and the first class of eight students met in the vestry room of the school adjoining Trinity Church.

The college moved to Park Place in New York in 1760, and it remained there until 1857 when it was relocated on 49th Street between Madison and Park Avenues. In 1897 Columbia moved to its present location in Morningside Heights.

Funds for King's College were obtained from friends in England, members of Trinity Church and by means of a lottery. Equal opportunities were afforded to persons of all faiths; but when the vestry of Trinity Church deeded the land for the college, it provided that the president "should forever be a member of or be in communion with the Church of England. . . ." The curriculum included the liberal arts but also embraced surveying and navigation, geography and history, and commerce and government. The course of study, far more modern than others of the era, was to perfect youth and to "lead them from the study of nature to the knowledge of themselves, and of the God of nature, their duty to Him, themselves and one another."

On June 21, 1758, in St. George's Chapel on Beekman Street, President Johnson conferred the first Bachelor of Arts degrees on seven students. Four honorary degrees were also conferred. The exercises were conducted almost entirely in Latin. Soon thereafter Johnson was succeeded by the Reverend Myles Cooper of Queen's College, Oxford. Cooper came to America with a great reputation, having been recommended by the Archbishop of Canterbury, but he soon became engaged in political controversy. His Tory sentiments reacted against the college and hastened his return to England.

After receiving dire threats, Dr. Cooper is reported to have escaped half-dressed over the college wall on May 10, 1775. He found refuge in the home of a friend and soon slipped aboard a ship bound for England. Needless to say, there was no formal commencement at King's College in 1775. Shortly thereafter the college was occupied by American troops and it was not reopened until 1784. While at King's, President Cooper introduced several Oxford customs, including the wearing of caps and gowns. With the exception of the Revolutionary period Columbia students wore

George Washington brought his stepson John Parke Custis to King's College in 1773. They made the trip from Mount Vernon, Virginia, to New York in about two weeks. COURTESY COLUMBIA UNIVERSITY.

caps and gowns daily while in residence and this practice continued until the Civil War.

Students of King's who later achieved fame were Alexander Hamilton, John Jay, Gouverneur Morris, and William and Robert R. Livingston. George Washington enrolled his stepson, John Parke Custis, in King's College in 1773, after considering a

European education for the lad. The local tutor had convinced Washington that King's was not only an excellent college but that it was situated in New York, "the most polite and fashionable place on the continent."

Following the Revolution, the legislature of New York granted a new charter and the former King's College prospered as Columbia College. The charter provided for a self-perpetuating board of trustees. Although church dominance was ended, several of the presidents were Episcopal clergymen. In 1787, Dr. William S. Johnson, son of the first president, was elected president of Columbia. At his second Commencement on May 6, 1789, in St. Paul's Church, ten seniors appropriately robed delivered orations and received degrees. The event was of national importance because President Washington, Vice-President John Adams and several members of Congress were in attendance.

The College of Philadelphia, later to become the University of Pennsylvania, evolved from the Charity School established in 1740. In 1751, the Philadelphia Academy was organized and it took over the property and students of the Charity School. Benjamin Franklin was president of the trustees of the new academy, and he employed a brilliant young graduate of the University of Aberdeen, the Reverend Dr. William Smith, to assist in converting the academy into a college. Smith had published progressive ideas for a college in his work, *General Idea of the College of Miranda.* These men and their associates, in 1755, obtained a charter for the College and Academy of Philadelphia.

Mention should also be made of the Reverend George Whitefield, minister of the Church of England, and a one-time member of the Oxford Holy Club, which provided leaders for the early Methodist Church. He preached widely throughout the colonies in the eighteenth century and is credited by Franklin as the man responsible for the Charity School, ". . . the beginning of the University of Pennsylvania." A monument honoring Whitefield on the campus of the University of Pennsylvania has bronze tablets affixed with Franklin's tribute.

Although there was little mention of religion in connection with the establishment of the College and Academy, its first sessions were held in a building erected for Whitefield's congregation and three fourths of the trustees, including Franklin, were members of the Church of England. There was no regular financial support by any church group but Anglican influence was dominant until the momentous Day of Independence in Philadelphia.

William Smith headed the new college with the title of provost. In a manner characteristic of hundreds of succeeding American college presidents, he became a solicitor of gifts at home and abroad. He had considerable success in England, receiving donations from King George III, Lady Curzon, Thomas Penn, William Pitt and other notables. While the provost sought funds and students, the resourceful trustees of the college helped meet operating expenses with income from a lottery.

Provost Smith, as was customary for all early college leaders, doubled as minister and professor. Among other subjects, he taught "logick, Rhetorick, Ethicks and Natural Philosophy." The emphasis at the College of Philadelphia, probably due to Franklin's practical outlook and the business needs of the city, veered from the classics and religion to preparation for vocations and various professions. Courses in English and citizenship were encouraged, and instruction was urged for the many rather than the few. Tutors guided the few students assembled in the original buildings at Fourth and Arch Streets. College life was influenced by the environment of a growing political and commercial city. The first commencement was held on May 17, 1757, without benefit of academic costumes, and the degree of Bachelor of Arts was conferred on seven graduates.

The dreams of Dr. Smith and his colleagues for an ideal faculty and curriculum were cut short by troubles leading to the Revolution. Also the provost had the misfortune to become involved in disputes with his former friend and champion, Benjamin Franklin. Following the Revolution, Dr. Smith was ousted by a new board less dominated by Anglicans. He became rector of a parish in Chestertown, Maryland, and the first president of the new Washington College established there in 1782. George Washington served actively on the first Board of Visitors and Governors of this school, the first college named in his honor while he was alive.

In addition to Smith and Franklin, the names of Thomas Penn, colonial proprietor; Benjamin Rush, physician; James Wilson, jurist; Thomas Wharton, governor; David Rittenhouse, astronomer; Thomas Mifflin, governor; John Dickinson, statesman and writer; and Robert Morris, patriot and financier, are associated with the development and early history of the college in Philadelphia. This institution established the first school of medicine in North America in 1765, and it pioneered with a department of botany three years later. Politics, taxes and tempers, however, fanned the patriot cause and war soon replaced education for faculty and students.

The college and academy were closed during much of 1777–1778. First, the Pennsylvania militia was quartered in college halls and later the British used the buildings as a hospital. Also loyalties were divided notwithstanding general support for the American cause. Following 1778, the state took over the college and operated it for a decade. Subsequently it was returned to private trustees and there were changes in the charter and name, with the institution becoming the University of Pennsylvania by Act of the State Assembly in 1791.

Like the College of New Jersey, Rhode Island College was a product of the Great Awakening, but the chief participants were Baptists. Roger Williams, William Coddington, Anne Hutchinson and other dissenters had located in the Providence area in the 1630's, and in 1663, Charles II granted the united settlements a charter that continued as the basic law of the state until 1842.

The Baptists believed in the separation of church and state, and seeing the fruits of Congregationalist, Anglican and Presbyterian colleges, it was natural that they should desire an institution of higher learning that would train ministers and educate youth "properly." A plan to this end was approved by the Baptist Association of Philadelphia in 1762, and steps were taken to locate a college in Rhode Island.

The Colonial Assembly in 1764 issued a charter for Rhode Island College that provided for absolute liberty of conscience and prohibited religious tests. First located in Warren, the college moved to Providence in 1770. Although the college was liberal for its time, the charter stipulated that twenty-two of the twenty-six trustees must be Baptists, and it required that the president should forever be a member of the Baptist Church.

The Reverend James Manning, a graduate of the College of New Jersey and a local school master, was elected president and professor of the college. Funds were raised principally in England, Ireland, South Carolina and Georgia. President Manning considered but resisted the temptation to raise funds through a lottery.

Rhode Island College held its first commencement in 1769 for a graduating class of seven. By 1775 the enrollment had increased

Brown University, 1825.

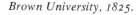

to forty-one. The college was forced to close during the Revolutionary War, the buildings being used as a barracks by American troops and later as a hospital for French soldiers.

Manning continued as president until 1791, and was succeeded by an alumnus of Rhode Island College, the Reverend Jonathan Maxcy. In 1802, Asa Messer of the class of 1790 became president, and it was during his administration that Nicholas Brown, an alumnus and treasurer of the college, made several substantial gifts to his *alma mater*. In 1804 the trustees voted to change the name of Rhode Island College to Brown University. Although the colonial history of Rhode Island College was limited to a dozen difficult years, the college had high standards and set an example of religious freedom. It was a beacon and source of pride for Baptists along the Atlantic coast, and it would be heard from in future years.

Each college developed its own campus and personality, but there were many common features in addition to the curriculum and emphasis on religion. The campus was an unfenced barren plot, generally overrun with livestock. The wood lot and well were centrally located, and the privies and pigpens were essential border features. Students purchased and often chopped their own firewood and all fetched water from the well. Bathing facilities were rare until the nineteenth century, and it was great sport for the students to turn over the privies or burn them.

Aside from "Old Main," most of the buildings were cheaply constructed, and candles were the chief source of light. Library resources were sadly lacking; Harvard possessed some 12,000 volumes by the time of the Revolution, and Yale claimed 2,600 titles. Literary societies were soon to supplement these collections. Travel to and from college was difficult and most students walked or rode horseback. Along with denominationalism, distance was a prime factor in the location of the early colleges.

Queen's College of New Jersey, which later became Rutgers College, Rutgers University and finally Rutgers—The State University, was established by royal charter in 1766. It was named in honor of Charlotte, the queen consort of King George III. The college was sponsored by members of the Dutch Reformed Church and located in New Brunswick.

Instruction at Queen's was begun in the fall of 1771, the classes meeting in the Sign of the Red Lion Tavern. The president and chief tutor was a young graduate of Princeton, Frederick Frelinghuysen. He inserted an advertisement in a New York newspaper inviting parents to send their sons to college in New Brunswick where ". . . the strictest Regard will be paid to their moral conduct . . . and to every Thing which may tend to render them a Pleasure to their Friends and an Ornament to their Species." The classical curriculum of the colonial period was followed at Queen's and the first baccalaureate was awarded in 1774. Some fifty years later the name of the school was changed to Rutgers College in honor of a benefactor Colonel Henry Rutgers.

The charter for Queen's was approved by Governor William Franklin, the Tory son of Benjamin Franklin and a graduate of Oxford. It clearly set forth the desire of the Dutch Reformed Church to establish a college wherein the "learned languages and other branches of useful knowledge may be taught and degrees conferred . . . and especially that young men of suitable abilities may be instructed in divinity."

The college was scarcely opened before unsettled conditions and military conflict forced changes and temporary moves. President Frelinghuysen resigned to study law, and he subsequently became a successful military and political leader. Colonel John Taylor and fellow tutors held the college together, moving to Millstone and to North Branch when the troops threatened New Brunswick. The college also suffered during this period from conservative-liberal disputes within the church.

By the end of the Revolutionary War, Queen's had graduated some thirty students. The first graduate was Matthew Leydt who delivered commencement orations in Dutch, English and Latin. Other students of this select group who later attained eminence were Simeon DeWitt and Jeremiah Smith. The former served as geographer for the American forces during the Revolution, and the latter became governor and chief justice of New Hampshire.

The last of the nine colonial colleges, Dartmouth, was established in Hanover, New Hampshire, in 1769. The charter, later to become famous in the history of higher education, was granted by the Province of New Hampshire by the authority of King George III. The college was an outgrowth of Moor's Indian Charity School founded at Lebanon, Connecticut, by the Reverend Eleazar Wheelock, a graduate of Yale. Financial support in England, contributed in part by Lord Dartmouth, enabled Wheelock to move the school and expand the scope of its work.

The trustees were "God fearing men," and the purposes of the college to Christianize Indians and others were clear, but the charter enforced no church requirements. Unfortunately, the Indians did not thirst for learning, and most of the students were soon colonials. Wheelock was assisted in meeting financial needs by Evangelist George Whitefield and a former Indian student, the Reverend Samson Occom. Gifts in England came from George III, the Countess of Huntingdon and the Marquis of Lothian. General support in New England came from leaders of the Great Awakening who were unable to make sufficient converts at Harvard and Yale.

Off to a good start, Dartmouth faltered with the coming of the Revolutionary War. Gifts from England ceased and attempts to raise money through a lottery failed. Eleazar Wheelock died in 1779, and he was succeeded as president by his son John. The latter was able to strengthen and advance the college after the war, but the contest between Federalists, largely Congregationalists, and Republicans, chiefly Presbyterians, for control led to his removal in 1815. The moves to make Dartmouth a state institution and the litigation ending in the Supreme Court will be discussed later.

Colleges generally commanded respect but not popularity dur-

Dartmouth College, 1850.

ing the formative period of our country. They had to contend with illiterate immigrants and the harsh influences of frontier life. They tended to serve the aristocratic elements of society and often suffered from denominational rivalries and political pressures. There being no common system of preparatory education, students were often poorly prepared; and, as in all periods of istory, there was never enough money. Other weaknesses of the olonial colleges were readily apparent. They were ill equipped and the curriculum was obsolescent when it was introduced from England and Scotland. Most of the students were natives of the colony where the college was located but a few came from other colonies, Europe and the West Indies. Many of the students were immature and the minutiae of regulations required a disportionate amount of time. Religious orthodoxy and discipline often ended in riot and anarchy. Instruction to the mind frequently entered through the seat of the pants, but somehow the system of Latin and Greek, harsh discipline, and public piety worked.

The curriculum, often described as liberal, was vocational. In most of the colleges the education of "learned, pious and orthodox" ministers came first. The emphasis of instruction was on orthodoxy and not on free inquiry. Students were warned against conversations with muses of loose morals and reading heathen writers. An early student of Yale reported that Tully and Vergil were recited as well as Ramus in logic. Continuing, he stated: "We recited the Greek Testament; knew not Homer; received the Psalms in Hebrew." Truly the "discipline and furniture of the mind" were the order of the day.

And yet if colleges are to be judged by their fruits, those in Colonial America were excellent institutions. Or, as is often the case, students later excelled in spite of, rather than because of, exposure to higher education. Without continuing or attempting to resolve this age-old debate, let us consider a few figures and the records of some of the college men who helped to win independence and establish the Federal Republic.

Today, when a small college enrolls 500 to 5,000 students, it is difficult to realize that the nine colonial colleges were very, very small indeed. Often a sizable proportion of the students were enrolled in pre-college classes. In 1775, Harvard graduated 40 students, Yale 35, King's 13, Dartmouth 11, and Pennsylvania 5. These figures are typical for the era and the other four colleges. The academic parades were truly short and the degrees prized possessions of the selected few.

Notwithstanding the fact that six of the nine colonial colleges were less than thirty years old when the Revolution began, seventeen of the fifty-six men signing the Declaration of Independence were graduates of American colleges. Three of the Committee of Five named to draft the Declaration were graduates of colonial colleges. Four of the five members of President Washington's first cabinet had mastered the antiquated curricula of pre-Revolution-

ary American colleges. In all there were some 3,000 living graduates of the nine colleges to help guide and build the new nation.
Only two of the college presidents, Cooper of King's and Smith
of Philadelphia, sided with the Royalist cause. This was an im-
pressive record, one which would inspire and challenge the numerous colleges to be founded in the eighty years between the
Revolution and the Civil War.

CHAPTER VI

❦❧❦

Experiment and Diversity, 1780–1862

THE LEGACY OF the American Revolution brought many changes to higher education. The establishment of new colleges was checked but not for long. The buildings, endowments and enrollments of existing institutions had to be repaired, but most important of all, the colleges were forced to redefine their purposes and adjust to new political and economic conditions.

As a result of the Revolution a man counted for more, and superiors in church and state were of less importance. The ideas of French deism were introduced into the country, students questioned and rebelled against authority, and state legislatures began to concern themselves with higher education. The belief became common that colleges had a new responsibility to a nation that must prove itself in a hostile world, and that young men should be prepared for lives of usefulness and responsible citizenship.

By 1800, seventeen new colleges had been established and twelve more were added by 1820. The number continued to grow as population increased in the north, south and along the western frontier. Some colleges were almost extensions of existing institutions, others were creations of the states, but by far the greatest number grew out of the rivalry of religious denominations. With new goals and new institutions, the curriculum responded, but very slowly. There were experiments in Virginia and Michigan, and the manual training movement had a wide following from New England to Georgia, but the basic liberal arts curriculum was far from liberal. In most places up until the Civil War, it was organized into four divisions: (1) the classics, (2) rhetoric and literature, (3) natural philosophy and mathematics and (4) mental and moral philosophy. Greek and Latin were required during the first three years and were the backbone of the course. Hebrew was generally included for ministerial students. Even after the 1860's students complained of verb forms and recitation by rote.

Yale, Princeton and Harvard were leaders in exporting this pre-Civil War curriculum to new colleges in the West and South. In some seventy-five institutions conferring degrees before 1840, thirty-six presidents came from Yale, twenty-two from Princeton and eight from Harvard. Horace Hadley, a graduate of Yale and president of Transylvania College in Kentucky, kept the basic curriculum but liberalized it through an undogmatic approach and by asking students to examine conflicting religious views. The Reverend Bethel Judd of Yale became president of St. John's College (1784), in Maryland, but his curriculum was quite different from the present pioneering Great Books course of this institution.

Josiah Meigs took the Yale curriculum to Franklin College (University of Georgia) at Athens. With encouragement from Thomas Jefferson, he was able to expand offerings in science. Perhaps the most radical changes in curriculum and college life following the Revolution were at the College of William and Mary, the University of Virginia and Oberlin College. These will receive separate treatment.

In 1828, the famous Yale Report defended the "dead lan-

Old well at the University of North Carolina, Chapel Hill, with Old East.   COURTESY UNIVERSITY OF NORTH CAROLINA PHOTO LAB.

guages," Latin and Greek. The faculty and administration recognized the need for improvement in various areas, but wrote convincingly of the "discipline and furniture of the mind." Inasmuch as Yale provided so many presidents and teachers for the new colleges of the South and West, this report delayed general curriculum reform until after the Civil War.

Following the Revolution the idea of a national university was debated, and it is still revived from time to time, but so far the federal service academies at West Point, Annapolis, New London, Kings Point and Colorado Springs are the closest approach. The need for a national university was discussed in the Constitutional Convention, and President Washington endorsed the idea in his first and last addresses to Congress. In 1961, the George Washington Memorial Foundation was formed to help establish a national university.

From the beginning of the nation, education at all levels has been the primary responsibility of the states and the citizenry. The first constitution of North Carolina, drafted in 1776, provided that "all useful learning shall be duly encouraged and promoted in one or more universities." The University of North Carolina was chartered in 1789, first instruction given in 1795, and the first baccalaureate awarded in 1798. Thus in terms of legal origin, first instruction, first degrees awarded and continuity under the same name, North Carolina is our first state university. It was located at Chapel Hill, and one of the chief founders was William R. Davie, Revolutionary soldier and subsequently governor of the state. From the earliest days the influence of Princeton was strong at this institution. "Old East," the first building to be erected on the campus of a state university in the United States, is still in use.

The University of Georgia at Athens, originally called Franklin College because its first building was named in honor of Benjamin Franklin, was chartered on January 27, 1785, making it the first chartered state university in the United States. Instruction, however, did not get under way until 1801, and the first student was graduated three years later. President Josiah Meigs, who had had trouble with Federalists at Yale because of his Republican sentiments, was forced by political opponents to resign in 1803. After additional buildings were constructed, the institution was called The University of Georgia.

Two other state universities were started before the end of the eighteenth century. The University of Vermont was founded by Ira Allen, brother of Ethan Allen, and chartered in 1791. It later became the land-grant college of the state. The University of Tennessee, originally Blount College, was established in 1794, before the state entered the union. It became a land-grant college in 1869, and the present name was adopted a decade later.

Several colleges claim to be the first west of the Appalachian Mountains, Allegheny Mountains or other mountain ranges. Inasmuch as dates for the establishment of colleges or their predecessor academies vary, and mountain names and boundaries are not clearly defined, it is difficult to present all claims, but the honor clearly belongs to Transylvania College, Lexington, Kentucky. This institution was chartered by the Virginia Legislature in 1780, when Kentucke, as it was then spelled, was a remote county in the western part of Virginia. It was part of Thomas Jefferson's ambitious educational program that he planned while serving as governor. Some of the early institutions with dates generally accepted are: Washington and Jefferson College (1781) originally separate institutions, Dickinson College (1773), Union College (1785), Tusculum College (1794), and the University of Tennessee (1794). Certainly the early minister-educators of the church-sponsored colleges were a pioneering lot, men determined to take learning, culture and religion to the advancing frontier.

When Thomas Jefferson became one of the Visitors of the College of William and Mary in 1779, he brought about fundamental changes. The preparatory school and department of divinity were abolished, and professorships of law and police, anatomy, medicine and chemistry, and modern languages were established. Inasmuch as the number of departments was limited to six, the department of moral philosophy was broadened to include fine arts, and the law of nature and of nations and natural history were added to mathematics and natural philosophy. But of greater importance were provisions abolishing Greek and Latin for entrance, permitting students to elect courses and making the time required for a degree dependent on the student's qualifications. These drastic changes foretold the curriculum of the University of Virginia mentioned in Chapter II, and placed William and Mary almost a century ahead of her sister institutions.

The University of Virginia at Charlottesville was chartered by the General Assembly in 1819, and first instruction at the college level was offered in 1825. As envisaged by Jefferson, it combined practical new subjects with an intellectual orientation of university breadth and depth. The university was divided into eight schools and each had the capacity to expand with the growth of knowledge. Students were free to elect studies in any of the schools, not as freshmen or seniors but as students of a free institution of learning.

At first Virginia gave no degrees, each school issuing its own diploma to students satisfactorily passing examinations. Jefferson had planned schools of commerce, manufacturing and diplomacy, but lack of funds curtailed these projects. The presidents of Harvard, Brown and other colleges visited Charlottesville in quest of ideas, but they were unable to convince their faculties of the need for curriculum reform. The Virginia system avoided compulsion and superficiality, evils that were associated with the classical program of the day and that were to lead to elective systems a half-century later. Virginia was one of the very few liberal colleges in America before 1850, and by the time of the Civil War it was larger than Harvard or Yale.

Beginning with its first name. Catheolepistemiad, the University of Michigan has been different. It was organized in Detroit by the Territorial Legislature in 1817, and moved to Ann Arbor in 1837, as a land-grant type of college on the frontier. Enrolling its first class in 1841, it had little to commend it at its beginning, but within thirty years after statehood it was one of the leading colleges of America.

Much of the credit for the growth and success of the University of Michigan belongs to President Henry P. Tappan. A graduate of Union College in New York, he had traveled in Europe where he came to know and admire the German universities. Upon his arrival in Ann Arbor he set about building the state university on the German model. He abolished dormitories and the age-old custom of *in loco parentis,* and used the buildings for a library, museum, and art gallery. He added departments of physics and civil engineering and inaugurated graduate courses.

Tappan discarded rote recitations from textbooks and introduced the lecture system with library readings. He taught a course in English literature and employed Andrew D. White, afterwards president of Cornell University, to teach history. President Tappan invited students to his home and urged them to browse in his personal library. He scandalized church folk by serving wine and his liberal views gained the ill will of demagogic newspapers. In 1863, he was discharged by the regents as being too "Eastern" and "Prussian" for the West, but he had pointed Michigan to true university status and his name ranks with the nation's great educators.

Most students of American history know that the Northwest Ordinance of 1787 promoted education by declaring: "Religion, morality and knowledge being necessary to good government and the happiness of mankind, schools and the means of education shall forever be encouraged." Not so well known, however, are the land grants from the federal government to the Ohio Company, which led to the establishment of Ohio University at Athens, Ohio, in 1804 and Miami University at Oxford, Ohio, in 1809. These institutions were prototypes of state universities in states thereafter admitted to the Union (excepting Maine, Texas and West Virginia where the United States never owned the public land).

Institutions of higher education sometimes initiate, encourage or retard movements such as the "Awakening" or "Enlightenment." In turn they are initiated or greatly affected by the social, economic and political upheavals of their time. Examples are abundant but one of the best is Oberlin College in Ohio, the product of Jacksonian democracy, religious revivalism and utopian dreams.

Oberlin was established as a collegiate institute in 1833, and it offered instruction at the college level the following year. The leaders primarily responsible for the college in the wilderness were the Reverend Charles G. Finney and the Reverend John J. Shipherd. They raised money in the East, cleared land, and provided for a college wherein the manual labor department would be an integral part of the academic department. Here was a return to the ancient Greek ideal of a sound mind in a strong body.

Along with religious zeal, Oberlin embraced with enthusiasm the various attempts of the era to form a "new and more perfect society." These included health fads, racial equality and equal rights for women. The perfectionism of the faculty and students, spurred by numerous revivals, helps to explain Oberlin's concern with peace, moral reform and the abolition of slavery.

Oberlin was distinguished more for its general philosophy and activities than for curriculum reform. It did not abolish the classics. It was not the first to admit Negro students, but it welcomed them in sizable numbers. Oberlin was coeducational in the preparatory department from the beginning, but in 1837, four young ladies were admitted to the regular college program, and on August 25, 1841, three of them received bachelor's degrees. They were the first women to graduate from a coeducational college. Up to this time colleges and universities were for men, and it was generally understood that women were not interested in higher education and that they did not possess the required mental capacity.

The first college in the world exclusively for women and the first to confer baccalaureate degrees on women graduates was the Georgia Female College of Macon (now Wesleyan College). This institution, sponsored by Methodists, was chartered in 1836, offered college level instruction in 1839, and conferred the first degrees on Catherine Brewer and ten fellow seniors at commencement in July 1840. The "Testimonial" of the college stated in English that "after having passed through a Regular course of study . . . embracing all the Sciences which are usually taught in the Colleges of the United States, with such as appropriately belong to Female Education in its most ample range" they were deemed worthy of the "First Degree" conferred by the institution.

The course of study included natural philosophy, mental and moral philosophy, astronomy, physiology, geology, history and ancient and modern languages. The final examination was oral and public and according to President George F. Pierce, "it made upon the assembled crowd a very decided impression—exhilarating to the friends of the Institution—substituting faith for doubt with those who had been sceptical—and affording to all practicable demonstration that the proposed plan of Education is feasible."

Catherine Brewer was able to qualify for her degree in a year and a half by virtue of the fact that Thomas B. Slade of the Clinton Female Institute brought two of his teachers and thirty students to the new college, and eleven, including Miss Brewer, qualified for advanced junior standing. The Georgia Female College became the Wesleyan Female College in 1843, and the name Wesleyan College was adopted in 1919.

Two other Methodist-related colleges in the South were pioneers in the higher education of women—Athens College at Athens, Alabama, and La Grange College at La Grange, Georgia. The former began as the Athens Female Academy in 1822, and in 1843 it was chartered as the Female Institute of the Tennessee Annual Conference of the Methodist Episcopal Church. It awarded the first baccalaureate in 1846. The La Grange Female Academy, chartered in 1831, became the La Grange Female Institute and it conferred its first degree in 1847.

Although colleges in the frontier states of Georgia and Ohio offered the first degrees in the world for women, most of the states had female seminaries prior to 1860, and some such as North Carolina, Texas, Illinois, Massachusetts, New York and Pennsylvania were well advanced in the education of women. Hillsdale College (1844), then called Michigan Central, was opened to women at the college level after 1850, and Antioch College in Ohio, under the leadership of Horace Mann, admitted coeds in 1853. Beaver College (1853) conferred its first degrees in 1856. Coeducation became fairly general after the Civil War, especially in state institutions. By 1895, colleges for women flourished in all parts of the country, and the new feminine degrees of Mistress of Arts, Maid of Philosophy, Sister of Arts and Laureate of Science gave way to the Bachelor of Arts degree.

In North Carolina, the Salem Female Academy was established by Moravians in 1772. This institution added college courses in 1866, and conferred its first degree in 1890. Queen's College in Charlotte, North Carolina, chartered as Charlotte Female Institute, offered college instruction in 1857 and conferred the B.A. degree the next year.

The first chartered institution for women in the Midwest was Rockford College (1847) in Illinois, originally the Rockford Female Seminary. Instruction at the college level began in 1851, and the first baccalaureate was awarded in 1882. It is often argued that academic requirements were not as high in the South and West as in the East, but this is a contested matter. Certainly, the younger states took the lead in advanced education for women.

Shortly before the Republic of Texas entered the union in 1845 as the state of Texas, the Baptist Educational Society established Baylor University for men. The Female Department of this insti-

Mount Holyoke Female Seminary, 1836, later Mount Holyoke College. From a lithograph by N. Currier. COURTESY MOUNT HOLYOKE COLLEGE.

tution, now Mary Hardin–Baylor College, first offered instruction at the college level in 1851 and conferred its first baccalaureate degree in 1855. These institutions bear the name of Robert E. B. Baylor, a native of Kentucky, who was a minister, congressman from Alabama, and associate justice of the supreme court of the Republic of Texas.

For two hundred years higher education in Massachusetts was exclusively for men, but in 1836, the women of the Bay State began to overturn ancient prejudices. In that year the Mount Holyoke Female Seminary was established at South Hadley and in 1837 it offered college courses. The name was changed to Mount Holyoke Seminary and College in 1888, and the first baccalaureate was awarded in 1889. Mount Holyoke is the oldest continuing institution of higher education for women in the United States.

The State of New York was one of the early centers of the suffrage movement in the United States. Education, temperance, peace and slavery engaged the minds of women as well as men. In 1848, in Seneca Falls, leaders in the campaign for woman's rights issued a ringing declaration of freedom modeled on the Declaration of Independence. The press and platform orators discussed this radical proposal pro and con. In less than a decade a movement was under way for the establishment of the Elmira Female College (1855), and that institution, now Elmira College, conferred its first B.A. degree in 1859. Vassar, Wells and other colleges for women were delayed by the coming of the Civil War.

In Pennsylvania, the Moravian Church established the Bethlehem Female Seminary in 1742. This became the Moravian Seminary and College for Women in 1863, and it awarded its first baccalaureate in 1870. The professional education of women was advanced greatly by the establishment of the Woman's Medical College of Pennsylvania in 1850. This was the first college in the world for the medical education of women, and despite the fact that its students were denied clinical advantages for many years, it achieved great success and continues today as the only medical school in the country exclusively for women. The dramatic expansion of educational opportunities for women will be recounted in a later chapter.

Any discussion of American colleges and universities between the Revolution and the Morrill Act of 1862 must take into account the activities of the various religious groups in establishing academies, seminaries and colleges. It is estimated that between five and six hundred colleges were organized and that about half survived until 1860. Of this number approximately 175 still exist. Financial difficulties, religious disputes and fires took a heavy toll. Many of the surviving institutions are under church patronage or are church-related, some became independent and a few were converted into state institutions. It is beyond the scope of this work to list all of the colleges and trace their history, but selected institutions and general denominational trends will be presented.

Many of the early church colleges began as academies or included preparatory departments. Public education was lacking in most states, and the various denominational groups met local educational needs while proclaiming their own "orthodox" views. Many of the colleges were manual training institutions, and this feature reduced costs and promoted the education of middle-class citizens. College assembly halls doubled as churches and they were centers of cultural and political enlightenment.

Columbian College, now George Washington University, was the first college founded by the Baptists after Independence. It was chartered by Congress in 1821 and located in the nation's capital. Although many Baptists favored humble men called to the ministry of God, many leaders such as Luther Rice and Adoniram Judson saw the necessity of higher education for ministers and others.

Columbian College soon became nondenominational, but before 1860 some ten colleges were founded by or related to the American Baptist Convention. The list of institutions from Maine to

Oregon includes: Bucknell (1846), Colby (1813), Denison (1832), Franklin of Indiana (1834), Kalamazoo (1833), Linfield (1857), Ricker (1847), Stephens (1833), and William Jewell (1848). Hillsdale (1844) and Bates (1855), originally Free Will Baptist, later joined this group. Colgate University (1850) and the University of Rochester (1850), both now nonsectarian, were established by Baptists in this era of experiment and diversity.

Southern Baptist colleges established before the Civil War include: Baylor University (1845), Tift College (1849), Carson–Newman (1851), Furman University (1826), Georgetown, Kentucky (1829), Howard, now Samford (1842), Judson (1838), Mary Hardin–Baylor (1845), Mercer (1833), Mississippi (1826), Union, Tennessee (1834), Richmond (1830), and Wake Forest (1834). Hollins (1845) in Virginia and Limestone (1845) in South Carolina, originally Baptist seminaries for women, are now independent colleges.

The Congregational church may proudly claim a large number of educational institutions. Some of these were established in cooperation with the Presbyterians and other groups. Many of the colleges were founded or assisted by its American Missionary Association. We have discussed Harvard, Yale, Dartmouth, Oberlin, Mount Holyoke, and California. Other institutions founded by or historically related to this church before 1860 are Amherst (1821), Beloit (1846), Berea (1855), Bowdoin (1794), Grinnell (1846), Illinois College (1829), Knox (1837), Marietta (1830), Middlebury (1800), Milwaukee–Downer (1851), Olivet (1845), Pacific (1849), Ripon (1851), Rockford (1847), Western Reserve (1826), Whitman (1859), and Williams (1793).

The Disciples of Christ entered the educational field in the first half of the nineteenth century under the leadership of Thomas Campbell and his son Alexander. They took over Transylvania College (1780), which had been started by the Presbyterians, and before 1862 they had established Bethany (1840), Butler (1850), Chapman (1861), Culver–Stockton (1853), Eureka (1855), and Hiram (1849).

Adherents of various branches of the Lutheran Church have established many fine colleges in the United States. They will be considered as one group, and those established between 1780 and 1862 include the following: Augustana, S.D. (1860), Capital (1850), Carthage (1846), Gettysburg (1832), Gustavus Adolphus (1862), Luther (1861), Muhlenberg (1848), Newbury (1856), Roanoke (1842), Susquehanna (1858), Valparaiso (1859), Wartburg (1852), and Wittenberg (1842).

Following the historic Christmas Conference in Baltimore in 1784, which led to the establishment of the Methodist Church, men of "piety and learning" set forth in all directions to establish colleges and universities. Those founded by or related to this church or its divisions are numerous. The list of institutions organized before 1862 includes: Adrian (1845), Albion (1835), Allegheny (1815), Athens (1822), Baker (1858), Baldwin–Wallace (1845), Birmingham–Southern (1856), Boston University (1839), Centenary (1825), Central (1854), Cokesbury (1785), University of the Pacific (1851), Columbia, South Carolina (1854), Cornell College (1853), De Pauw (1837), Dickinson (1773), Emory (1836), Emory and Henry (1838), Evansville (1854), Greensboro (1838), Hamline (1854), Houghton (1833), Huntingdon (1854), Illinois Wesleyan (1850), Iowa Wesleyan (1842), La Grange (1831), Lawrence (1847), MacMurray (1846), McKendree (1834), Mount Union (1846), Northwestern (1851), Ohio Wesleyan (1842), Randolph–Macon (1830), Simpson (1860), Southwestern, Texas (1840), Tennessee Wesleyan (1856), Trinity–Duke (1839), Wesleyan College (1836), Wesleyan University (1831), Wilberforce (1856), Willamette (1842), and Wofford (1845). Cokesbury College, named for Bishops Thomas Coke and Francis Asbury, was destroyed by fire, but it was the beginning of a vast missionary and educational movement.

Presbyterian colleges following the Civil War were divided into Northern (U.S.A.) and Southern (U.S.). Also there are independent institutions that had their beginnings under Presbyterian auspices or in cooperative projects of the Presbyterians and Congregationalists. Most of the schools are indebted to Princeton, which became an independent university, for their early leadership.

Colleges established before 1862 and affiliated with the Presbyterian Church, U.S.A., include: Beaver (1853), Blackburn (1857), Carroll (1846), Centre (1819), Coe (1851), Dubuque (1852), Hanover (1827), Illinois (1829), Lafayette (1826), Lake Forest (1857), Lindenwood (1827), Maryville (1819), Waynesburg (1849), and Westminster, Missouri (1853).

The Presbyterian Church U.S.A. was also involved in the establishment of colleges that later came under the auspices of other groups or became public or independent schools, such as Allegheny, Dickinson, Hamilton, Elmira, Knox, Lincoln, Wabash, Washington and Jefferson, Union, New York University, and the state universities of Delaware, Kentucky and California.

In the South the following colleges predating the Civil War were founded by or are related to the Presbyterian Church in the United States: Centre (1819), Davidson (1836), Hampton–Sydney (1775), Mary Baldwin (1842), Queens (1857), Southwestern at Memphis (1848), and Westminster, Missouri (1853). Two of these, Centre and Westminster, are related to both groups, Washington and Lee, long independent, had its origins in the Augusta Academy in 1749 under the leadership of Presbyterians.

Other early Presbyterian colleges founded by or related to the United, Cumberland, Associated Reformed, or Reformed groups are: Monmouth (U, 1853), Muskingum (U, 1836), Westminster, Pennsylvania (U, 1852), College of the Ozarks (C, 1834), Cumberland (C, 1842), Bethel (C, 1842), Erskine (AR, 1839) and Geneva (R, 1848).

The largest single group of colleges and universities in the United States, more than 300, is related to the Roman Catholic Church. Most of these institutions are under the control of various teaching orders of monks and nuns. The majority of the colleges were established after the Civil War.

The first Catholic college in the United States, Georgetown, was founded in the District of Columbia in 1789 by the Most Reverend John Carroll, S.J., first Bishop and subsequently Archbishop of Baltimore. This institution was referred to by Pope Paul VI as the "Alma Mater of Catholic Colleges in the United States." In 1815, the college received a charter from Congress and its name was changed to Georgetown University. The first baccalaureate was awarded in 1817, and the M.A. degree was offered in course during the 1820's. Other colleges soon followed, the next Jesuit institution being Spring Hill College (1831), in Alabama.

The following Roman Catholic colleges and universities were active in the several states before 1862 (no attempt has been made to indicate the ownership or control by various religous orders): Clarke (1843), Dayton (1850), Fordham (1841), Holy Cross (1843), Loras (1839), Loyola, Baltimore (1852), Manhattan (1853), Manhattanville (1841), Mount St. Joseph (1854), Mount St. Mary's (1808), Niagara (1856), Notre Dame (1842), Quincy (1860), Seton Hall (1856), Santa Clara (1851), San Francisco (1855), Saint Benedict's (1859), Saint Bonaventure (1856), Saint Francis, New York, (1858), Saint John's (1857), Saint Joseph's, Maryland, (1809), Saint Joseph's, Pennsylvania (1851), Saint Louis (1818), Saint Mary's, Indiana, (1844), Saint Mary's, Texas, (1852), Saint Mary-of-the-Woods (1840), Saint Vincent (1846), Villanova (1856), and Xavier (1831).

Colleges that had been related to the Church of England in the colonial period became independent during the Revolution or soon thereafter. The successor to the Anglican Church in the United States, the Protestant Episcopal Church, was organized in Philadelphia in 1785. This denomination sponsored several colleges and seminaries before 1862: Bard (1860) Hobart (1822), Kenyon (1824) Trinity, Connecticut (1823), and the University of the South (1857).

Other colleges of note that were founded between the Revolution and the Civil War, with their sponsoring or affiliated churches, are: Evangelical and Reformed: Catawba (1851), Franklin and

Marshall (1787), Heidelberg (1850), Hood (1893), Mission House (1862) and Ursinus (1832); United Brethren: Albright (1856), North Central (1861) and Otterbein (1847); Society of Friends (Quakers): Earlham (1847), Guilford (1834) and Haverford (1833); Moravian: Moravian college (1807), Moravian College for Women (1742) and Salem (1772); Reformed: Central College, Iowa (1853) and Hope College (1862).

Other religious groups, notably the Adventists, Brethren, Church of Christ, Mormons, Church of God, Church of the Nazarene, Mennonites, and the Y.M.C.A. founded colleges, but most of these are of recent origin. Churches were particularly concerned with the establishment of a large number of colleges for Negroes in the South but they came after the Civil War and will be named later.

Mention has been made of church colleges that became independent institutions. Not so well known, however, is the fact that several church colleges became public universities and some public institutions became church related or independent. Some of these changes follow: East Alabama Male College (Methodist) became Auburn University; Florence Wesleyan College (Methodist) in Alabama became Florence State College; Henderson–Brown College (Methodist) in Arkansas evolved into Henderson State Teachers College; College of California (Presbyterian-Congregationalist) became the University of California at Berkeley; Episcopal University (Methodist) evolved into the Colorado School of Mines; Newark Academy (Presbyterian) grew to be the University of Delaware; Washburn College in Kansas (Congregationalist) became Washburn University of Topeka; Fairmont College (Congregationalist) is today the Municipal University of Wichita; and Bellevue College (Presbyterian) in Nebraska became the Municipal University of Omaha.

The University of Kentucky grew out of early church efforts, principally Presbyterian and Christian; in Maryland, the Morgan State College was sponsored by Methodists; the Jackson State College in Mississippi was established by Baptists; the University of Akron was founded as Buchtel College by Ohio Universalists; Central State College in Ohio evolved from Wilberforce University with Methodist support; and Marshall College in West Virginia received early support from the Presbyterians and Methodists.

Rutgers University, previously noted, became independent and later became the State University of New Jersey. The College of William and Mary, after many financial difficulties, was taken over by the Commonwealth of Virginia. Also it should be noted that church leaders were instrumental in establishing Blount College (Presbyterian), later the University of Tennessee, and the College of Charleston (Episcopal), originally municipal and subsequently independent. But on the other hand, the Methodist-related Centenary College of Louisiana, the Baptist-sponsored Mississippi College and the independent Tulane University of Louisiana had their origins as state-supported institutions.

Colleges and universities in the United States have reached a larger percentage of the citizenry than in any other country. They have truly gained strength through experimentation and diversity. In this summary account, some of the earlier colleges may inadvertently have been overlooked, but enough have been named surely to indicate the vitally important role of the several faiths and states in providing a collegiate experience for Americans in the formative period of the nation's history.

CHAPTER VII

❦

A Potpourri
of Higher Education

As the lives of numerous eminent men and women attest, one can study at home and be well educated. Certainly, the experience of going to college and of campus life supplements the lecture hall, library and laboratory and makes for a college education. It is not necessary to dwell on the well-rounded student, or debate the merits of education versus training, but it will be apparent that American colleges and their students before the Civil War were concerned with more than "book learning." The ivy towers possessed little ivy, and even at colleges that were deliberately located far from the "evils of the city," life was never completely isolated.

Curricula at most colleges looked to the past, but an ever-present awareness of life on the farm or in the village and the knowledge that they would have to make their way in the world made students aware of the realities of life. Then, too, there were lectures by others beside revivalists, speeches and debates by candidates for public office, musical entertainments, and, above all, the literary or debating societies to awaken their interest.

Literary Society Halls at Emory College. Phi Gamma Hall was built in 1851, Few Hall in 1853.   COURTESY EMORY UNIVERSITY.

Usually there were two societies on each campus, and students were elected or assigned to membership. Names ranged from Athenian, Cliosophic and Demosthenian to Philolexian, Phi Gamma and Philanthropic. The rival groups maintained rooms and often separate halls, which provided some of the comforts of a present-day student union. Often there were initiations and secret passwords similar to those of Greek fraternities, which later replaced the societies. Each group excluded the members of the other except on very special occasions. They taught public speaking, parliamentary law and schooled members in manners.

The literary societies purchased current books, and at times their libraries were better than those of the college. They operated student loan funds, some of which are part of college trust accounts today. Most important of all, the societies held debates on the questions of the day and sponsored oratorical contests on ancient and modern subjects. These joint affairs were usually a feature of commencement and with enthusiastic cheering sections and prizes for the winners, they provoked as much excitement as a championship football game today. They also sponsored magazines for the publication of original essays and poems. It would be difficult to overemphasize the educational importance of these groups, although they were gradually replaced by other organizations. Their place in college life has never quite been filled by other student activities.

If the literary societies had rugs, curtains and comfortable chairs, the dormitories were usually crude, cold in winter and without modern plumbing. The dining hall or commons, which often doubled as an assembly hall and chapel, was generally lacking in amenities. The wooden tables were often bare and benches were generally used instead of chairs. Pewter mugs and platters were in common use until well into the nineteenth century. Complaints were numerous and frequent concerning poor food and service, and "bread and butter" riots were familiar occurrences on most campuses.

Cooks and bakers were difficult to find and keep. The bill of fare seldom changed. At one institution, students, fearing more bully beef, drove the college bull into the river where the poor animal drowned. There are many stories of wormy salt pork and slimy leftovers. Food, such as it was, was generally plentiful and cheap. Some administrations continued their dining halls notwithstanding the annual rebellions with resulting breakage, and others leased their commons or permitted students to patronize local eating houses or clubs.

Although there were rules against going to town without permission, students ate out when possible and fellow students and peddlers sold pies, cakes and sweets in the dormitories. Fruit was available in season. After the 1830's ice cream became popular and there were many varieties of homemade soft drinks in addition to cider. Most of the colleges served tea and coffee, but these along with condiments and meat were moral issues for a time at Oberlin. The college butler often operated a sort of commissary and sold food, stationery and candles.

The dormitories were places for sleeping, study, prayer and polite conversations. They were also places for riots, duels, card playing, and boisterous noises. There are records of conversions and killings, accidental and deliberate fires and all manner of life not described in the catalogues or textbooks.

The colleges had proctors and often faculty families lived in dormitories, but these did not extinguish the stink bombs or eliminate the breakage of doors and windows. Princeton experienced six serious rebellions between 1800 and 1830 against the established system of "diligent study, of guarded moral conduct and of reasonable attention to religious duty" as the catalogue stated. Numerous other institutions apparently failed to provide for the "rites of spring," the animal energy of youth, and the instincts of the coerced to challenge authority. The problems of student dormitories raised questions that are debated today without satisfactory answers.

A great deal of college life in former years centered around chapel, and much of this was wholesome, but, as with the dormitories, there were problems. Initially, daily morning and evening prayers and two church services on Sunday were required. In time these were replaced by compulsory weekday chapel services with attendance at church on Sunday expected. All too frequently the services were of a routine nature, and for many the routine became a nuisance to be flouted.

There are innumerable stories relating to chapel services—absenteeism, dodging proctors, passing notes, rolling buckshot, throwing corn, shuffling feet and ogling lady visitors. Livestock and sometimes wild animals greeted the first arrivals, and stink bombs and firecrackers were not unknown. In some places public worship was turned over to religious societies, and later the Y.M.C.A. and Y.W.C.A. became active on many campuses.

Various forms of compulsory chapel lingered on into the twentieth century when the chapels and churches were no longer large enough to seat the student body. A few church-related institutions still retain compulsory chapel, quite a few hold voluntary assemblies, but for most, long before the Supreme Court entered the picture, the problem was solved by abolishing the requirement. A similar commentary could be made concerning required courses in Bible.

If churches and groups within churches established colleges and occasionally fought over their ownership and control, the same was true of communities and political parties. The chamber of commerce spirit between rival towns was strong, and after the Revolution, the Federalists and Republicans contended for educational institutions as well as public office. This is illustrated by the famous Dartmouth College Case.

In 1816, the Jeffersonian Republicans won the elections in New Hampshire, charging that the self-perpetuating board of Dartmouth followed aristocratic principles. The legislature changed the name from Dartmouth College to Dartmouth University and took the college away from trustees chosen according to its charter and placed it under effective state control.

The original trustees decided to take their case to the courts, and meanwhile two rival colleges were operating in Hanover.

When the case was heard before the Superior Court of New Hampshire, it was clear that the contest was one of public *versus* private control. In 1817, the court decided that Dartmouth was a public corporation and subject to legislative control. The court rejected the argument that the original charter was a contract, stating it could find no precedent and that such an idea would place an instrument of the people beyond public authority.

The case was appealed to the Supreme Court of the United States, and on March 10, 1818, a graduate of Dartmouth, Daniel Webster, won fame by defending his *alma mater* and Federalist principles. He contended that the original charter was a contract and that no legislature could "take that which is not their own, to turn it from its original use, and apply it to such ends or purposes as they, in their discretion, shall see fit." He concluded with the often quoted emotional plea: "It is, sir . . . a small college, and yet there are those that love it. . . ."

On February 2, 1819, Chief Justice John Marshall, speaking for the court, handed down a decision in favor of the old board of trustees, declaring that charters given to private corporations were contracts and inviolable. The decision held that Dartmouth College was not a civil institution and that its property was private, recognized it as a private eleemosynary institution with an object of public benefit, but not as a corporation of the state subject to public control.

This landmark decision voided the act of the New Hampshire Legislature. It also demonstrated for the first time the method by which the sovereignty of the states could be limited by the Federal Constitution. Since this decision, it has been the custom of states in granting charters to corporations to insert clauses reserving the right of amendment to the legislature.

Even though the New Hampshire Legislature lost control over Dartmouth, democratic principles were at work in higher education. We have noted trends in curriculum reform and these were advanced by the coming of manual training schools, polytechnical institutes, professional schools and municipal colleges. The ferment for education and training suited to future farmers and industrial workers, in addition to education for the learned professions, would lead inevitably to the Morrill Act of 1862, which provided Federal support for the education of the sons and daughters of the working class.

The Era of Jacksonian Democracy witnessed the establishment of several manual labor colleges. Inspired by the work of Phillip Fellenberg and Johann Pestalozzi of Switzerland, these schools enabled students to finance all or a substantial part of their education through constructive work programs. Attention was given to farming and elementary mechanics, and this embraced the concept of physical exercise and work-study education. Assigned work periods were integrated with class instruction, and many colleges urged their students to work during summer vacations. Students had worked at odd jobs since the establishment of Harvard, but the new programs were different. They sought to dignify labor and make education meaningful in terms of daily life and, incidentally, the work reduced disciplinary problems.

In 1831, in New York, the revivalist and antislavery leader, Theodore D. Weld; George W. Gale of the Oneida Colony; and Lewis Tappan, merchant and antislavery advocate, formed the Society for Promoting Manual Labor in Literary Institutions. Weld traveled and lectured in all parts of the country in support of his religious ideas, temperance and manual labor.

Among the colleges using some form of work-study curricula were Dartmouth, Oberlin, Oneida Institute, Davidson, Emory, Knox, Lafayette, Marietta and Randolph–Macon. The movement was soon checked by the Panic of 1837, and it gradually died out.

Manual training was a great idea, but its champions did not reckon with all of the obstacles. The public was not convinced by the efforts of colleges to dignify labor, and many conventional educators opposed the scheme. The farming operations were not profitable, and the market for workshop products such as chairs and brooms was limited. Furthermore, wage scales of from two to ten cents an hour were so low that both students and teachers soon discovered that this type of labor was an unprofitable way to finance an education. Possibly the real doom of the movement was sealed when some colleges put professors to work in the fields to set a proper example.

Vastly more important and lasting innovations in American higher education in the half-century following the Revolution resulted from the establishment of municipal colleges, Federal service academies, technological institutes, and professional schools at existing colleges. The College of Charleston in South Carolina was the country's first municipal institution of higher learning. It was established in 1770, chartered in 1785, and the first baccalaureate was awarded in 1794. Louisville College in Kentucky, evolving from the Jefferson Seminary (1798), was established by an ordinance of the city council in 1837, and it became the University of Louisville in 1846. Cincinnati College was chartered in 1819, and in 1870 it was taken over by the city and named University of Cincinnati. New York University, chartered as the University of the City of New York in 1831, awarded its first degrees in 1834. This progressive institution offered parallel curricula, one in classics and one in English and science. It also established a distinct program for an earned M.A. in 1835. The City College of The City University of New York was founded as a free academy in 1847. Instruction at the college level began in 1849, and the degree-granting privilege was gained in 1853. These institutions, public, private and mixed, have always been closely identified with their areas while serving students from all quarters.

The United States Military Academy at West Point was opened in 1802, and the United States Naval Academy was established in 1845. These served the nation well but enrollments were small and most of the graduates had required duties for several years along the frontier or at sea. West Point engineers helped survey the rivers and railroad routes, but there was always a shortage of men with technical training to build the industries, canals and various public works. Also agricultural societies, state boards of

agriculture and speakers and journalists of the day were demanding education for the masses according to the needs of everyday
life.

In 1824, the Rensselaer Polytechnic Institute was founded to
train teachers who could help farmers apply scientific knowledge
to agriculture, and ten years later a program was offered in
engineering. This institute, established by Stephen Van Rensselaer,
was a prototype of subsequent land-grant colleges. In New York,
the Polytechnic Institute of Brooklyn was incorporated in 1854,
and the Cooper Union was chartered in 1859. About the same
time definite movements for the establishment of separate state
colleges of agriculture were under way in Michigan, Maryland and
Pennsylvania. In 1861, the Massachusetts Legislature incorporated
the Massachusetts Institute of Technology for the purpose of
instituting and maintaining a society of arts, a museum of arts and
a school of industrial science.

The demand for practical courses did not go unheeded by the
private colleges and state universities. Courses in chemistry,
physics, mineralogy and natural history were offered early in the
nineteenth century by such institutions as Harvard, Yale, Princeton, Columbia and the universities of North Carolina, South
Carolina and Georgia. In 1843, Amherst College listed in its
catalogue a "lecturer on agricultural chemistry and mineralogy,"
and in 1846, John Pitkin Norton was appointed professor of
agricultural chemistry and vegetable and animal physiology at
Yale. Newer colleges that were being established in the West, and
state universities like those in Virginia, Ohio, Illinois, and Wisconsin, tended to break away from the classical tradition by
offering courses on the application of science to agriculture and
the useful arts. The practical courses in the various private colleges and state universities were almost entirely theoretical and,
generally speaking, they lacked financial support and were viewed
with considerable disdain by the older departments of the institutions in which they were offered.

Thus far this study has dealt primarily with undergraduate
education. The professions such as theology, medicine, law and

teaching, especially theology and teaching, were served by the early colleges but standards in these fields were low and far from uniform. In practically all fields the apprenticeship system was widely followed, often without the requirement of a college course, and practitioners learned in the school of life.

The early professional study of medicine at the University of Pennsylvania and the study of law at the College of William and Mary have been mentioned. These were soon followed by schools of medicine and law at other institutions and by new ones in theology, science and engineering and agriculture. No complete listing will be attempted in this fascinating story of professional education, but the following institutions were pioneers in medical education: Pennsylvania (1765), Columbia (1767), Harvard (1782), Dartmouth (1797), Maryland (1807), Brown (1811), Yale (1813), Cincinnati (1819), Virginia (1825), George Washington (1825), Medical College of Georgia (1828), Louisville (1833), Tulane (1834), Ohio State (1834), St. Louis (1836), Union (1839), New York University (1841), Western Reserve (1843), Michigan (1850) and Georgetown (1851).

Schools of medicine, possibly more than other professional schools, resulted from mergers. Many were moved to new locations and annexed to existing colleges. They advanced the profession from the "bleeders" and "herb doctors" to the coming of hospitals, public health services and modern scientific medicine.

The first separate law school in the United States was the Litchfield Law School. It was established in 1784 by Judge Tapping Reeve at Litchfield, Connecticut.

Other early professional schools of law were: William and Mary (1779), Harvard (1817), Yale (1824), Virginia (1825), North Carolina (1845), Louisville (1846), Cumberland (1847), Union (1851), Pennsylvania (1852), Columbia (1858), Georgia (1859), and Michigan (1859). The law schools were largely "hornbook" courses until the 1890's. Most candidates for the bar "read law" in the office of a local judge or attorney, and they graduated in the school of experience.

Theological training for the most part was continued at the

church-related colleges. Separate or professional programs were started by Harvard (1816), Yale (1822) and Boston University (1839). Standards for the ministry were not uniform, and many were just "called to preach." Theology aside, the circuit riders, men of God on horseback, were educational pioneers in America.

In addition to the science and engineering programs at West Point and Rensselaer, curricula in these fields were inaugurated at Harvard (1847), Michigan (1850), Yale (1852), New York University (1854), Pennsylvania (1855), Virginia (1861), and the Massachusetts Institute of Technology (1861). The spread of the industrial revolution and the technical developments and demands during the Civil War advanced science and engineering tremendously.

Agriculture was basic in the manual training schools. More advanced work was offered by the following institutions before the passage of the Morrill Act: Rensselaer (1824), Pennsylvania State (1855), Michigan State (1855) and Maryland (1856). Agricultural societies promoted better farming, livestock and marketing. Courses in forestry and conservation were to come much later.

In the era before the Civil War, training in dentistry, optometry, pharmacy, nursing and veterinary medicine was generally related to the study of medicine. As separate fields these and the newer professional programs in architecture, art, music, social work, teacher training and library science came later and are usually associated with the general development of postgraduate studies.

The American college, however, was far from being all curriculum and intellect. The religious revivals stirred the emotions, the literary societies supplemented the formal course of study and provided entertainment, and after 1825, the Greek letter fraternities came to promote friendship and social activities. Using the example of Phi Beta Kappa, initially a social club at William and Mary, and strongly influenced by Freemasonry, which was popular and influential throughout the country, college groups at

Union, Hamilton, Washington and Jefferson, Miami and other centers organized secret societies. Most existed openly and included college officials and faculty members, but the anti-Masonic movement of the 1830's forced some to operate *sub rosa*. Few colleges and universities were untouched by the fraternity movement which flourishes today. In some of the Eastern colleges the class-club system prevailed. In fraternities undergraduates found fellowship, relief from routine and strength in organization. The fraternities established a new social system on the campus and were an unofficial educational force for good or ill depending on tradition, leadership and point of view. They came to dominate social and political life, gradually replacing the literary societies because some purposes were similar but more importantly because they created and demanded a higher loyalty.

The fraternities pledged the more sophisticated and they were adept in schooling those of promise who had rough edges in manners befitting gentlemen. They did not invent diversions that went back to the Middle Ages and beyond, but they gave new meanings to drinking, card-playing, smoking, singing and girls in the life of American college men. Despite criticisms of snobbery, anti-intellectualism, discrimination, high jinks and the like, the fraternities flourished, and generally led in scholarship, campus activities, and the production of successful alumni. The sorority movement came later, closely paralleling the organizations for men in the new coeducational institutions and colleges for women.

Fraternities founded before 1910 with more than seventy-five chapters each include: Alpha Phi Alpha (1906), Alpha Tau Omega (1865), Beta Theta Pi (1839), Delta Sigma Phi (1899), Delta Tau Delta (1858), Delta Upsilon (1834), Kappa Alpha Order (1865), Kappa Sigma (1869), Lambda Chi Alpha (1909), Phi Delta Theta (1848), Phi Gamma Delta (1845), Phi Kappa Tau (1906), Phi Sigma Kappa (1873), Pi Kappa Alpha (1868), Sigma Alpha Epsilon (1856), Sigma Chi (1855), Sigma Nu (1869), Sigma Phi Epsilon (1901), Tau Kappa Epsilon (1899), and Theta Chi (1856). The Kappa Alpha Society, organized in

1825 at Union in New York, is the oldest social fraternity to have maintained continuous existence. Some groups have been liberal and others very conservative in their expansion policies. Their common interests are coordinated through the National Interfraternity Conference.

Almost from their beginning, stories have circulated that fraternities would not last, but there are more chapters and more members than ever before in history. Like the colleges that have made them possible, they have changed with passing years. Most fraternities have dropped discriminatory membership provisions, and many have replaced Hell Week with Help Week. In times of mass enrollments and multiversities, small groups of congenial students, howsoever labeled, will be of greater and not less importance. Sororities came after the Civil War and are discussed in the next chapter.

The structure of college student life has never been uniform. Whereas the seniors were above all and the sophomores hazed the freshmen, the Greeks cut across class lines and generally dominated the Barbarians or Independents. Also there were rivalries between dormitories and the in and out of state boys. Distinctions between the Easterners and Westerners and Northern and Southern men were well defined before the Civil War. Differences on the campus, however, did not impair strong institutional loyalties and these were important in town and gown relations and in dealings with rival institutions.

In the earlier period most colleges tended to dominate the communities where they were located, and relations between the students and local citizens were generally harmonious. There were times, however, when local rowdies attacked students returning from social calls on young ladies or crashed picnics and fraternity parties. Retaliation usually followed and the faculty had another disciplinary hearing.

Intercollegiate athletic contests were not yet in vogue and transportation was so difficult that most disturbances were usually local. Halloween, commencement and "spring fever" days were favorite occasions for village raids, ringing the fire bell, removing the pump handle, placing the mule in the assembly hall or painting the parson's fence. Immediately after graduation, when no fines could be collected or punishment enforced, many dormitories suffered broken doors and windows, and sometimes mattresses and chairs were burned in a farewell bonfire to assure better furnishings for the next group of students. Even to this day many colleges and universities collect damage fees, which are not refunded in whole or in part until well after the end of the term.

By the 1850's, largely as a result of the immigration of numerous Germans who brought the *Turnverein* with them, several institutions began to experiment with gymnasiums. These proved far more satisfactory than the manual labor programs in permitting students to work off excess energy. Students and alumni often constructed their own gymnasiums, associations were organized, and athletic instructors and foreign tumblers were employed to give instruction.

By 1860, numerous buildings had been completed and college administrations were assuming responsibility for gymnastics. Amherst led in establishing a department of hygiene and physical education, but soon there were criticisms of exercises that were hard work and demands for games and sports that were fun such as baseball, cricket matches, boat races, ice skating and similar activities. Football and basketball were to come later, and the fame of Amelia Jenks Bloomer with her modified Turkish trousers for co-eds belongs to a later period.

The first intercollegiate contest was a boat race on Lake Winnipesaukee in New Hampshire in 1852 between Harvard and Yale. Boating became popular, but baseball was the first sport of universal appeal to college students. Bat and ball games have an ancient history and Washington's soldiers were reported to have played a type of baseball at Valley Forge. Rules were not perfected before the 1830's, however, and the game was not widely played before the 1840's.

In the decade before the Civil War, baseball gained momentum and there were amateur teams in dozens of cities. College students cleared diamonds and made their own balls, bats and mitts. Those who did not excel as players cheered their class or fraternity and a new phase of college life was on its way. On July 1, 1859, Amherst and Williams played the first intercollegiate baseball game at Pittsfield, Massachusetts. This and other sports were soon checked by the requirements of war, but baseball was to hold its supremacy as a campus game until the twentieth century.

If college education and training were preparation for life, commencement, public day or degree day was the gateway sought by virtually all students. It was the well-marked date on the academic calendar when scholars would parade and students would be certified to the world as having satisfactorily met all requirements of a prescribed course of study. The requirements were moral as well as intellectual according to the policies of the college, and those with "character deficiencies" were usually weeded out before the final semester.

Commencements were considerably changed from those at Oxford and Cambridge. Academic costumes were worn at a few of the older colleges in the East, but gowns and mortarboards were not in general use until the 1890's. Most presidents wore the tail coats of ministers or the clerical garb of their religious group, and the graduates wore their Sunday best, usually dark suits, stiff white collars and ties for the men, and long white dresses for the young ladies. Commencement invariably followed the baccalaureate sermon, and the speaker was usually a clergyman, literary figure or public official. With few exceptions in the period before the Civil War, the degree conferred was the Bachelor of Arts, and the magic words were usually in English, but some of the older colleges retained Latin. Most exercises were held in the college chapel or a local church.

The commencement disputations of the colonial period were gradually replaced by the oratorical contests and championship debates of the literary societies. These displayed members of the senior class at their best and gave an indication of what they had learned. These pre-exercises were often long and tedious, but they were pleasing to parents, sweethearts and friends, who made a real occasion of commencement week. Picnics and social engagements were mixed with the more scholarly activities, and in the South and West horse races and cock fights were often side attractions. In many places special marshals were appointed to keep things under control.

The graduation exercise was the grand finale, a memorable experience. Popular speakers included Ralph Waldo Emerson, Henry Ward Beecher, Daniel Webster, Wendell Phillips, Rufus Choate, George Ticknor, Philip Lindsley, James Marsh and Theodore Weld. Often the speeches were long and there were distractions of crying babies, runaway horses and occasional pranks by the town boys. Sometimes there were serious disruptions such as storms and fires, and on one occasion at Oberlin the program was cut short so that students and townsmen could rescue some Negroes from the slave catchers.

Commencement day lacked the cheering sections, which were part of the student programs, and the songs that kept everyone up late the night before; but the large parchment diplomas that would grace many walls for years to come were evidence of accomplishment. Graduating classes were small and as the names were called by the dean or senior professor, each graduate walked to the center of the platform to receive his degree and words of personal commendation from the president. The service was closed with a benediction and the singing of a hymn, often "Blest Be the Tie That Binds." In later years the *Alma Mater* became the closing song before the recessional.

The graduates of the early colleges were men of distinction in a society that was predominantly agricultural. Many of them would fight over states rights, slavery and secession. Some would achieve success in the growing cities of the industrial era. Others would help build new colleges in the West. They had learned much from the formal and informal curriculum, and their education had cost approximately $100 to $300 for each year in college. As college men they would have to prove the worth of their education in a society that generally extolled the virtues of self-made men.

Well-established and endowed colleges and public universities generously supported by state and federal funds are prone to forget their humble origins in the camp meetings, forests and corn fields. The blandishments of early promoters included everything from rich soil, pure air and healthful water to orthodox religion, sound learning and morals beyond reproach. It was no accident that towns were named Athens and Oxford because the people of the growing republic were determined to build, grow and succeed. If the Methodists had a college, surely the Baptists or Presbyterians must have one, and if Vermont and Tennessee could boast of state universities, every other new state admitted to the union must by lottery, taxes or the sale of public land establish a citadel of learning atop a hill to serve as a lighthouse for the future.

Colleges were part of the scheme of Americanization. They were social investments, and those students privileged to attend were obligated to exert their talents for the public good. The American people and their government were on trial before the world, and, therefore, institutions had a national purpose. Colleges also promoted personal economic advancement by contending that "a degree is worth money—education is better than a farm"; and success in church, professions and politics would be advanced if one had the "mark and manner of a college man." Some of the claims were premature and the boasting changed with changing conditions, but the practice of promoting education for God, country and self-advancement was well established by the mid-nineteenth century.

Knox College of Galesburg, Illinois, chartered as a manual labor college in 1837, was typical of frontier schools concerned with the realization of "the American dream." It also emphasizes the fact that small colleges participate in national life in many

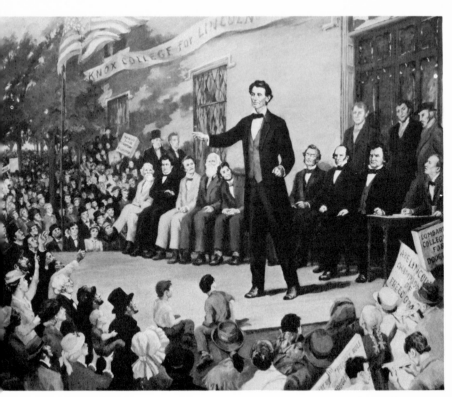

Lincoln-Douglas Debate, Knox College, 1858. From a painting by Ralph Fletcher Seymour. COURTESY KNOX COLLEGE.

ways. It was here on the afternoon of October 7, 1858, at the east side of Old Main, that Stephen A. Douglas and Abraham Lincoln engaged in one of their famous debates. It is estimated that some 15,000 people came on foot, by wagons and carriages and on the new railway to see and hear the contenders for the United States Senate. During his speech at Knox College, Lincoln emphasized the moral evil of slavery. He lost the election to Douglas but won the presidency two years later.

By 1860, the questions on every farm and in every city and village were: did God prefer one country or two, the North or the South, and did country mean a union of states or the state where one lived? During this period of crisis and conflict, how could a college man or woman most effectively serve? These questions and many related issues were to disrupt the nation and the colleges and universities for four or more years. They would bring many changes including greater federal participation in higher education and a shift from the dominance of church-related and independent colleges to state universities and land-grant institutions.

CHAPTER VIII

❦

Democracy in
Higher Education

With the firing on Fort Sumter by Confederate forces, April 12, 1861, academic processions rapidly gave way to military operations. At colleges north and south drill companies were organized, flags were displayed, and patriotic songs echoed at night. Men from practically every college class from 1845 to 1862 volunteered or were called to serve with the Blue or the Gray. It has been estimated that 23 percent of the graduates of New England colleges served the Union, and a larger percentage of college graduates from southern states were in the Confederate army. Some 75 percent of the graduates of Emory College in Georgia saw military service, and the new University of Michigan furnished 1,200 men to help save the Union.

During the war virtually all colleges in the North carried on with reduced enrollments and younger students. In the South, many colleges were closed after the second year of the conflict and buildings were often occupied and in many cases destroyed. On May 15, 1864, the 247 younger cadets remaining at the

Virginia Military Institute at Lexington took part as a unit in the battle of New Market, repelling a superior force and sustaining 57 casualties. A month later their college was burned by Federal troops. Long after the war the federal government voted partial compensation for some of the damages to colleges in the former Confederacy.

General losses in the South were such that it was not until 1900 that economic conditions were restored to the level of 1860. Aid of the kinds granted to a defeated Germany after World Wars I and II and to Japan after World War II was not extended to the Confederate states, which had fought for independence or engaged in rebellion. All church-related colleges, those for whites and the new ones for Negroes, led a hand-to-mouth existence. Land-grant colleges evolved slowly to strengthen public higher education. The four decades of blight and poverty left a legacy of major importance in the development of the nation.

The coming of peace was reluctantly accepted by the South, but years of reconstruction lay ahead. In the North victory was welcomed and the colleges and universities began to share in a new industrial prosperity. Reaction to the news of the collapse of the Confederacy at Ohio Wesleyan University was typical of many throughout the North. On April 10, 1865, President Frederick Merrick issued the following proclamation:

> ALL HAIL! LEE HAS SURRENDERED!!
> Let the day be given to rejoicing!
> There will be no recitations to-day.
> Students will meet at 5 o'clock for prayers.
> Let God be praised!

In the enthusiasm of war, many colleges had given credit and diplomas to seniors reporting for military service. The classes of 1860–1863 furnished particularly large quotas of soldiers, and later a sizable number who had seen service at the front returned to the campuses. At many colleges the seniors of 1868 were known as the "soldiers' class," and former officers and men without arms or legs were a common sight. The large number of

veterans returning to college surprised many and their maturity
and seriousness of purpose pleased teachers and administrators
alike.

While the Civil War was in progress, President Lincoln had
signed the Morrill Act, a law of greatest significance to higher
education, first in northern states and ultimately throughout the
country. This act was the culmination of a long series of demands
to make higher education responsive to the needs of the sons and
daughters of the industrial classes, farmers and mechanics. It
marked the real beginning of continuing federal support for
colleges and universities and it led to a democratization of higher
learning. It forced curriculum reform and eventually broke the
dominance of church-related and independent colleges.

Prior to 1860, there were experiments in several states with
manual training schools, courses in applied science, science clubs
and programs in agriculture and technological education. As early
as 1841, Alden Partridge of Norwich, Vermont, a founder of
Norwich University and a friend of Justin S. Morrill of Strafford,
Vermont, prepared a petition to Congress requesting aid for
practical education from the sale of public lands. The motion was
tabled, but Partridge undoubtedly had hastened the land-grant
idea.

In Illinois, Jonathan Baldwin Turner, a member of the Yale
board and a former professor at Illinois College, was working
effectively to aid the farmers and mechanics of his state. He held
that society was made up of two classes, the professional and the
industrial. He noted that the small professional class had ample
colleges, and that the numerous industrial class had practically
none. To remedy this condition, he urged the creation of an
industrial university in which a system of education in agriculture
and the arts would be offered to meet the needs of all farmers,
artisans, mechanics and merchants. Turner did not believe the
existing classical colleges could offer this sort of education, and
he was opposed to industrial education becoming an incidental

appendage to an established institution. Turner's ideas led to the University of Illinois with its colleges of agriculture and engineering, and his name is associated with the land-grant movement because of his plan to establish an industrial university in each state with funds to be obtained from the sale of public lands.

In the South, agricultural and industrial education found a champion in Thomas G. Clemson, the able and versatile son-in-law of John C. Calhoun. While serving as a diplomat in Europe during the 1840's, Clemson was a keen observer of agricultural methods and technological instruction. Upon his return to the United States he settled on a farm near Bladensburg, Maryland, where, during his leisure hours, he wrote articles on scientific farming and agricultural education. He was a leader in the movement that culminated in the establishment of the Maryland Agricultural College in 1856. Three years later he was appointed by Jacob Thompson, Secretary of the Interior, as Superintendent of Agriculture of the United States. In this position he urged the establishment of an independent bureau of agriculture and the founding of agricultural colleges by means of federal land grants.

During the Civil War, Clemson served the Confederacy, and following that conflict he made his home at the Fort Hill homestead of John C. Calhoun in South Carolina. The cause of agricultural education having been championed nationally by others, Clemson determined to help the farmers and mechanics of his adopted state. In his will he gave the bulk of the Clemson holdings to South Carolina for the founding of a scientific and technical college. His monument is Clemson University, which was opened as a land-grant institution in 1893.

Although he was undoubtedly influenced and aided by Partridge, Turner and Clemson, it was Justin S. Morrill who fought the long battle in Congress which led to the successful land-grant act. During his first term in the House of Representatives in 1856, he introduced a resolution requesting the Committee on Agriculture to inquire into the expediency of establishing one or more agricultural schools along the line of the military and naval academies. This resolution failed, but a year later Morrill introduced his first land-grant bill in Congress. It was adversely reported by the Committee on Public Lands, but this did not end the matter.

A few days later Morrill delivered an impassioned speech in behalf of colleges for the people and the country, and he submitted a substitute bill. After considerable delay and political jockeying, the land-grant bill was approved by the House and Senate by narrow margins. This hard-won victory was vetoed by President James Buchanan on February 26, 1859, on the grounds that the measure was extravagant, impolitic and unconstitutional.

Unable to overrule the President's veto, Morrill and his friends continued the fight in the next administration. Both Abraham Lincoln and Stephen A. Douglas had endorsed the land-grant idea during the presidential campaign of 1860. Following Lincoln's election, Morrill reintroduced his bill and again it was reported unfavorably. Meanwhile, a similar measure introduced in the Senate by Benjamin Wade of Ohio was reported favorably to that body. Morrill championed this bill in the House and after various delays it was finally passed. The long struggle to obtain direct federal aid for agricultural and industrial education triumphed when President Lincoln signed the bill into law on July 2, 1862.

This act is the most important ever passed by Congress in support of higher education in the United States. It emancipated learning from the classical and aristocratic ideas of the past. It broke a logjam in the advance of learning by recognizing that the everyday affairs of life are fit subjects for a program of higher education for ordinary citizens. The influence of this act and subsequent federal laws supporting research and extension programs and higher education generally cannot accurately be measured.

Briefly stated, the Morrill Act appropriated to each state 30,000 acres of public land for each senator and representative in Congress, under the census of 1860. The land could be sold or held as endowment, and all sums received were to constitute a perpetual fund to support at least one college in each state, which would teach courses in agriculture, the mechanic arts and military science in addition to other scientific and classic studies. All of this was "to promote the liberal and practical education of the industrial classes in the several pursuits and professions in life."

In 1860, there were twenty-one state colleges. Following the war several new land-grant colleges, generally known as agricultural and mechanical colleges, were started. In several instances land-grant colleges were attached to existing state universities or incorporated with new public universities. With the coming of peace in the North and following Reconstruction in the South, the movement for public higher education made rapid progress. For several years there was considerable opposition from and rivalry with the church and independent colleges, but the dual system operated to the benefit of education generally.

The state universities and A. and M. colleges were particularly strong in the West and South, and new ones were established as western territories were admitted to the union as states. Among the state land-grant institutions we find: Auburn University (1872), University of Arkansas (1871), Colorado State University (1870), University of Florida (1884), Georgia Institute of Technology (1885). University of Illinois (1867), Iowa State University (1868), Kansas State University (1863), University of Kentucky (1865), Louisiana State University (1870), University of Maine (1865), Michigan State University (1855), University of Minnesota (1851), Mississippi State University (1878), University of Missouri (1839), University of Nebraska (1869), University of New Hampshire (1866), North Carolina State University (1887), Ohio State University (1870), Oregon State University (1858), Pennsylvania State University (1855), Purdue University (1865), Texas A. and M. University (1871), Washington State University (1890), West Virginia University (1867), and the University of Wisconsin (1848). In New York and Massachusetts, the land-grant funds were attached to the private institutions, Cornell University (1865) and the Massachu-

setts Institute of Technology (1860). Also there were other variations between institutions within states, particularly for state
colleges for Negroes in the South.

As a result of Lincoln's Emancipation Proclamation and the
adoption of the Thirteenth, Fourteenth and Fifteenth Amendments
to the Federal Constitution, the education of Negro citizens at
all levels became a matter of pressing concern. Several church
groups started colleges in the South, Negro land-grant colleges
were organized, and Howard University (1867) was chartered in
the District of Columbia. The work of many public and private
institutions primarily for Negroes struggling against prejudice with
meager funds is a heroic development of the past century.

Some of the institutions making significant contributions to the
higher education of Negroes are: Wilberforce University (1856),
Atlanta University (1865), Fisk University (1865), Shaw University (1865), Lincoln University, Missouri (1866), Rust College (1866), Howard University (1867). Morehouse College
(1867), Morgan State College (1867), St. Augustine's College
(1867), Talladega College (1867), Lincoln University, Pennsylvania (1868), Hampton Institute (1868), Philander Smith College (1868), Claflin College (1869), Clark College (1869),
Dillard University (1869), Tougaloo College (1869), Bennett
College (1873), Wiley College (1873), Knoxville College (1875),
Meharry Medical College (1876), Prairie View A. and M. College
(1876), Philander Smith (1877), Stillman College (1876), Spel-
man College (1881), Tuskegee Institute (1881). Virginia State
College (1882), Central State College (1887), Florida A. and
M. University (1887), A. and T. College of North Carolina
(1891), South Carolina State College (1895), Bethune–Cookman
College (1904), Miles College (1905), North Carolina College
at Durham (1909) and the Tennessee A. and I. State University
(1909).

Many colleges in various parts of the country have long accepted qualified students of all races, and since 1954, colleges and
universities generally have removed labels and barriers to educa-

tional opportunity. Today there are some 111 predominately Negro colleges and universities, 72 private and 39 public. Of the total, 76 are fully accredited by regional associations and several more will qualify before 1970. It is estimated that about 60 percent of all Negro college students attend these schools.

The institutions primarily serving Negroes have done so much with limited financial resources that it is difficult to discuss one without commenting on all. Howard University in Washington, D.C., Fisk University and Meharry Medical College in Nashville, Tennessee, and Tuskegee Institute in Alabama, to name four, have served the country ably in times of peace and war, and they have added numerous men and women of distinction to the growing parade of scholars. Many individuals, church groups, private foundations and government agencies have assisted higher education for Negroes. In recent years the work of the United Negro College Fund has been particularly helpful.

Most of the new institutions following the Civil War and several older ones admitted women, but prejudice lingered in many places against females, and the curricula and, to a considerable extent, the facilities were primarily for men. At the same time the industrial revolution was opening selected jobs for women, expanding public school systems were demanding more and more qualified teachers, and a democratic society was requiring women to accept greater responsibilities. These conditions and needs, with the tradition of preparatory schools and seminaries for young ladies, gave rise to the belief that there should be more separate colleges for women. The idea was soon championed by wealthy individuals, churches, and state legislatures influenced by the Populist movement.

Many able leaders were engaged in the crusade for women's rights, of which higher education and separate colleges for women were a part. Among these were Lucy Stone, Emma Willard, Margaret Fuller, Mary Lyon and Catherine Beecher. The latter was a sister of the Reverend Henry Ward Beecher, and her sister, Harriet Beecher Stowe, had written *Uncle Tom's Cabin*. Catherine became one of the most effective proponents of female education, and she had the backing of the American Woman's Educational Association, which had boldly declared for endowed colleges "to aid in securing to American women a liberal education, honorable position, and remunerative employment. . . ." The program of the society closely followed Catherine Beecher's book, *True Remedy for the Wrongs of Women*.

That Catherine Beecher influenced Matthew Vassar, the Poughkeepsie brewer, Henry Durant, the father of Wellesley, and Sophia Smith, who gave generously to Smith, is beyond question. Miss Beecher's leadership led to the establishment of colleges that gave emphasis to curricula including physical education, teaching and domestic science. Her position in society and writings and speeches on the practical elements of education as related to day-to-day life helped to win the support of men who heretofore had thought that "the Mrs." was the only appropriate degree for a woman.

The first great surge for the establishment of modern, college-level institutions for women came during the last four decades of the nineteenth century. These colleges were independent and church-sponsored, and some of them subsequently changed titles and relationship with founding groups. Several colleges for women became coeducational. Some of the institutions for females, the term generally used at that time, became coordinate divisions of existing colleges for men. Also there were several tax-supported colleges for women, chiefly in the South.

Among the independent and church-sponsored colleges were: Vassar College (1861), Wells College (1868), Chatham College (1869), Wilson College (1869), William Woods College (1870), Wellesley College (1870), Chestnut Hill College (1871), Maryville College of the Sacred Heart (1872), Smith College (1871), Ursuline College (1871), Lander College (1872), Blue Mountain College (1877), Shorter College (1877), Brenau College (1878), Bryn Mawr College (1880), College of the Holy Names (1880),

Goucher College (1885), Mills College (1885), Colorado Woman's College (1888), Converse College (1889), Agnes Scott College (1890), Keuka College (1890), Loretta Heights College (1891), Meredith College (1891), Randolph–Macon Woman's College (1891), Hood College (1893), Maryhurst College (1893), Western College (1894), Trinity College (1897), Our Lady of the Lake College (1897), Lake Erie College (1898), Principia College (1898), College of Saint Elizabeth (1899), Simmons College (1899), Finch College (1900), and Sweet Briar College (1901).

Coordinate colleges for women were related in various ways to established institutions for men. They were based on the plan of Queen's College at the University of London and Girton College at Cambridge. Among those founded in this period were: Radcliffe College (1879), Harvard; Newcomb College (1886), Tulane; Flora Stone Mather College (1888), Western Reserve; Barnard College (1889), Columbia; Pembroke College (1891), Brown; Jackson College (1892), Tufts; and William Smith College (1908), Hobart.

Several other institutions for men debated the wisdom of adding colleges for women but for various reasons, chiefly financial, they decided to keep their bachelor status. Some colleges for men admitted women as day students or during the summer session or for special courses of instruction. In 1968, California Institute of Technology, Colgate, Princeton, Trinity College, Vassar, Wesleyan University and Yale joined several traditional colleges for men and women and became coeducational or voted to change as soon as practicable. Undoubtedly other institutions will also soon become coeducational.

Tax-supported institutions established for women in the 1880's and 1890's include: Longwood College, Virginia, (1884); Mississippi State College for Women (1884); Winthrop College, South Carolina, (1886); Hunter College, New York (1888); The Woman's College of Georgia (1891); University of North Carolina at Greensboro (1891); Alabama College (1893); and the

Belles of Newcomb College, about 1900. COURTESY TULANE UNIVERSITY.

Texas Woman's University (1901). Some of these schools now admit men on a coeducational basis and others permit them to register for special programs.

One of the oldest institutions for women in the nation, the Moravian Seminary and College for Women (1742), merged with the Moravian College and Theological Seminary (1807), under the name Moravian College in 1954. This school has offered college level work for women since 1863. Mount Holyoke College, previously mentioned, first offered college courses in 1837 and conferred its first baccalaureate in 1889. A few colleges for women offered graduate and professional programs, but most serve undergraduates only.

Although late to enter the field of higher education, the numerous colleges for women made remarkable progress. Most of their early moralistic philosophy and missionary zeal has faded, and the special pleas and defenses for their existence are no longer heard. Women graduates have added charm and intelligence to society and the on-going procession of scholars.

Today when women go to college, work in factories, engage in business, own property, vote and hold public office and generally engage in the affairs of the world, it is difficult to comprehend their low status within the memory of persons still living. Their successful revolution cannot be overemphasized, and the world and higher education will never return to the old order.

Colleges for women and coeducation helped men as well as women; they added educated and trained womanpower to the betterment of home, industry and society. Coeducation helped to save several men's colleges from the competition of state universities, and it made men aware of scholastic competition and of women as citizens. The coeds, of course, were not accepted without a struggle but they made their way on merit as well as charm. They organized athletic teams, provided cheer leaders for football games, and, whether on campus or at a sister college, they added a feminine plus to higher education, which had generally been lacking for a thousand years.

The women had their literary and debating activities, usually separate from men, May Days and daisy chains, and they were quick to organize sororities, sometimes called fraternities. Among the female Greek letter societies organized before 1910 that now have more than seventy-five chapters each are: Alpha Chi Omega (1888), Alpha Delta Pi (1851), Alpha Gamma Delta (1904), Alpha Kappa Alpha (1908), Alpha Omicron Pi (1897), Alpha Phi (1872), Alpha Xi Delta (1893), Chi Omega (1895), Delta Delta Delta (1888), Delta Gamma (1873), Delta Zeta (1902), Gamma Phi Beta (1874), Kappa Alpha Theta (1870), Kappa Delta (1897), Kappa Kappa Gamma (1870), Pi Beta Phi (1867), Phi Mu (1852), Sigma Kappa (1874), and Zeta Tau Alpha (1898). These social groups are not to be confused with the numerous college honor, professional and recognition societies. Most sororities are members of the National Panhellenic Conference, and despite occasional stories of their demise, they are growing in numbers of chapters and members.

While women were demonstrating their capacity for higher education, professors and administrators were debating problems of postgraduate education. These were related to curriculum reform but they went far beyond. It was not enough to perpetuate knowledge; true universities should increase it through research and diffuse it through publications and demonstrations for the benefit of mankind. Graduate and professional programs were needed in addition to the study of medicine, law and theology; concerted demands were made for graduate schools of arts and science wherein scholars could earn master's and doctor's degrees.

Until 1875, there was no real university in the United States. Most M.A. degrees were honorary, or they were conferred on the basis of a modest thesis without resident work. The Ph.D. degree, widely respected in Europe and hailed by American scholars returning from abroad, was first conferred by Yale in 1861. This degree appeared ideally suited for postgraduate needs and steps were taken at several of the eastern colleges to offer doctoral programs. The inauguration of advanced earned degrees required considerable reorganization in higher education, and it raised the goals and services of many colleges to university level. Briefly stated, the transformation of the last quarter of the nineteenth century included a general overhauling of the undergraduate curriculum with the introduction of the elective method, and the addition of a German type of research school on top of the traditional English type of college.

The bold thinking and reforms changed the entire course of higher education in America. New universities were founded to emphasize graduate research; charters were broadened and the names of colleges were changed to universities. Classics gradually gave way to science, social studies and practical courses; endowments were raised; and laboratories and libraries were constructed. There was a general intellectual ferment mingled with debates over A. and M. colleges, the role of women in university life, the place of fraternities and sororities on the campus, the dangers of football (the new popular sport), and the destiny of the United States in world affairs.

Following the Civil War, the earlier efforts of Jefferson at Virginia and Tappan at Michigan to reform the curriculum bore fruit on many campuses. Their ideas for university greatness and the graduate research programs of the new German universities were carried forward by Charles W. Eliot, who became president of Harvard in 1869. There he inaugurated an elective system that permitted undergraduates to choose their own studies, and later he and his colleagues transformed Harvard from a provincial college into a great university. He sought to develop character and scholarship, not by petty rules and required archaic courses but by holding each student responsible for his own conduct and intellectual development. Eliot's influence over forty years extended to other colleges and universities and to high schools. His famous Five-Foot Shelf of *Harvard Classics* became a symbol of self-education to millions of Americans and advanced the correspondence education movement, which gained momentum after 1890.

The founding of The Johns Hopkins University in 1876, on the German model, and the work of Daniel C. Gilman there meant that the true university as contrasted with the college was firmly established as a vital part of American higher education. His work and the efforts of Eliot at Harvard and Frederick A. P. Barnard at Columbia were greatly augmented by those of the leaders of the new public and private universities.

Cornell University (1865) moved forward under the presidency of Andrew D. White, who had served with Tappan at Michigan; Clark University (1887) was founded as a graduate school under the leadership of Granville S. Hall, a member of the first faculty of Hopkins; the Catholic University of America (1889) under the Hierarchy of the United States was chartered by Pope Leo XIII as a graduate center; the University of Chicago (1890), endowed by John D. Rockefeller, obtained the services of the dynamic President William Rainey Harper; and Stanford University (1885) in California rapidly won renown under the presidency of David Starr Jordan, a graduate of Cornell and a noted naturalist. At Minnesota (1851), the distinguished President William Watts

Commencement at Princeton College, 1878.   CULVER PICTURES, INC.

Folwell urged a federation of professional schools as opposed to a graduate school on top of an undergraduate college. Yale, Columbia, Princeton, Pennsylvania and other private colleges retained their undergraduate schools but endorsed the view that institutions of higher learning had an obligation to increase knowledge and they rapidly moved to university status, generally following the Hopkins plan.

Several of the state universities, particularly in the Midwest and West, established graduate schools of arts and science, and soon they were supplying a large number of M.A. and Ph.D. graduates for education, scientific research, government and industry. Leaders in this group were the Universities of California, Wisconsin, Illinois, Michigan, Ohio State and Minnesota. Later they were joined by land-grant colleges, and the types and numbers of graduate degrees, often far removed from the traditional arts and sciences, multiplied rapidly. The spirit of democracy was affecting subject fields as well as the increasing numbers seeking higher education. It was only a short time until the graduate schools became the most important shapers of education. In 1900, the leading universities of the country with Ph.D. programs organized the American Association of Universities to advance postgraduate study and research.

The establishment of graduate schools across the nation in the last quarter of the nineteenth century led to the widespread use of academic costumes. This cannot be called a revival because most American colleges and universities had never adopted caps and gowns. A few, such as Harvard and Columbia, had adopted the British custom for special occasions in the years before the Revolution; but in general, college officials, professors and graduating classes of practically all institutions dressed in civilian clothes for convocations until well after the Civil War.

The time was ripe for a change in style. The frontier was passing and college teachers and students were more affluent. The chief factor promoting European styles of gowns, hoods and caps, however, was the new Ph.D. degree. This became a badge of

Senior class, University of Texas, 1891.　　　CULVER PICTURES, INC.

distinction and every faculty had to have a few. Since older professors could not earn them, many were conferred *honoris causa*
by leading universities of the country. Regardless of the type of
degree, the dress for academic occasions became important and
a new day had arrived for scholars on parade.

There were attacks on sham doctorates and earned doctorates
at the turn of the century. The U.S. Bureau of Education and
new learned societies, along with the American Association of
Universities, struck out at honorary Ph.D.'s, and teachers such as
William James, the Harvard philosopher, decried the new "octopus
degree" as an advertising resource that would decorate college
catalogues without improving teaching. Charges of academic
snobbery were tied in with debates over the stratification of departments and ranks of teachers, professors, associates, assistants and
instuctors, a factor that had not existed when faculties were small
and knowledge was more related.

Valid research degrees carried the day, but not until reputable institutions had set a bad example for jerkwater colleges and degree mills. Also, the question of whether limited funds should be used primarily for undergraduate instruction or postgraduate research became an important question on many campuses. Both are essential to the true university, but the de-emphasis of classroom teaching and size of classes and student bodies go to the heart of problems that plague higher education today.

Other changes in an era of change included the beginning of separate teacher training colleges and divisions, agricultural experiment stations under the Hatch Act, the establishment of professional schools in the newer disciplines, and the expansion of church-related, independent and municipal colleges in the rapidly growing urban centers. Some of these were traditional institutions with various modifications of the elective system and others were more specialized.

Urban and regional schools, established in the late nineteenth century, under various auspices and often with national patronage included: University of Akron (1870), Syracuse University (1870), University of Toledo (1872), Brigham Young University (1875), University of Detroit (1877), Case Institute of Technology (now Case Western Reserve University) (1880), University of Denver (1880), University of Southern California (1880), Drake University (1881), Marquette University (1881), Newark College of Engineering (1881), Temple University (1884), College of Saint Thomas (1885), University of Chattanooga (1886), Pratt Institute (1887), College of Puget Sound (1888), Drexel Institute of Technology (1891), Illinois Institute of Technology (1892), University of Tulsa (1894), Lowell Technological Institute (1895), Birmingham College later Birmingham-Southern (1898) and De Paul University (1898). Virtually all of the junior or two-year community colleges developed later, in the twentieth century.

Although many colleges and universities are affluent today, most have experienced dire poverty at some stage of their history.

All, in one way or another, have assisted poor students. The number of young men and women who have been helped with scholarships, work-jobs, and loan funds will never be known. Before the existence of federal and state loan programs, the G.I. Bill and other forms of assistance, many students arrived on campus without funds and the number taking degrees is a tribute to their enterprise and the resourcefulness of dedicated college administrators and teachers. Several grass-roots citadels of learning could be mentioned, but two in the Appalachian area have grown strong through distinctive types of self-help programs, Berea College (1855) in Kentucky and Berry College (1902) in Georgia. Their scholars, chiefly from mountain towns and hillside farms, have joined ranks with those from all sections in building a better society.

Following its establishment, Berea admitted Negro students from time to time. This liberal policy was finally challenged in the courts under a Kentucky school segregation law of 1904. In the case of Berea College vs. Commonwealth of Kentucky (211 U.S. 45), the Supreme Court of the United States upheld the state law and thus forced Berea to operate as a segregated institution. The tide began to turn, however, when the Maryland Court of Appeals in Pearson vs. Murray (169 Md. 478) directed that a qualified Negro must be admitted to the University of Maryland Law School.

Higher education, like nature and society, has its strong and weak points, and some qualities and conditions are more desirable than others. Many a battle has been fought over the curriculum, standards for admission and graduation, student conduct in and outside of fraternities, undue influence by alumni and professional groups, and academic freedom. There have been occasions when the church, government, business and other agencies sought and for a time dominated the scene. The true university, the great college, however, must have the greatest possible freedom to achieve its purposes. Existing knowledge may be preserved and passed along under various controls but the pursuit of truth and

Freshmen vs. sophomores, University of Pennsylvania.

CULVER PICTURES, INC.

the discovery of new knowledge involves risks and change. This is particularly true of their dissemination.

Those matters and their importance to a free society are not always understood. True scholars understand them and accept all dangers and responsibilities in the discharge of their duties. A lamentable few who claim to be scholars discover little that is new or true, talk much of freedom and all too often forget their responsibilities. The new universities with their graduate and research programs brought these issues into focus as never before in history, and their record of responsible advocacy of intellectual freedom on and off the campus is a bright new chapter in the long history of higher education.

The same, unfortunately, cannot be said of the handling of athletic contests, commercial events that, separate from physical education and sports for fun, have little relevance to scholarship. Mention has been made of the popularity of baseball and the coming of gymnasiums. The great universities provided large audiences for athletic contests that soon proved to be camels in the academic tent. The most popular game of all, football, came into prominence along with the graduate schools and both have achieved great if not compatible success.

All too often faculties have turned this problem over to the administration, the athletic committee and the alumni-citizens quarterback club that has helped recruit players and sell tickets. The coaches are often caught in the middle, and their tenure is seldom defended by the faculty or the American Association of University Professors after a second losing season. Certainly, football on most campuses is big business. A redeeming feature is that many outsiders who support big-time athletics also support various drives for academic programs, while the critics in many cases support neither.

Actually, football, like curricula in agriculture and mechanic arts and graduate research, is a part of American society. The game is interesting, popular and it has many desirable features. It has helped to break snobbishness based on race, religion and social class, and star athletes are welcomed in society and business organizations headed by college men. Perhaps more universities will in time limit the evils and utilize the worthwhile qualities found in the sport of football. Meanwhile, a brief outline of one of the major activities of institutions of higher education will be helpful.

American football is a descendant of British rugby, but the game is rougher and involves more bodily contact. Like baseball, it evolved in terms of balls, playing fields and rules. It was played on village greens in colonial days and as an intramural sport on college campuses in the early nineteenth century. It became so rough at Harvard and Yale about the middle of the century that it was temporarily abolished. The first intercollegiate game, involving features of soccer, was played in New Brunswick, New Jersey, on November 6, 1869, between Rutgers and Princeton. Rutgers won under its rules 6 to 4, but Princeton won the second game a week later 8 to 0 under Princeton rules. The faculties of the two colleges forbade the paying of a third game. Columbia played its first football game in 1870, and Yale followed when it defeated Columbia at New Haven in 1872. Harvard delayed uniform rules for a time by insisting on a rugby style of game imported from Canada. Soon compromises were reached, rules agreed upon, and the first Ivy League of Yale, Princeton, Rutgers, and Harvard was formed.

From the older colleges of the East, football spread rapidly to the interior, to the Midwest and South and thence to the Far West. Early leaders in the sport were Michigan, Notre Dame, Centre College, Lehigh, Lafayette, Trinity (later Duke), North Carolina, Vanderbilt, Stanford and California. Yale soon emerged as the first great football university, having nine undefeated seasons between 1883 and 1901. Princeton, Harvard and Pennsylvania followed in prowess, and finally Michigan, Chicago and the Carlisle Indians entered the league of national champions. The football fever spread to high schools, and soon small colleges were recruit-

First intercollegiate football game, Rutgers vs. Princeton, at New Brunswick, N.J., November 6, 1869. From a painting by M. W. Boyd.
COURTESY RUTGERS—THE STATE UNIVERSITY OF NEW JERSEY.

ing players and defeating the large universities. The game rapidly got out of hand and became a profession, and colleges and universities lost much of their moral leadership.

The names of coaches and star players were better known than those of eminent presidents and scholars. Some of the early greats were Walter Camp, Glenn Warner, Clark Shaughnessy, Percy Haughton, Fielding Yost, James Thorpe and Alonzo Stagg. They and others such as John Heisman, William Alexander, Knute Rockne, Frank Thomas, A. C. Moore, Bud Wilkinson, Earl Blaik, Robert Neyland and W. W. Hayes produced crowds and parades in the fall never equalled by the commencements in the spring.

Virtually all colleges and universities have chosen names for their teams which indicate prowess, stamina, and speed. Typical of these are the Razorbacks of Arkansas, the Bisons of Bucknell, the Golden Bears of California, the Indians of Dartmouth, the Blue Devils of Duke, the Gators of Florida, the Yellow Jackets of Georgia Tech, the Tigers of Grambling, the Wildcats of Kentucky, the Jayhawks of Kansas, the Wolfpack of North Carolina State, the Fighting Irish of Notre Dame, the Cowboys of Oklahoma State, the Boilermakers of Purdue, the Fighting Gamecocks of South Carolina, the Rockets of Slippery Rock, the Huskies of Washington, and the Bulldogs of Yale.

Animals and birds tend to predominate among the names of teams and they add to the colorful jargon of sport pages. There are also names such as the Presidents, Statesmen, Diplomats, Bishops, Generals, Colonels, Cadets, Braves, Moccasins, Mountaineers, Buccaneers, Musketeers, Roughriders, Spartans, Trojans, Titans, Tar Heels, Vikings, Saxons, Scots, and Zips. The half-time parades and shows honoring these and other teams are joys to behold.

Professional football has taken some of the edge off the college game, but the role of athletics has by no means been finally resolved. Some 30,000 "Big Men on Campus" report for pre-season practice each fall to the coaches of the country's more than 600 football-playing colleges and universities. The cheer leaders, bonfires, pep rallies, bands, alumni homecomings, special trains and shirttail victory parades continue to enliven the academic year. Conference victories open doors to all manner of post-season and bowl games far removed from ivy halls. The lament of Princeton's Woodrow Wilson that "those who perform in the main tent must often whistle for their audiences. . . ." is generally true today notwithstanding the de-emphasis or abolition of football by several institutions. Each year more than 25,000,000 individuals attend games played by the 600-odd football-playing colleges and universities. In an age when education was becoming democratic it was perhaps natural, although unplanned, that town, gown and countryside would be united in the university's most imposing structure, the stadium.

Democracy's educational offspring, a mixed breed, will be discussed in the next chapter. From student glory on the battlefield for the preservation of the Union to scrimmage on the football field to win a trophy, from colleges for the industrial classes and for women to the reformation of the curriculum, new professional schools, and Ph.D. programs, the last half of the nineteenth century was truly a remarkable and fruitful era. With the passing of the frontier, the arrival of modern industry, and the successful conclusion of the Spanish-American War, higher education and the nation came of age.

CHAPTER IX

The Contemporary Scene

HIGHER EDUCATION IN the United States in the twentieth century has been characterized by tremendous growth and variety. Colleges that had 1,000 students or less in 1900 have from 10,000 to more than 40,000 today. Professional schools and degrees multiplied; teacher education programs and normal schools became numerous; adult education, extension and home study courses joined the ranks of higher education; summer schools and evening colleges became common; junior colleges entered the field in force; R.O.T.C. units were established to help train men for peace and war; and industrial and government research came to stay.

Learned societies and professional organizations of teachers, alumni associations, college and university associations, accrediting agencies and foundations have become part of the academic procession. As free enterprise support increased and then wavered and state revenues proved inadequate, the federal government has come to the rescue of higher education with a vast array of special grants and continuing appropriations. Church groups have lost many colleges and lessened their control over others. The lines between private and public institutions have become blurred, but the public sector has moved into ascendancy. Higher education has come to touch almost every facet of life, and it has entered the world scene as never before in history.

An understanding of this development requires a glance at federal legislation dating from the original Morrill Act of 1862. The states did not manage their land-grants equally well, and over half of them failed to obtain the regional price of $1.25 an acre. State appropriations were not sufficient in most cases to operate first-class colleges, so Morrill sponsored another bill for additional federal support, which failed. Meanwhile, in 1887, Representative William H. Hatch of Missouri persuaded Congress to appropriate $15,000 a year for agricultural experiment stations. The second Morrill Act was then passed in 1890, and it appropriated $15,000 to each state and territory and provided for annual increases of $1,000 for ten years after which the yearly appropriation would be $25,000. In 1907, the Nelson Amendment increased federal grants for instruction in agriculture and mechanic arts to $50,000 a year.

Although teacher training was not specified in the Morrill Acts, the land-grant colleges began to incorporate departments and schools of education into their programs. With the growth of elementary education and the coming of public high schools, which replaced many of the private academies and seminaries, the new schools of education flourished. Most states established one or more two-year normal schools for the training of teachers. Some of these offered high school programs. Most of the normal schools evolved into four-year teachers colleges after World War I, and following World War II most broadened their functions and became state colleges. As extensions of the land-grant concept, teacher training institutions of the twentieth century were useful, accessible, and tuition charges were low.

In 1914, Congress voted the Smith-Lever Act, named for Senator Hoke Smith of Georgia and Representative A. F. Lever of South Carolina. It provided for cooperative extension work by the U.S. Department of Agriculture and the land-grant colleges in the fields of agriculture and home economics. This law carried the colleges to the people through extension agents and made family welfare a matter of national concern.

Realizing that many students for one reason or another did not go to college and that trained vocational teachers were necessary for any well-rounded educational program, the Congress in 1917 passed the Smith-Hughes Act. This measure, named for Senator Hoke Smith and Representative D. M. Hughes of Georgia, provided for vocational education in secondary schools and for the training of vocational teachers by the A. and M. colleges. These laws, long since augmented by other federal legislation, particularly the Vocational Education Act of 1963, indicate the continuing concern of Congress for wider educational opportunities.

The agricultural extension system was a great stimulus to extension programs generally. Off-campus classes for adults were supplemented by numerous correspondence courses at the college level. Following the lead of the British extension movement and proprietary schools in Europe and the United States, Chicago under William Rainey Harper, Wisconsin under Charles R. Van Hise, Columbia under Nicholas Murray Butler and other institutions, chiefly state universities, offered a variety of credit and noncredit home study courses. This activity led to the establishment of the National University Extension Association in 1915. Later off-campus centers and branch universities were started, and, after World War II, radio and television instruction was utilized extensively. The next moves of public and private education undoubtedly lie in the areas of electronic, intercontinental and interplanetary instruction. Adult education generally has been advanced by the Adult Education Association of the United States of America.

After the turn of the century, summer schools, evening colleges, special institutes and workshops became common. Several institutions inaugurated cooperative work-study programs, especially in engineering and business, and others perfected "three-two" programs, especially in engineering, with professional schools. More recently, colleges began experiments with independent study and advanced standing by means of equivalency examinations. The junior year abroad programs are now permanent features of numerous liberal arts colleges, and several universities have research institutes and centers in various parts of the world.

The federal government has sponsored numerous cooperative arrangements between American universities and those in developing nations. The East-West Center of the University of Hawaii was established in 1960 to promote greater understanding among the peoples and countries of the Pacific area. The exchange of students has grown tremendously since World War I. In 1967–68, according to figures of the Institute for International Education, this country was host to more than 110,000 students from 172 foreign countries and territories, most of them receiving substantial public and private financial assistance. During the same period, American universities and colleges were host to some 10,700 professors, researchers and senior academic personnel from 118 distant lands. Rockefeller, Ford and other foundation grantees, Fulbright scholars, Technical Assistance and Peace Corps volunteers have made American education known to all parts of the free world.

The most important structural unit of higher education to emerge since 1900 has been the two-year college. William Rainey Harper first used the term junior colleges, and in 1901 he was influential in establishing the oldest public two-year community college in the United States at Joliet, Illinois. The first privately supported two-year colleges were established in the late 1800's. Initially these institutions were to offer instruction parallel and equal to the first two years of standard liberal arts colleges. Such instruction is still generally available, but purposes have been expanded to include technical training and terminal vocational courses.

These uniquely American institutions are public, independent or church-related in control. They have grown rapidly in urban centers where they are often connected with public schools and systems of higher education. Through a variety of methods and curricula the junior college is expanding and extending opportunity for education beyond the secondary school. Approximately 85 percent of the students enrolled in two-year colleges are attending public institutions. Since World War II, community colleges of various types have increased in number; by 1968, some 950 were serving the public with additional ones planned for the near future. In the fall of 1967, about 30 percent of the first-time opening college enrollments were in two-year institutions. Total enrollments in 1967 were 1,671,440 and it is estimated that more than 2,500,000 students will be attending junior colleges, technical institutes and community colleges by 1975.

The rapid expansion of two-year institutions in all states, particularly in states like California, Florida and New York, has broken the old barrier between high school and college. James Bryant Conant, former president of Harvard, has suggested that the time is not far distant when state educational authorities will plan a fourteen-year course of study for almost all youth, which will be virtually free to the student or his parents. It is believed that such public education will help overcome remaining inequities in our educational system and produce graduates who will fit effectively into a democratic society. By any standard the two-year institutions, public and private, are on the move, sometimes defining goals as they progress. Many have grown into four-year colleges and several four-year schools have concentrated their resources on quality and returned to the two-year curricula. All have added to the number and variety of associate degrees, with appropriate academic costumes.

With population growth, educational advances and the further division of labor into specialized professions and vocations, new professional schools have been added to existing universities and special-purpose institutions have been established. Beside the traditional fields of medicine, law and theology, we have noted the growth of engineering and teacher training departments and schools of education. Some of the latter introduced the doctor of education degree to distinguish the practice of teaching from research in various subject fields. Other professional programs include architecture, art, business administration, dentistry, forestry, home economics, journalism, landscape architecture, library science, music, nursing education, osteopathy, pharmacy, public health, religious education, social work and veterinary medicine. There is no end to what may be studied, and subject specialists and accrediting agencies are kept busy defining areas and agreeing on standards. Most accrediting bodies in the field of higher education are members of the National Commission on Accrediting.

Special-purpose institutions include Catholic, Jewish, Protestant and other religious seminaries; schools of fine arts, conservatories of music, schools of dance and drama; institutes of aeronautics; schools of electronics and computing sciences; and special business programs in banking, insurance, real estate, retailing and the like. Many industrial firms, labor unions, and trade and professional associations conduct training and research programs. In many respects private and special-purpose education has been more innovative and flexible than the programs and methods of traditional institutions. Business has entered the field of education to develop new instructional materials and systems that are both educationally sound and profitable.

The federal government operates many educational and training programs for members of the armed forces. Among these are: the National War College, the Industrial College of the Armed Forces, the Armed Forces Staff College, the Army War College, the Naval War College, the Air University, the Marine Corps Schools, the Naval Postgraduate School, the Air Force Institute of Technology and the Defense Language Institute. The United States Coast Guard Academy was established at New London, Connecticut, in 1876, and it offered its first baccalaureate in 1940. The United States Merchant Marine Academy at Kings Point,

New York, was authorized by Congress in 1942. In 1954, the United States Air Force Academy in Colorado joined the other federal service academies. These institutions confer standard B.S. degrees, and their commencements with their own special uniforms add military precision to the academic procession.

American civilian colleges and universities have always made significant contributions to the nation's defense efforts. Students and teachers alike participated in both World Wars as many a memorial marker or building attests. Action at the front was backed by numerous training programs and science research projects. Technological warfare made the universities and their talented professors essential. The Morrill Act provided for military training at land-grant colleges. The National Defense Act of 1916 called for Reserve Officers Training Corps at colleges but few were in operation before they were replaced by the Student Army Training Corps during World War I. The latter program was not successful, but the college R.O.T.C. units, reinstated in the early 1920's, made valuable contributions to victory in World War II. During the early 1940's, a variety of training units were located on campuses across the country, and the indispensable role of the professor in projects ranging from languages, intelligence work and oceanography to aviation, electronics and the atom bomb is well known.

World War I raised serious questions on many campuses concerning the right of dissent, the limits of academic freedom, and the patriotism of German-Americans. The damage to democracy at home while saving it abroad is an unhappy chapter in our national history. Several professors were summarily fired for voicing unpopular opinions. Charles A. Beard, the historian, made history when he resigned from Columbia in opposition to the administration's policy backed by a "few obscure and willful trustees." In addition to championing constitutional rights for teachers, he was raising the issue of outside lay control *versus* the professional competence of faculty members.

Some of the experiences of World War II showed that earlier lessons involving academic freedom and teachers as citizens had been learned, but far too much of Attorney General A. Mitchell Palmer's "Big Red Scare" following 1919 was repeated in the Joseph R. McCarthy episodes of the early 1950's. The sacrifices and hardships of World Wars I and II taught all citizens that the world is a unit and that freedom and responsibility at home cannot be separated from these issues abroad. Korea and Vietnam underscore the point, and future historians will record the extent to which scholars and others have mastered the lesson.

The reconciliation of liberty with authority is an age-old problem. Universities by their very nature are places of dissent, but this cannot properly be equated with disloyalty. Heresy is proper and to be expected if joined with reason and common sense, but conspiracy is an abuse of academic and other freedoms. Those with zeal for reform should never forget the values of the present, and change should bring progress and not retrogression. All too often the issues are not clear-cut and personalities and emotions blur sound judgment. Leaders in various areas of higher education must speak out for truth and justice, and they must know that men of integrity often disagree and that those who claim the greatest freedom must bear the heaviest responsibilities. Certainly, if centers of learning were ever isolated from the problems and contentions of society, that luxury no longer exists. The academic man is part of the work-a-day world, and to the gain and loss of the campus, he is essential in industry, business, scientific research and affairs of state.

The need for international understanding was dramatically stated by Winston Churchill in his Iron Curtain address at Westminster College in Fulton, Missouri, on March 5, 1946. Speaking under the auspices of the John Findley Green Foundation Lectures and accompanied by President Harry S Truman and Governor Phil M. Donnelly of Missouri, Mr. Churchill described the wall of secrecy behind which the Soviet government operated. He also gave timely warning to the non-Communist world of the aggressive intentions of Joseph Stalin.

A little over a year later at Harvard University's commencement,

General George C. Marshall, then serving as Secretary of State, presented a bold proposal for European recovery, which became known as the Marshall Plan. In his efforts to assist the war-torn nations of Europe to help themselves, he helped stem the tide of Communism on many fronts. A graduate of the Virginia Military Institute, this five-star general became the first military man to receive the Nobel Prize for Peace.

The addresses of Churchill and Marshall from platforms at educational institutions underscore the fact that colleges and universities, large and small, are part of the mainstream of life. The significant policy statement of President John F. Kennedy at The American University, the address of President Lyndon B. Johnson at Johns Hopkins and the meeting of President Johnson and Premier Aleksei Kosygin of the Soviet Union at Glassboro State College in New Jersey in 1967 recall similar events going back to the founding of the country. Halls of Ivy are and have always been places of ideas and action.

Both World Wars displaced teachers and students, and life was never the same after Château-Thierry, Bougainville or months of service in jungle or arctic regions or even behind a desk in strange cities or distant camps. Most colleges accelerated their programs, and various arrangements were made to award credits and diplomas to those engaged with the armed forces. The greatest assistance to veterans and colleges, however, came with the enactment by Congress of the so-called G.I. Bill. This was not a pension of the type granted to veterans of previous wars, but an educational benefit based on length of service and not related to disabilities. It was a recognition of value to the nation, culturally and professionally, of educationally trained persons.

Many believed that the G.I. Bill would be a waste of money and time, but to the agreeable surprise of most citizens the returning veterans settled down, took their education seriously and their scholastic marks averaged higher than those of the younger civilian students. Older faculty members found World War II students superior in scholarship and conduct to their World War I predecessors. The mature students enriched the intellectual life of the campus while flouting freshman regulations and often ignoring fraternity social life. Many of the students were married and this introduced special problems, but the colleges and universities quickly learned to adjust, most realizing that they were entering a new era. The program costing millions was an excellent investment for the federal government, and the Veteran's Administration merits high praise for its administration of the G.I. Bill's provisions.

College life underwent many changes before the veterans arrived. The literary societies disappeared on most campuses, glee clubs and drama groups increased in quality and prestige, student publications multiplied, and visiting lecturers and artists gradually replaced many of the required chapel services and revivals. Voluntary Protestant religious clubs, Catholic Newman clubs, Jewish Hillel foundations and Y.M. and Y.W.C.A. groups appeared in many college communities across the country. Athletics prospered and huge stadiums and fieldhouses were constructed. Football replaced baseball as the major sport, and after World War I basketball emerged from the Y.M.C.A.'s as a popular game. Track, swimming, and other sports involved both men and

Winston Churchill and Harry S. Truman at Westminster College, 1946.
COURTESY WESTMINSTER COLLEGE.

women but nothing captured town, gown and alumni like the rough and ready football that not even President Theodore Roosevelt could tame. The automobile entered academic life, off-campus dances became popular, and the prohibition era brought its special problems. One reading F. Scott Fitzgerald will have a better understanding of why the offices of Dean of Men and Dean of Women were created. Coonskin coats and bell bottom trousers had best be forgotten with the observation that little is new in present-day student dress and conduct.

Business prosperity brought signs of affluence to the campus. New libraries, laboratories and dormitories were vast improvements over anything known before. Endowed chairs and faculty clubs came into being and these were followed by student unions or commons buildings. General endowments grew rapidly but there was never enough money to be dispensed by trustees and administrators. By this time college and university presidents had long since ceased to be clergymen and teachers of moral philosophy, that wonderful course that united all disciplines and related them to life and religion, and they were becoming plant managers, public relations experts and fund raisers.

With all the changes and diversions, the quality of scholarship improved. This was not always true of undergraduate classroom teaching, but allowances must be made for new knowledge, new social and world relationships and the pressure of greatly increased enrollments. The body of knowledge and man's world in the twentieth century is a far cry from anything experienced in the previous thousand years, and this only underscores the increasing importance of all education at all levels.

The scholarship of the new universities with emphasis on research led to learned journals, professional societies and university presses. Faculty appointments, promotions and status came to rest on original scholarship as evidenced by publications and creative works. Most of this was salutary at the graduate level, but the "publish or perish" philosophy did not always produce the best undergraduate teachers and counselors. Professors in the small colleges were at a distinct disadvantage because of heavy teaching loads, the lack of library resources and the absence of sabbatical leaves. Before the development of the large universities, many professors could teach most of the subjects in the college catalogue, but after 1900 they did well to keep abreast of the reviews and abstracts in their major fields. Specialization added depth, but knowledge became fragmented and the elective system tended to provide a cafeteria mental diet. The students probably adjusted better than many teachers, but all were aware of a new day with new values and loyalties.

For years scholars had known of the general purpose journals of the American Philosophical Society, the American Academy of Arts and Sciences and the American Association for the Advancement of Science. Under the leadership of Johns Hopkins, Chicago and Columbia, these journals were joined by scholarly reviews of mathematics, chemistry, sociology, history and virtually all of the other subjects offered. To keep pace universities had to publish their own journals, and libraries to be respectable had to purchase and bind all publications for reference. Special lists were required for doctoral dissertations and university presses were established to print them. Now such information is being stored in computers.

The last quarter of the nineteenth century witnessed the organization of the American Historical Association, American Economic Association, American Mathematical Society, Geological Society of America, Modern Language Association, American Chemical Society, American Physical Society, American Psychological Association, American Academy of Political and Social Science and others. All of these learned groups, as well as education generally, have been assisted by the American Library Association. Once the departments and specialties were organized, it was only natural to have other college and university groups such as the American Association of University Professors, the American Federation of Teachers, the American Association of University Women, and the National Student Association.

College administrators were no less ingenious in the mechanics of organization. The Association of American Universities was soon followed by the National Association of State Universities and Land-Grant Colleges, Association of American Colleges, American Council on Education, Association of Urban Universities, Association of State Colleges and Universities, American Association of Junior Colleges, Association of Governing Boards of Universities and Colleges and the American Alumni Council. There are organizations of church colleges, teacher colleges, trustees, deans, business officers, registrars, librarians, physicians, lawyers, engineers, athletic coaches and others almost without limit. The Association for Higher Education, affiliated with the National Education Association, was organized to help bridge the gap between professors and administrators through the joint consideration of current problems. Possibly in more ways than he realizes or cares to admit, the professional college man is an organization man from the day he dons his freshman beanie until he joins the Retired Professors Registry and receives his annuity from the Teachers Insurance and Annuity Association.

Much of the organization phenomenon was a part of the maturity of higher education, some resulted from a need to advance courses or causes and to protect special interests, but most became essential because of the bigness of the enterprise. Higher education remained intellectual, cultural, and social, but it now was definitely big business. With many ancient purposes outlived and new goals often poorly defined, the forced growth of colleges and universities required organizations for psychological comfort and to help point directions if not to find solutions. If the organized president, professor or student lost part of his independence, dignity and status, he gained protection from the group and he could take pride in being part of a vast army that was fighting ignorance and advancing frontiers of knowledge in virtually all areas of life.

Administrators and professors often define the university or college as a community of scholars, but since the early days in Bologna when the students controlled the universities, students

James B. Conant, Secretary of State George C. Marshall, and members of the Board of Overseers at Harvard Commencement, 1947.

have never been accorded full membership in the academic community. Generally, under the doctrine of the university being *in loco parentis,* they have been apprentice scholars governed by all manner of rules and regulations, and until recent years subject to stern faculty discipline. Time brings changes, however, and perhaps as a result of the permissive spirit of modern society or the protests and arrests at Berkeley and on other campuses across the country, students have demanded full academic citizenship.

In 1967, a new code of student rights and obligations was hammered out by representatives of the National Student Association, the American Association of University Professors, the

Association of American Colleges, the National Association of Student Personnel Administrators, and the National Association of Women Deans and Counselors. The bill of rights will undoubtedly be ratified by the various organizations but considerable time will be required to implement it. The document provides that "the student body should have clearly defined means to participate in the formulation and application of institutional policy affecting academic and student affairs," and that students can be disciplined only for violating rules that they helped draft through "significant student participation." The code has long been needed. It will clarify but not end continuing campus struggles for power.

To lessen campus tensions and assist students in obtaining informal and prompt settlement of their problems, Michigan State University in 1967 appointed Dr. James D. Rust as its first Ombudsman. This office is patterned after the system operating in Scandinavian countries. It affords competent guidance through the maze of administrative bureaucracy and protection against abuses of authority. As a conscience of the university and a friend and counselor of those aggrieved or with problems, the ombudsman relies on equity, diplomacy and public opinion to resolve problems and prevent difficulties. The success of the office in helping maintain a campus atmosphere conducive to learning will be watched with interest by the academic world.

Major national groups assisting universities and scholars in the pursuit of high academic standards and scholarly research are the American Council on Education, the National Commission on Accrediting, the National Research Council, the Social Science Research Council and the American Council of Learned Societies. All five have their headquarters in Washington, D. C. The American Council on Education is a private organization of some 1,500 national and regional educational associations, institutions of higher education and affiliated organizations. Its members cooperate in studies of educational problems and they seek the improvement of educational standards, policies and procedures. The National

Commission on Accrediting, also private, represents and serves as a clearinghouse for the major voluntary, regional and national accrediting agencies that are primarily concerned with higher education. It advocates high professional standards and opposes the proliferation of accrediting agencies. The commission sponsors studies in depth of various disciplines as related to standards and accrediting procedures.

The National Research Council, largely supported by federal funds, has as its purpose the advancement of science and its applications to the benefit of mankind. It supports conferences, research projects and fellowships. As its name implies, the Social Science Research Council seeks to advance work in the social studies. It administers grants and fellowships and assists faculty re-search projects. The American Council of Learned Societies repre-sents some thirty national groups in the social sciences and humanities. It encourages research through grants and fellowships, and, through its membership in the International Union of Acad-emies and other relationships abroad, it promotes cooperation among scholarly groups around the world.

With all the growth and organization, there were rivalries and tensions on the campus, and often there was friction with the business community, government agencies or accrediting bodies. Industrial leaders, frequently college graduates, were expected to endow chairs or build Gothic halls but not to understand the academic mind. Legislatures were useful in providing tax dollars, but they too were not qualified to pursue funds into what was taught or researched. The voluntary regional and national accredit-ing agencies were not so voluntary, and they were viewed as stern proctors in virtually all areas except intercollegiate athletics. Also, there were the forces of organized religion with various points of view, newspaper editors, liberal and conservative leagues and countless others who knew what should be taught and how a university should be operated in a democracy.

Despite enrollment increases, explosions of knowledge and pres-sure from within and without, it is a tribute to colleges and universities that virtually all of them have gone about their business and outlived their critics. Recent emotional outbreaks and disregard for law are far from typical, despite the publicity received, nor are such activities condoned by those who value freedom and scholarship. Definite figures are lacking, but some 2 percent of the students are probably hard-core activists, usually members of or affiliated with the New Left, the Students for a Democratic Society, or Black Power groups. At times they are aided and encouraged by 8 to 10 percent of their fellow students and a few outside "hangers-on," depending on the institution and the issues involved.

The world of learning, including debate, dissent and campus autonomy, depends on academic law and order, not anarchy. Perhaps it should be added that institutions of higher learning can and do change and that, after ten centuries, they have learned to persevere and "roll with the punches." They have survived wars, plagues, changes of governments, depressions, religious reformations, evolution controversies, civil disobedience, teach-ins and riots. Like the country which nurtures them, they are strong enough to tolerate many human and physical deficiencies because always there is the ideal of truth, justice, service to mankind and a better tomorrow.

In higher education today, many inheritances from the medieval university remain including the spirit of the eternal quest for knowledge. These take tangible form at hundreds of commencements when gowns reminiscent of old are worn and ancient titles are conferred. The quest for knowledge is present in state systems of colleges and universities, regional cooperative programs of associated institutions, experimental colleges and scholarly societies. The spirit of learning, the pursuit of excellence, is encouraged by numerous honors programs and independent study, and it is rewarded by hundreds of prizes and membership in honorary and recognition societies. It is assisted by all manner of scholarships, fellowships and government grants and loans. An understanding of the history, structure and facets of the higher education about us is a key to present-day colleges and universities and an indicator for the future.

Colleges and university contacts and organization memberships do not end with the completion of undergraduate or professional courses of study. In fact alumni loyalty, activity and financial support are highly developed in America, and these are major distinguishing factors from institutions in other countries. To a considerable extent an individual's college has replaced his home and church in the status world. There are alumni clubs and university clubs in many major cities. The several fraternities and sororities have numerous alumni chapters. The American Association of University Women is active through its several chapters and its national headquarters in Washington, D.C. In numerous ways the college stamp follows a student from matriculation as a freshman until death is recorded in the necrology column of the alumni magazine. And, hopefully, he or she may have remembered *alma mater* in the last will and testament.

Harvard has been growing for more than three hundred years, but Hopkins, Chicago and Stanford are essentially institutions of the past eighty years. The same is generally true of the great universities in the Midwest and West. In the South, Virginia, North Carolina, Duke, Vanderbilt, Emory, Tulane, Louisiana State, Texas and Rice came of age in the twentieth century. Numerous other institutions have made significant gains in size and quality and many of them offer the doctorate. Money has enabled educational statesmanship to flower, and money from individuals, corporations, foundations and especially the federal government will advance or retard the universities of the future.

Most private colleges and universities have endowments and many public institutions benefit from trust funds. Endowments range in market value from zero to approximately $1 billion for Harvard. Universities with $200 million or more of trust funds in decreasing order are Harvard, Texas, Yale, M. I. T., Rochester, Princeton, Chicago, California, Rockefeller and Cornell. Approximately 58 percent of the various endowment funds are invested in common stocks. As financial pressures have increased, more and more institutions have been buying glamour issues. The management of these funds plus bonds and real estate is part of the big business of higher education.

The benefactions of the captains of industry in support of higher education—Cornell, Vassar, Hopkins, Stanford, Vanderbilt, Rockefeller, Carnegie, Eastman, Rice, Candler and Duke, to mention only a few—are well known, and persons of means still give generously. Tax burdens and the rise of corporate wealth, however, have shifted much of the responsibility for stewardship to business and industrial corporations. In recent years these corporate citizens have taken great interest in higher education, but their giving is usually limited to percentages of earnings under tax laws. Organized alumni contribute millions annually for current support and special projects through relatively small gifts. Foundations plant "seed money" and help with matching grants, but needs have outpaced foundations and their resources. Tuitions and fees have been increased substantially and legislative appropriations have grown, but the problems of finance for institutions and students have increasingly become the responsibility of the federal government.

Before discussing the magnitude of federal aid, the great philanthropic foundations that have so greatly influenced higher education merit consideration. Their role has generally been helpful and constructive, but they would probably be the first to admit mistakes and some unintended results of their grants and policies. The mere existence of the foundations with their generally stated objectives and fields of interest has encouraged thousands of trustees, presidents, deans and professors to seek help from them with high hope and many have received generous grants, but, of necessity, most applications are rejected. There have been charges of favoritism, and the tax-exempt status of foundations has been questioned, but despite all criticisms their trusteeship of private funds for public good constitutes a remarkable record. Colleges

Columbia President Grayson Kirk conferring an honorary degree on Nelson A. Rockefeller. COURTESY COLUMBIA UNIVERSITY.

and universities as the chief beneficiaries of foundation grants have been greatly assisted in their endeavors.

Today there are approximately 16,000 foundations in the United States with assets of $100,000 or more. The larger foundations with assets of $10 million or more hold approximately three-fourths of the assets of all foundations and account for the majority of the grants. Trust funds range up to approximately $3 billion held by the Ford Foundation. Among other giant foundations and endowments with more than $150 million each of market-value assets are: the Rockefeller Foundation, Duke Endowment, Kellogg Foundation, Mott Foundation, Hartford Foundation, Lilly Endowment, Carnegie Corporation, Sloan Foundation, Moody Foundation, Pew Trust, Kresge Foundation, Longwood Foundation, Rockefeller Brothers Fund, Commonwealth Fund and the Danforth Foundation. The existence of these agencies has given rise to the cynical statement that they are "islands of money surrounded by outstretched hands."

With grants ranging from a few hundred dollars to millions, the foundations have helped to improve existing programs and to pioneer new and experimental projects. Recent areas of interest have included faculty salaries, graduate instruction, medical research, educational television, Negro education, international affairs and the nature and future of higher education. Foundations will undoubtedly continue to play an influential part in the development of higher education, but President McGeorge Bundy of the Ford Foundation recently warned that ". . . there is no solution to the problems of the private colleges and universities in simply giving away the Ford Foundation." "The present needs of deans and presidents, strung end to end," he said, "would go three times around the present endowment of the Ford Foundation, without a pause for breath."

Sparked by Sputnik, the federal government, long a friend of the colleges, gave renewed attention to higher education. The U.S. Office of Education was expanded greatly, and billions, over and beyond the G.I. Bill and military education, were voted for research, buildings and equipment, teacher education, student support and international educational programs. The National Defense Education Act of 1958 and the Higher Education Facilities Act of 1963 were major steps in the evolution of the relationship of the federal government with higher education. Coming almost a century after the Morrill Act, NDEA constitutes a bench mark for the future historian.

Inasmuch as the Congress has never been empowered to exercise direct legal or administrative control over education in the country, most assistance has been in the form of grants of land or money, and justification has been grounded on need, the general welfare and national defense. The need for assistance from any and all sources is seldom questioned, but the constitutionality of federal aid, particularly for private and church-related institutions, awaits a clear cut decision of the Supreme Court.

President Lyndon Johnson stated on April 27, 1967, "Once we considered education a public expense; we know now that it is a public investment." And he continued, "Not many people really realize how swiftly times have changed in federal support for education. Four years ago, your federal government was spending a little over $4 billion—$4.2 billion—for education and related training programs. The budget for the coming year calls for $12.4 billion—almost three times as much." The President stated that the gains made, over and beyond all other forms of support by the states and private agencies, constituted only a beginning. He predicted that the extra billions spent for education "will pay the greatest returns of any investment that our country has ever made."

In addition to the U.S. Office of Education, which administers the general appropriations, several other federal agencies, departments and foundations support education in various ways. The Veterans Administration dispenses millions of dollars for the education of veterans and their dependents under various acts of Congress. The Vocational Rehabilitation Administration is concerned with educational programs to increase the training and employment of disabled citizens.

The Department of Defense, the Department of State and the Agency for International Development, the Department of Agriculture, the National Institutes of Health, the Atomic Energy Commission and the National Aeronautics and Space Administration invest several hundred million dollars annually in research, much of it with major universities. The Library of Congress with its vast resources is a haven for scholars from all over the world, and many projects are financed by the National Science Foundation and the recently established National Foundation on the Arts and the Humanities. The total outlay for education of various types from all sources in the United States is more than $50 billion annually, and the figure may reach $75 billion by 1975. The total expenditures for higher education now exceed $20 billion and the trend is ever upward.

Federal aid for institutions of higher education increased from $1.6 billion in 1962 to $4.6 billion in 1967. Although more than 2,000 institutions share in these funds, approximately 75 percent of the total is disbursed to 100 major universities. The leading recipients of more than $50 million each in decreasing order are: the University of Michigan, M.I.T., Stanford, Illinois, Harvard, U.C.L.A. and California. Most of the money is spent for research, and the programs are so varied and the activities so new that evaluations in terms of education and stated university objectives are not possible at this time.

Federal aid to education may not lead to direct federal control but it necessarily involves regulations, fiscal accounting—and almost irresistible influence. No college or university today, regardless of its size or distance from Washington, can escape the impact of federal largesse. If the funds were suddenly withdrawn, thousands of professors and students would be displaced, thousands of research projects would cease and numerous institutions would face bankruptcy.

About 90 percent of public independent and church-related institutions of higher education participate in one or more projects financed in whole or in part with federal funds. The remaining 10 percent, including Southern Baptist and Seventh Day Adventist colleges, must compete with the majority. Uncle Sam has moved from the role of a minor stockholder to that of a dominant partner, and basic changes will result and directions will be influenced notwithstanding disavowals and debates over control.

The chief threat is not direct control; rather, it is the impalpable influence of big government with virtually unlimited resources. The categorical grants, and most federal aid is categorical, are a form of control, and shared or matching costs divert institutional funds needed for other purposes. The courtship between the federal government and education, which has been going on since 1787, is now a marriage of financial necessity. It involves the dangers of classified research for institutions and individual faculty members, crash programs and political grants to all Congressional districts, and it holds forth the promise of new centers of excellence. The success of the program will depend on court decisions, educational statesmanship and a reconsideration of the objectives of the partners. The new Interstate Compact for Education may help the states present a united front in federal aid programs.

In 1967, the Department of Defense announced fifty new research programs under Project THEMIS to develop centers of excellence capable of solving defense problems in the future and to provide a wider geographical distribution of defense research funds, "favoring institutions which have not heretofore received substantial opportunity and financial support in the field of defense research." Numerous institutions not favored will desire some of the easy money, and undoubtedly many of those receiving defense funds would prefer the freedom to engage in research projects of their own selection. Only time will tell whether higher education in the United States has passed the point of no return in the control of its destiny. Certainly, the academic community in its eagerness to receive federal aid will have to bear most of the blame for not using its freedom and wisdom to point out to Congress and to various federal agencies the changes being worked in the structure and purposes of American colleges and universities.

Public concern with the financial strain and direction of colleges and universities is forcing consideration of these matters. A Carnegie Commission on the Future of Higher Education, headed by Dr. Clark Kerr of the University of California, is presently studying the relationship of the functions and structure of American higher education to the changing needs of society. This study is a long range examination of where our institutions are now, where they should be headed and how they can best reach projected goals.

The last chapter on higher education, we hope, will never be written. Experiments and trends today point direction for tomorrow. Just as the Jacksonian period pioneered for the common man and woman, we must pioneer for the better American at home, in the world and in outer space, a man at peace with himself and mankind. We shall watch the trend of private gifts and state and federal appropriations and note the accomplishments of colleges that dare to be different; we will profit by their successes and failures, and move education and the country forward. It is safe to predict that funds will become available to the extent that educators can define needs and show where they are going and why.

From time to time there will be new Harvard reports on "General Education in a Free Society," and good will come from White House and Williamsburg conferences on education. The success and failures of innovative programs at Antioch College, California State Polytechnic College, Central Washington State College, Chapman College, St. John's College (Maryland), Farmington State College, Sarah Lawrence College, Rollins College, Bennington College, Goddard College, Stephens College, Bard College, Mankato State College, Santa Cruz, Oklahoma Christian College, Oakland University, San Francisco State, California Western University, Western Washington State College, Richmond College (New York), Kirkland College and others will be studied, as will those of the experimental colleges at Wisconsin, Minnesota, Chicago and Michigan State. There will be new schools and experiments when the New School for Social Research in New York and New College and Nova University in Florida are as old as New College, Oxford.

Individuals interested in change and growth correctly turn to the great state and land-grant universities. Some fifteen of these public institutions currently enroll over 30,000 full-time students each. Persons may well be startled by the phenomenal development of the superb new units of the University of California or the sixty-eight units of the State University of New York. Other twentieth century additions to the university firmament include Carnegie-Mellon University (1900), the University of Puerto

Rico (1903), the University of Hawaii (1908), Southern Methodist University (1911), Memphis State University (1912), University of Alaska (1915), Ball State Teachers College (1918), Texas Technological College (1923), Claremont Graduate School and University Center (1925), University of Miami (1925), University of Bridgeport (1927), University of Houston (1927), Hofstra University (1935), Farleigh-Dickinson University (1941), Roosevelt University (1945), Portland State College (1946), Brandeis University (1948) and the University of South Florida (1960). In 1966, Congress voted to establish the Federal City College and the Washington Technical Institute in the District of Columbia. It also voted a National Sea-Grant Program to help establish colleges and programs of education, training and research in the marine sciences and related fields. The Public Broadcasting Act of 1967 recognizes the present and future importance of radio, television, computers and satellites to the entire field of education. Two-year community colleges and technical institutes are growing at the rate of about fifty each year, and they along with the many public and private colleges and universities bring higher education within reach of millions of students.

Compared with earlier periods of history, Protestant groups did not establish many colleges in the twentieth century, the number being approximately fifty. They were strengthening the numerous institutions founded earlier and raising several to university status. Various Roman Catholic orders, however, founded some 120 colleges in populous areas after 1900, chiefly in the northern and western states. Catholic educational activities generally are coordinated through the National Catholic Educational Association. A few independent institutions were established in the twentieth century, but the trend definitely favored tax-supported institutions of higher education. It should also be noted that hundreds of proprietary business, correspondence, trade, technical and vocational schools offer post-secondary instruction to more than five million students annually.

The majority of the Protestant church-related colleges are virtually independent secular institutions. Present-day teachers and students know little of the history that brought their college into being, and little attention is given the Bible, Chapel and courses in moral philosophy. The decline of the old-style "Christian college" has given rise to several fundamentalist institutions and these are often long on piety and short on scholarship. Protestant church-related colleges are served by the Council of Protestant Colleges and Universities in Washington, D.C.

Catholic colleges, sometimes suffering from what has been called "pluralism verging on anarchy," are facing changes in areas of control, academic freedom, declericalization and adaptation to the mainstream of educational life. Change for individuals and institutions is often painful, but universities throughout history have been resilient and as they seek identity and absorb the good things in secular education, let us hope they will avoid its mistakes and retain some of those qualities that in the past made private colleges of all faiths distinctive. Considering the temper of the age, value judgments of professors and research scholars will have to replace the moral neutrality prevalent in many quarters.

A few years back several critics of the small church-related and liberal arts colleges predicted an early demise for most of them. Fortunately, these institutions have not succumbed and most are far stronger than in previous years. Many have been assisted by the Council for the Advancement of Small Colleges, The United Negro College Fund, the Council for Financial Aid to Education and the Federation of State Associations of Independent Colleges and Universities. While it is true that public institutions today enroll the majority of college students, the casualties requiring major state relief have been the large independent urban institutions such as Buffalo, Pittsburgh and Temple. Many large institutions have been trying to reorganize into smaller units and clusters of colleges to avoid the problems of bigness. The nation sorely needs all of its colleges and universities with the highest degree of excellence.

In some respects education has almost traveled the full circle and is compounded of inconsistencies. Counterparts of Bologna professors and students are found at Berkeley; lotteries have re-

President John F. Kennedy delivering a major address on foreign policy at American University, 1963.

COURTESY THE AMERICAN UNIVERSITY.

turned to finance education; private institutions receive public funds; public institutions receive private support; liberal arts colleges offer vocational courses; technological institutions include the humanities; nonprofit schools occasionally make a profit; land-grant colleges for farmers have moved to town; and urban universities serve the countryside. The changes and contrasts reflect society and changing times and they are all part of the mosaic of higher education.

Trends and happenings of the contemporary era are so much

with us that it is difficult to isolate those differing from earlier periods. Some developments are new and others represent growth or a change of emphasis. Some of the happenings apply to colleges generally, and others to types of schools or to a few institutions. The summary following is by no means complete, but higher education in the United States since 1900 has been characterized by: greatly increased enrollments, College Board examinations, integrated and core curricula, testing and guidance, R.O.T.C. units and education for veterans, international programs, foreign students, the growth of fraternities and sororities, expanded research-oriented facilities, graduate and professional programs, fine arts programs, greatly improved libraries, professional organizations for professors and administrators, accrediting agencies, experimental colleges, two-year colleges, government and industrial sponsored research, state systems of higher education, cluster colleges and regional groups of cooperating colleges and universities, alumni associations, large endowments, foundation support, development offices, federal aid, improved physical plants, big-time

President Lyndon B. Johnson and Russian Premier Aleksandr Kosygin meeting at Glassboro State College, 1967.

athletics, independent study, programmed instruction, civil rights and peace demonstrations, teach-ins, a lessening of church control, new degrees and mammoth outdoor commencements, professors in government, and a much greater freedom for students. Colleges and universities have become makers and shapers of society, joining forces with business and government.

Scholars have been in government at various levels since colonial time and before, but never on the widespread scale existing today. Beginning with Woodrow Wilson during the World War I period and continuing through Roosevelt's New Deal into World War II and beyond, key professors have been drafted as administrators, research leaders and consultants. This has been necessary because of the dynamics of modern society. It is good for government to have talent and fresh ideas and for intellectual activists to gain practical experience, but unlike the graduate school, government must emphasize correctness and success rather than originality.

The new action scholar may have roots in any part of the nation, but he tends to join kindred spirits in the centers of learning and research such as those which have developed in Massachusetts, Michigan, Illinois, California, North Carolina and Washington, D.C. A few of the many halls of ivy may be considered halls of power, but there is no danger of a brain cartel taking over the country. Knowledge is power and it is for constructive use. The American people need and respond to inspiration and new ideas. Their instincts, however, are those of free citizens. Along with true scholars, they resent secret C.I.A. involvements and they do not like to be manipulated or told what to think.

Of all changes characterizing higher education today, the greater freedom of students, the teachers and builders of tomorrow, is of greatest portent. More and more society is composed of young people; and what they learn or fail to learn, think, say and do in a democracy is of the greatest importance. By 1975, about half of the citizens of the country will be twenty-five years old.

Contemporary man has witnessed, often without understanding, a change of pace and a change of values. Alienation has become a common term in America's complex urban society, and the colleges and universities that helped to bring the country to the point of alienation in history offer the best hope of salvation. The problems and needs are such that individuals on each side of the age of thirty will perforce learn to trust and cooperate for the common welfare.

In our own secular age there is no Christian mission such as that which gave the early colleges a sense of unity and identity. Lacking the old ideal, teachers and students tend to drift with their splintered departments and subjects. Old creeds have been eroded, political and economic shibboleths are looked at askance, the new knowledge is overwhelming, computer technology is impersonal and confusing, and individuals must be educated and trained for unknown jobs in an unknown future and possibly on unknown planets. We are on the threshold of a cybernetic age. Faced with such factors, the threat of anonymity in corporate life, and the immediate prospect of war in an age of rockets and atom bombs, youth wonders about the world it has inherited.

Young people have always had to grow up, but standards tend to become permissive, guidelines are confused and the goals of life in home, school and church are often not attractively presented or they are not acceptable. Our secular age desires change and novelty, and many are unable to make decisions based on traditional moral or ethical standards. It is understandable, then, that citizens of all ages are confused and that youth turns to fads, rebellious acts and idealistic causes. It is reassuring, however, to remember that the lament of elders is not new except as to time and place. Over 2,400 years ago Aristotle wrote of young people: "They have exalted notions because they have not yet been humbled by life. . . . They would always rather do noble deeds than useful ones; their lives are regulated more by moral feeling than by reasoning—all their mistakes are in the direction of doing things excessively and vehemently."

Numerous alumni, remembering the good old days on the campus, find it difficult to accept many of the changes, new doctrines and attitudes as progress. Many forget the frivolous days of their youth and express nostalgic views for college experiences of fact and fiction. Astute alumni associations recognize the problems and seek to educate the old grads with all manner of seminars and panel discussions on class days. On most campuses the reunions of the present are a great improvement over the alumni binges of former years. Also it must be remembered that the public relations image of *alma mater* is most important and that, notwithstanding federal aid, she desperately needs annual gifts and large bequests. The contemporary scene, therefore, must reckon with former students as well as with those on campus and those knocking at the admissions office door.

Society can ill afford a half-educated nation. This does not mean that all students should seek academic degrees; rather, certificates in the vocational, trade, and specialized fields should also receive acceptance as evidence of accomplishment. The revised college curricula should be relevant, with greater emphasis on independent learning. The college calendar, which grew out of an agricultural economy, should be revised to meet the needs of an urban population and to assure the maximum utility of buildings and facilities. Commencement should lead to programs of continuing education along with useful employment. And, finally, institutions of higher education must find new and better ways to inspire, guide, instruct, and train oncoming generations in the paths of truth, justice, peace, and honorable industry to the end that free men and women, under God, may have personal dignity and enjoy their pursuit of happiness. This is the chief unfinished task of our colleges and universities.

CHAPTER X

❧❀❧

Academic Costumes
and Emblems

WITH THE POSSIBLE exception of military personnel, scholars have participated in more parades than any other professional group. Since the rise of the University of Bologna a thousand years ago, they have assembled and marched in prescribed dress in countless religious and academic formations. From the installation of rectors and special days of saints to the dedications of buildings, anniversaries and conferring of degrees, pomp and circumstance have added color and dignity to the world of learning. New schools and larger enrollments increase the number and length of academic processions because students must graduate and commencement is a cap-and-gown occasion.

Modern academic dress evolved from caps and gowns worn in the medieval universities, and, as noted in earlier chapters, these institutions were agencies of the church. Fine raiment has characterized leaders of church and state throughout history. The ancient Chinese and potentates of the East wore robes of many colors. In the Bible, Exodus 28, the story is told of the dress of the

Jewish high priests: their garments, "for glory and for beauty," were of gold, blue, purple and scarlet—"fine twined linen, skillfully worked"—and their breastplates were set with precious stones. The Popes of Rome and Avignon wore beautiful robes, as did prelates of the church; the custom of wearing distinctive garments was followed by bishops and their vice-chancellors as they became heads of universities. The costumes of doctors and lesser clerics were not as elaborate as those prescribed for officials, but they were subject to regulations. Academic gowns were formal and informal, and they distinguished university personnel from townspeople who also wore gowns for daily dress.

The styles of clothing for men and women have undergone drastic changes since the medieval period, but academic costumes for formal events, even with the new materials, colors and methods of fabrication, have changed but little. Scholars of past centuries would mix well in academic processions today, but the secular nature of commencements and the use of the vernacular would raise questions of concern to them. Emblems and regalia of office would look familiar and many words such as baccalaureate, master and doctor would readily be understood. And rightly so, because higher education in the United States, which has undergone so many changes during the past several decades, has sought to recapture much of the dress and pageantry of past centuries.

The limited and sporadic use of academic costumes during the late eighteenth and early nineteenth centuries came to a halt with the Civil War. During the 1870's and 1880's, there was a renewal of interest and several institutions began to experiment with caps and gowns. This interest was occasioned by more frequent contacts with European universities and the coming of graduate schools and Ph.D. degrees. Also, seniors desired a costume of distinction to replace Sunday suits and tailcoats at commencement. Harvard gave considerable encouragement to the movement by using caps and gowns on the occasion of its 250th Anniversary in 1886. Once the idea of academic dress took root, the custom spread rapidly with little regard for what was proper or what

Academic procession at Rutgers during the university's bicentennial celebration, 1966.

COURTESY RUTGERS—THE STATE UNIVERSITY OF NEW JERSEY.

sister institutions were doing. If British usage, previously discussed, lacked logical order, the array of caps, gowns and hoods worn in the United States was even more confusing, and some of the colored hoods were bizarre. At some institutions during the transitional period, seniors wore mortarboards and civilian dress without gowns.

At the University of Michigan, the class of 1894 of the College of Literature, Science and Arts was the first to wear academic gowns at commencement. The students of the Law School and Medical School opposed the idea, and the matter was resolved between the "gownity" and the "medics" and "laws" in a school "rush." The "lits" won and the next day the fraternity houses on State Street were aflutter with streamers torn from the backs of the enemy. In addition to establishing academic costumes as the proper graduation attire, this was the beginning of the famed nightshirt parades at Michigan. These were finally abolished after students invaded the library with distressing results.

By 1890, thirty or more colleges and universities were using some kind of ceremonial costume for public occasions. Leaders of several of the institutions became concerned about the styles and advocated greater uniformity. Much of the credit for formulating a standard system of academic apparel, however, belongs to Gardner Cotrell Leonard of Albany, New York. In 1883, the graduating class of Williams College used caps and gowns at commencement but Leonard, a freshman, thought they were unsatisfactory. He designed costumes for his graduating class of 1887, which were made by the family dry-goods firm in Albany. Following college, he researched university costumes and heraldry in Europe, and after his return he designed caps and gowns that were made by the Cotrell and Leonard Company for numerous seniors and faculty members in the East.

Leonard published articles on academic heraldry and became a spokesman as well as a designer in the field. He made hoods to distinguish between earned and honorary doctorates. The master's gown was adapted by him from the Oxford doctor's informal gown, and the American doctor's gown was taken partly from an Oxford bachelor of arts gown with trim from Cambridge undergraduate gowns. During the early 1890's, Leonard worked informally with various university officials to establish uniform regulations for academic dress.

On May 16, 1895, representatives of several institutions met at Columbia University to consider an academic costume code. Among them were President Seth Low of Columbia; John J. McCook, a trustee of Princeton; the Reverend Charles R. Palmer, a trustee of Yale; and Chancellor Henry M. MacCracken of New York University. Leonard served as technical adviser, and he displayed numerous colored pictures of suggested gowns and hoods for the several degrees. The discussions of this group produced, with slight subsequent changes, the Academic Costume Code that is in use today. In 1902, the Regents of the University of the State of New York chartered the Intercollegiate Bureau of Academic Costumes to serve as a source of information and guidance in such matters, and the firm of Cotrell and Leonard was designated to serve as a repository. About 98 percent of the several hundred institutions of higher education in the United States follow the standard code.

In 1932, a committee of the American Council on Education reviewed the 1895 regulations and approved minor changes that were incorporated into the Costume Code. In 1959, another Council committee was named to study the code and this group recommended several modifications later endorsed by the Intercollegiate Bureau of Academic Costume. The new code applies only to articles manufactured after 1960; all caps and gowns in existence at that time that met the requirements of the 1932 code were deemed correct if in good condition. The 1959 committee also prepared an Academic Ceremony Guide, which is followed by most colleges and universities throughout the country.

In 1967, the Commission on Academic Affairs of the American Council on Education issued a memorandum to its members concerning dress for graduates of two-year colleges, six-year specialist programs and for the recipients of bachelor's and master's degrees in physical therapy and comparable fields. These are listed as an addendum in Appendix IV. The Commission also recommended that institutions provide suitable dress for guests participating in academic ceremonies.

Inasmuch as the Academic Costume Code and Academic Ceremony Guide are printed as appendixes, only a brief description will be given of American collegiate gowns, hoods and caps. This will be preceded by a discussion of colors since they are basic in academic heraldry.

For all academic costumes, including trimmings, edgings and tassels, colors associated with the different subject fields are as follows:

Agriculture	maize
Arts, Letters, Humanities	white
Commerce Accountancy, Business	drab
Dentistry	lilac
Economics	copper
Education	light blue
Engineering	orange
Fine Arts, including Architecture	brown
Forestry	russet
Journalism	crimson
Law	purple
Library Science	lemon
Medicine	green
Music	pink
Nursing	apricot
Oratory (Speech)	silver gray
Pharmacy	olive green
Philosophy	dark blue
Physical Education	sage green
Public Administration, Foreign Service	peacock blue
Public Health	salmon pink

Science	golden yellow
Social Work	citron
Theology	scarlet
Veterinary Science	gray

In addition to the twenty-five subjects and colors listed in the code, there are others in use such as:

Optometry	sea green
Osteopathy	green
Podiatry-Chiropody	nile green
Social Science	cream
Statistics	light rose
Textiles	rose

Some of the colors are symbolic, some have historical associations, and others are related to the colors of older academic disciplines. Maize representing agriculture relates to Indian corn and the color calls to mind ripe grain. The white border for arts, letters and humanities is based on the white fur trimming of the Oxford and Cambridge B.A. hoods. Scarlet for theology has often been held symbolic of the blood of Christ or the robe he wore just before his crucifixion (Matthew 27:28). The royal purple of the crown represents law. Green, the color of living things, especially medicinal herbs, signifies medicine. Blue, the color of heaven, stands for wisdom and truth—philosophy. The golden yellow of science is an indication of the wealth that research has given to the world. Pink, long used by Oxford for degrees in music, was continued as an appropriate color for that subject. Olive, closely related to the green of medicine, was selected for pharmacy; and the russet of forestry may represent leaves in autumn or serve as a tribute to the dress of ancient English foresters. Similar meanings may be read into other colors, but some of the choices were undoubtedly arbitrary.

The academic gown is the basic garment of attire and by tradition it is black for all degrees and ranks. In recent years, several universities conferring the doctorate have established a trend for optional gowns in school colors for Ph.D. candidates. These and related exceptions will be considered following an outline of the prevailing system.

The bachelor's gown is of simple design, falling in straight lines from the yoke to within about six inches of the floor. It is usually made of black poplin, rayon or silk with pointed sleeves, and it is designed to be worn closed. Trimmings are not authorized for this or the master's gown. The thickness of the material should be selected with general climatic conditions in mind.

The prescribed gown for the master's degree has oblong sleeves open at the wrist and these are designed to hang down in the traditional manner. The back part of the sleeve is square-cut and the front has an arc cut away. Black is the recommended color and the material is usually synthetic or silk. The gown is supplied with buttons, hooks or a zipper and may be worn open or closed. The sleeves of this costume were materially changed by the 1959 code, and one may still see older gowns with arms emerging through sleeves slit at the elbows. Like that of other academic gowns, the length should be approximately six inches from the floor.

Academic dress for the doctoral degree. From The Doctorate, A Handbook *by George K. Schweitzer.*

COURTESY CHARLES P. THOMAS, PUBLISHER, SPRINGFIELD, ILL.

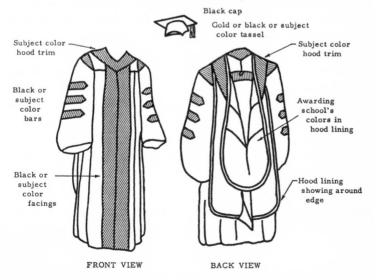

FRONT VIEW   BACK VIEW

The more elaborate gown for doctors is full-cut and usually black. The material is generally rayon, dacron, or ribbed silk, wool being too heavy for most May-June commencements. The doctor's robe is distinguished by its large full-length, bell-shaped sleeves, and it is designed to be worn open or closed. It is faced down the front with velvet and three bars of velvet are affixed across the sleeves. The facings and crossbars are usually black but may be velvet of the color authorized for the subject to which the degree pertains. In the latter case the color should match the binding of the hood and be appropriate to the particular doctorate.

Hoods are distinctive, colorful and useful. Far better than caps and gowns, they identify the subject field, level of the degree, and the institution conferring it. Originally, the hood served as a head covering, but it has also served as a shoulder cape and a bag for alms. Since the hood is no longer used as a covering for the head, the small end has remained as a neck band connecting the two halves of the cape.

The material of hoods is usually the same as that of gowns and the basic color is black. The length is three feet for the bachelor's degree, three-and-one-half feet for the master's degree, and four feet for the doctor's degree. The edging of hoods is usually velvet or velveteen, and the width is two inches for the bachelor's, three for the master's and five for the doctor's degree. The doctor's hood has panels at the sides. Hoods are lined with silk in the official colors or color of the institution conferring the degree. Academic colors are usually but not always the same as the school's athletic colors. A list of selected colleges and universities with their academic colors and a guide to doctoral gown and hood trim and tassel colors appear in the appendix.

Academic caps, hats and bonnets have varied widely throughout history. They have ranged from skullcaps and birettas to top hats and mortarboards. The history of the Oxford mortarboard, the headcovering most frequently worn today, is far from clear. Some authorities state that it was made to resemble a hard-cover book.

others believe it may derive from the skilled workman's mortar board and one writer believes it was adapted from the English college quadrangle. Whatever its origin, it was a prescribed part of the academic dress at Oxford in the sixteenth century and was imported to the American colonies before the Revolution. In the eighteenth century, the tuft was replaced by the modern tassel.

The collegiate code recommends black mortarboard caps for men and women, but states that soft, square caps are permissible for women. The material should match the gown, but velvet caps may be used for the doctor's degree only. Caps should have long tassels fastened to the top center point of the mortarboard. Tassels may be worn on either side, but it is customary for candidates to change them from right to left when the degrees are awarded to them. This custom is possibly a substitute for the practice of bestowing individual hoods for undergraduate degrees.

Permissible exceptions listed in the uniform code state that members of the governing body of a college or university may wear doctors' gowns with black velvet regardless of their degrees, but hoods, if worn, should conform to the degrees actually held or to those especially prescribed for them by the institution. Presidents, chancellors or chief officers may wear specially designed costumes similar to those used by the heads of foreign universities. The chief marshal may also wear a special costume approved by his institution. A person holding a degree from a foreign university may wear the entire appropriate academic costume of his university or he may use a black gown with the hood of the foreign university showing appropriate subject and school colors. In like manner, members of religious orders, military personnel and civil officials having special attire may wear the habits, uniforms and robes customary to their profession and rank. In many large institutions the custom of wearing bachelor hoods at commencement no longer obtains.

The Academic Costume Code is a helpful and influential guide, but there are no sanctions. A few institutions including Harvard, Berkeley Divinity School, General Theological Seminary, St. John's

College, (Maryland), Trinity College, (Connecticut) and The University of the South never adopted the code, but their costumes are distinctive and in good taste. Some colleges, such as Antioch, Carson–Newman, Coker, Furman, Goddard, Harvey Mudd, Mac-Murray, Maryknoll, Mississippi State College for Women, Ohio Northern, St. Augustine's and South Texas, use caps and gowns but do not have hoods. The several academic costume companies have complete information on approved colors and hoods and they provide reliable guidance to individuals or institutions ordering costumes.

The crimson gown of Harvard is well known, as is the crow's foot design for subject color worked into the lapel. This device is double for earned degrees and triple for honorary degrees. Harvard doctors' caps are worn with black tassel only. The Columbia gown is slate gray. The doctoral gown, with facing of black velvet, has sleeve bars in the color of the wearer's subject and a Columbia crown is embroidered at chest height. The cap is a four-cornered tam of soft material with a gold tassel.

Several institutions in addition to Harvard and Columbia have authorized costumes in their school's colors as alternate dress for their doctors. Among those are Boston University, California, Chicago, Cornell, Emory University, Farleigh–Dickinson, Fordham, Hawaii, Rutgers, Tufts, Union Theological and Yale. In some cases special officials have adopted the doctor's bonnet, which is usually made of velvet in one or more of the institution's colors. Occasionally, cap tassels have been used to indicate persons graduating with honors, but the practice has little to commend it since, in theory at least, the cap should be part of a lifetime costume.

The code recommends that only a single degree from a single institution be indicated in one garment. Faculty members should wear the costume of their highest degree, and the hood should reflect the institution that conferred the degree. Persons participating in academic processions should use dark colors for shoes and other visible attire so that a harmony of color will prevail. Decorative jewelry and flowers are not worn with academic gowns.

The color used as a border on gowns and hoods is determined by the subject color of the field of concentration and not by the degree. For example, all degrees in agriculture fall under maize, be they in animal husbandry, pomology or horticulture. Degrees in science have the subject color of golden yellow and this includes such fields as astronomy, biology, chemistry, geology, mathematics and zoology. In like manner philosophy, represented by dark blue, usually includes history, languages, literature, political science, psychology and sociology. Most of these subjects also fall under arts and letters or the color white, but since white is easily soiled, blue is usually used. The chief exception here is for honorary degrees in literature and humane letters where white borders are used. For some majors such as religious education a choice of colors is available, scarlet or light blue. Another choice would be orange or golden yellow for engineering physics. In most cases, color problems and hood designs were resolved long before current graduates entered college.

Along with subject colors for degrees, scholars and laymen are interested in the identification of the degree-granting institutions represented by the hoods worn on special occasions.

Although the American system of identifying schools by the lining of hoods is logical and a vast improvement over European methods, it presents several interesting problems. Some institutions do not follow the uniform code, several do not have hoods, and a few have two or three different hoods, using one for each degree. Furthermore, the number of basic colors for hoods are limited, and with several institutions out of more than 2,000 having the same colors, duplication occasionally occurs. To lessen the possibility of conflicts, academic colors and degrees are registered with firms manufacturing costumes.

Theoretically, conflicts could be avoided by the use of heraldic designs, but the details could not be seen at a distance and the cost of manufacturing such hoods would not make them practicable. A great deal of heraldry is involved in American academic hoods as well as coats of arms. Single-color patterns are used by several schools, but dual colors and chevron designs are by far the most popular. The chevron may be single, double, or triple with points down or reversed with points up. There are single, double and triple bars or horizontal stripes and pales or vertical stripes. Crosses, party designs and tartans are also used.

Among the schools using a single-color hood are Beloit, Bowdoin, Brandeis, Chicago, Dartmouth, Davidson, Fordham, Florida Southern, Hebrew Union, Holy Cross, Iowa, Kenyon, New York University, Oregon State, Mount Holyoke, Rochester, Rutgers, Stanford, Syracuse, Wisconsin, Yale and Yeshiva. It is easy to identify these hoods in a commencement procession, but with basic colors limited, chevrons and other designs are required to lessen the possibility of duplication.

Examples of heraldic hood designs currently used are given

Class of 1967 at the United States Military Academy takes the oath of office during graduation ceremonies at West Point.

U.S. ARMY PHOTOGRAPH.

in the following list. Those of some 200 institutions conferring earned doctorates are listed in Appendix II.

American University	red, white chevron, blue
Carleton College	maize, royal blue chevron
Carnegie-Mellon University	Carnegie tartan
Catholic University of America	lemon yellow, white bar
Cornell College	purple, three white chevrons
Detroit University	cardinal above white, per chevron
Emory University	blue, gold chevron
George Peabody College	garnet, light blue chevron
Hamilton College	Continental blue, Continental buff chevron
Illinois Wesleyan University	per chevron, green, white
Kansas State University	purple, two white chevrons
Loma Linda University	gold, purple chevron
Loretto Heights College	white, green chevron
Loyola University of Los Angeles	gray, crimson chevron
Mercer University	orange, two black chevrons reversed
Midland College	per pale, black, orange
Oberlin College	cardinal, two yellow chevrons
Ohio Wesleyan University	red, black chevron
Park College	wine, canary chevron
Roanoke College	mandarin yellow, national blue chevron
Scripps College	sage green with deep V-shaped silver stripe
Sweet Briar College	dark green, pale pink chevron
Tulane University	olive green, light blue chevron
Tuskegee Institute	crimson, gold chevron
University of Chattanooga	old gold, royal blue chevron
University of Denver	crimson, gold chevron
University of Illinois	navy blue, two orange chevrons
University of Miami (Florida)	orange, white chevron, green
University of Missouri	old gold, two black chevrons
University of Montana	copper, double bar (silver, gold)
University of Nevada	royal blue, silver chevron

University of North Carolina	light blue, two white chevrons
University of North Dakota	pink, green chevron
University of Puerto Rico	scarlet, white chevron
Vassar College	rose, gray chevron reversed
Washington and Jefferson College	party per chevron, red, black
Whittier College	purple, bright gold chevron
Worcester Polytechnic Institute	light gray, crimson chevron

The University of the South, at Sewanee, Tennessee, has a special academic code derived from Oxford and Cambridge usage, and it has an Order of Gownsmen, which recognizes scholastic achievement and good conduct. Established in 1857, the University has offered college-level work since 1868. Its costume code applies to faculty and students and prescribes rules for their daily use as well as for special occasions. All faculty members and graduate students, except first semester theology students, have always worn gowns to classes, chapel and certain official functions. Before 1873, all undergraduates wore gowns, but after the organization of the Order of Gownsmen in that year rules became more restrictive with respect to undergraduates other than seniors. At Sewanee the present regulations exclude freshmen but grant eligibility to sophomores with a 3.0 grade average, to juniors with an average of 2.25 and to seniors with an average of 2.0. The gown and the privileges that go with it are conferred at a special ceremony of investiture each semester and they may be revoked for cause.

Junior or community college costumes, now widely used, are not as well standardized as those of the older colleges and universities. The Academic Costume Code recommends that "collegiate institutions that award degrees, diplomas, or certificates below the baccalaureate level use caps and gowns of light color, e.g., light blue for teacher training, and light gray for other types of institutions."

The degrees generally conferred by the two-year institutions are associate in arts and associate in science, but there are also

Cadet Wing at the United States Air Force Academy stands at order arms during Graduation Week festivities. U.S. AIR FORCE PHOTOGRAPH.

associate degrees in business, education, engineering, fine arts and other fields. Gowns of the bachelor type are generally light blue and light gray, but black, white, maroon and other colors are used. Hoods, when worn, are usually the traditional bachelor's hood without the two-inch velvet border. Sometimes a smaller version of the regular bachelor's hood is used, and many institutes have recently adopted wide paneled velvet hoods displaying colors in a V pattern across the back.

Academic gowns are widely used by clergymen, jurists, officers of medical and dental societies and high school seniors. Each year about three million high school graduates receive diplomas in gray, black, blue, green and white gowns. Specially designed gowns are

Newly commissioned ensigns celebrate at commencement at the United States Naval Academy.   OFFICIAL U.S. NAVY PHOTOGRAPH.

used by the American College of Surgeons, College of Hospital Administrators, American College of Dentists and other professional groups. A few institutions have experimented with lightweight "throwaway" caps and gowns, but these are not recommended.

When a student has met all of the requirements for a degree and has purchased or rented the proper academic costume, and the designated time has arrived for commencement, he or she is ready to join fellow scholars on parade. The nature of the institution, size of the graduating class, type of program, place of the exercises, weather and other factors govern the details of the ceremony. Careful planning allows institutions to meet these conditions and usually a few cherished local customs are included.

Descriptions of typical commencement exercises, baccalaureate services and inauguration ceremonies are given in Appendix IV. Features discussed in the first chapter need not be repeated here. Suffice it to say that the conferring of degrees reflects a wealth of history, and the colorful ceremony is far more meaningful when the significance of degrees, costumes, emblems and regalia are understood. Forms, words and colors are charged with meanings all too often hidden or taken for granted.

The diploma is a written or printed document given as evidence of the degree and its rights and privileges. It names the recipient, states the degree, gives the date, includes the signatures of the certifying officers—usually the president and registrar—and it is imprinted with the official seal of the college or university. Often the school colors are attached to the seal. The diploma is made of parchment or heavy rag paper, and most are placed in leather or plastic folders.

In former times diplomas were hand-lettered in Latin on large sheets or scrolls of parchment generally called sheepskins, but today most are printed in English on small sheets of parchment or quality bond paper. When colleges were small, the president, chairman of the board of trustees, dean and all members of the faculty signed the oversized documents. Some institutions today provide graduates with pocket-size replicas of their diplomas.

Few graduates other than professional persons frame and display their diplomas.

Numerous institutions in the past, including some state schools, presented each graduate with a copy of the Bible, but the practice has largely died out. Orations in Latin by valedictorians and salutatorians have, with rare exceptions, been discontinued. The citations of *cum laude, magna cum laude* and *summa cum laude* have generally been replaced with "honors" and "highest honors." Graduates today are so numerous that most prizes and awards are announced at separate Honors Day Convocations. The names of those receiving major honors, including scholars elected to Phi Beta Kappa, are often printed on the commencement program.

In passing it should be noted that the big business of higher education has given rise to allied industries. Manufacturers of academic costumes have been discussed, but there are a host of others, including textbook concerns and athletic equipment houses. Each year hundreds of thousands of diplomas are printed with names and dates lettered thereon; the manufacture of class jewelry, particularly senior rings, is a major industry; graduation invitations are important; and yearbooks or annuals, with their numerous photographs, are the mainstay of several printing firms. Some companies manufacture and sell several lines and others specialize in jewelry, printing or costumes. Many Ph.D. graduates purchase academic costumes, but the rental, renovation and storage of hundreds of thousands of collegiate caps and gowns is a growing and profitable business.

Occasional mention has been made of the use of university seals, coats of arms, flags, maces, rings, and collars or chains of office. Seals are common to all corporate bodies, and flags or banners are well known. Most European and British universities, however, have a rich heritage of academic regalia that is little known to Americans. It is only recently that some items, such as the mace and collar of office, have come into occasional use in this country. As did academic dress, this custom will spread and special emblems merit consideration.

Seals have been used since ancient times to authenticate documents. They constituted the official signatures of emperors, bishops and corporations. Papal bulls were sealed, and some cathedrals had seals. One of the earliest English seals belonged to King Edward the Confessor. In subsequent years many private individuals possessed seals and often these adorned rings or were attached to watch chains.

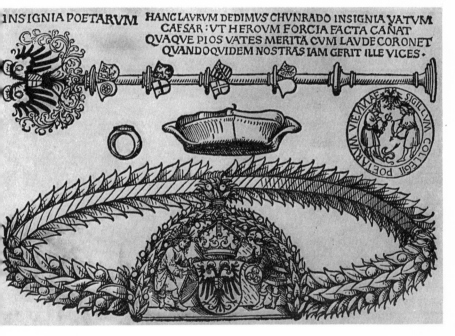

Insignia of the College of Literature, University of Vienna: mace, ring, cap, seal and collar.

COURTESY FRANZ GALL AND HERMANN BÖHLAUS NACHF., VIENNA.

University seals evolved from those of church corporations. Early ones extant show chancellors and masters in convocation. Seals of the individual colleges often picture their founder or patron saint. In Europe the early faculties and student nations possessed seals; some of these show doctors lecturing. In the United States since colonial days all colleges and universities have had seals, chiefly of round design; they are used in attesting official papers, deeds and diplomas. The school seal frequently appears on school pennants and class rings. It contains the name of the institution, date of establishment, and often mottoes, symbolic replicas and shields are included.

Institutional coats of arms are related to but quite different from seals. Whereas all schools have the latter, only a few have clearly defined armorial shields or coats of arms. All too often the two are confused, and the seal is displayed where arms or a banner would be more appropriate. Occasionally the official seal will include the arms as a centerpiece, but when arms are presented on a shield they are separate.

Before writing was generally understood, symbols such as dragons and eagles were placed on standards to distinguish tribes and nations. During the Crusades the cross appeared on shields as a means of identification. Mounted knights in tournaments and battle required shields for identification and protection because one galloping knight in full armor looked like another. In time colors and intricate designs were adopted and crested helms and mottoes added. Coats of arms, generally granted by the king, became prized possessions, handed down in families from generation to generation. Governments, the church and universities adopted or were authorized to use coats of arms, and the science of heraldry, little known and often improperly applied in democratic America, developed to delineate and safeguard family and institutional hereditaments.

College and university flags, banners and pennants are much better known than shields, and they often include the latter or the official seal. Flags, banners and ensigns were originally used in warfare. The Knights of St. John carried a flag consisting of a white cross on a field of red during the Crusades. European universities have ancient banners with heraldic insignia long since approved by proper officials. In the United States each institution usually designs and adopts its own flag. These are of various sizes and patterns. Some schools that have only one color place the seal in the center of the flag in a contrasting color, and two-color schools divide the field in various horizontal and vertical patterns to obtain the best color effect. The flags of some institutions resemble state banners. When carried in processions or used for decorative purposes at convocations, the school standard is subordinate to the state and national emblems. It is not to be confused with name-identification banners or pennants in school colors or with the R.O.T.C. standard. Aside from the colors, there is usually little relationship in design between the school's flag and its hood. Even though there is no official herald or board to prescribe insignia, most college and university flags are attractive and they add greatly to academic color and spirit.

In its 1967 commencement, Stanford University used heraldic banners to identify its professional school faculties and graduates. The banners combine the colors used on academic costumes for the various disciplines with special Stanford touches. Common to all of the banners is a stylized, three-pronged version of a redwood frond, which represents the organization, generation and transmission of knowledge. Stanford also has a special university banner and one for its president.

Graduates of medieval universities usually received rings representing a marriage of the truth of scholarship and the truth of religion. Some institutions still present rings to graduates, and this is undoubtedly the origin of American senior class rings. The heads of universities, usually bishops, had episcopal rings, or special rings of office were presented to them as part of the inaugural ceremony. The custom of presenting rings and chains of office to chief academic officers still obtains in historic centers of learning, and it is being adopted in the United States.

The precedent in the Bible for this practice goes back to the time when the Pharaoh installed Joseph as ruler of Egypt. In Genesis 41:42, it is stated: "Then Pharaoh took his signet ring from his hand and put it on Joseph's hand, and arrayed him in garments of fine linen, and put a chain about his neck." The use of rings by popes, kings, ambassadors and scholars throughout

Rector's chain of office, University of Utrecht.
COURTESY UTRECHTS UNIVERSITEITS MUSEUM.

history is well known. Roman senators and consuls received official rings, and the papal Ring of the Fisherman dates from the days of the earliest universities. In addition to adornment, rings serve as seals and symbols of authority.

Closely allied with rings and seals are the collars or chains of office worn by many officials including chancellors, rectors and

Rector's chain of office, University of Heidelberg.
COURTESY UNIVERSITY OF HEIDELBERG.

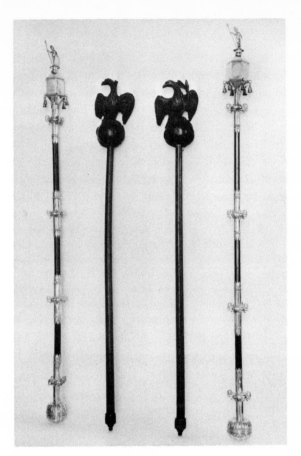

Groningen's four maces.   COURTESY UNIVERSITY OF GRONINGEN.

presidents of universities. The chains, usually of gold or silver, vary in length from choker design to two feet or more. Frequently they are ornate, set with precious stones, and they usually support a medallion inscribed with the seal or arms of the institution. The chain and seal of office may be personal to an individual, but usually they belong to the college or university and are presented to the president or chancellor at the time of his inauguration. The chain with seal is worn over the gown on public occasions, particularly at commencement when degrees are conferred.

The mace, which is now being used by several colleges and

universities in the United States, has an ancient history as a symbol of authority. Originally it was a weapon of offense, made of iron and capable of breaking armor. It was a giant club, which came to be associated with brave men who fought to protect the king's person. Maces were borne by sergeants-at-arms to protect Philip II of France and Richard I of England.

The use of maces for civic purposes began about the middle of the thirteenth century. By the sixteenth century or earlier they were covered with silver and used by several cities. In 1649, the

Rector and officials of Jagellonian University, Cracow, at the inauguration of the academic year 1964, the 600th anniversary of the founding of the university. The rector wears a red gown and biretta and an ermine cape; lying before him is the rector's verge, from the 15th century. The three proctors wear black gowns with red capes, birettas and their chains of office. To the right, an assistant proctor, wearing a green gown with dark green collar, carries the university's oldest verge, from about 1400. COURTESY DR. STANISLAW MOSSAKOWSKI.

House of Commons obtained a mace, and in 1756, a silver mace was made for the colony of South Carolina, which is still used in the state capitol at Columbia. The famous mace of the Lord Mayor of London is made of crystal and gold and set with pearls. As a symbol of authority, the mace usually has arms engraved on or near the top and these or a cross may be protected by a coronet or arched crown. In commencement processions the mace is carried before the president or chancellor and the dignitaries composing the platform party. The British term beadle, to mean mace-bearer, is not generally used in the United States.

The mace is but an additional note of pomp in academic life. Along with historic and colorful costumes, flags, and regalia of office, it stands for order and authority in the never-ending pageantry of scholars on parade.

CHAPTER XI

❦

Academic Degrees

EACH YEAR ALMOST a million Americans receive academic degrees from the various junior colleges, institutes, academies, colleges and universities of the country. Some institutions confer degrees two, three and four times a year, but June is the traditional month of graduation. The degrees vary greatly in level, nomenclature and inherent value. The significance of a degree depends on the level of educational attainment and on the quality of the institution that awards it.

An academic degree is a title awarded by an institution of higher learning for scholastic achievement or for various attainments. Most degrees are earned, and they are bestowed upon the satisfactory completion of prescribed courses of study. Honorary degrees recognize achievements and services not necessarily connected with institutions of higher learning. Degrees are special titles conferred by legally recognized bodies, and they are usually evidenced by a diploma under seal.

During the first two centuries of higher education in America, a very limited number of types of academic degrees were used. During the last century, however, they have multiplied rapidly with the expansion of curricula and specialized fields of study. Many of the new degrees, such as those in aeronautics, computer science and electronics, represent new fields of instruction, but many others are simply duplications. According to Walter C. Eells and Harold C. Haswell, recognized authorities in the field, more than 1,600 different academic degrees are currently conferred in the United States, and about 2,600 different abbreviations are used for these degrees. New titles are being devised from year to year, and the end is not in sight.

Some 800 degrees have been recognized in the past but are no longer awarded. Among the assorted obsolete titles are Associate in Philosophy, Bachelor of Accounts, Bachelor of Cement Engineering, Bachelor of Biological Chemistry, Bachelor of Domestic Arts, Bachelor of Library Economy, Bachelor of Elocution, Sister of Arts and Mistress of Classical Literature. At the master's level the following degrees were available at various times: Master of Applied Chemistry, Master of City Forestry, Master of Cosmetology, Master of Elements, Master of Polite Literature and Master of Science and English Literature. Among the discontinued doctorates we find Doctor of Accountancy, Doctor of Air Conditioning Engineering, Doctor of Arts and Sciences, Doctor of Anthropology, Doctor of Beauty Culture, Doctor of Christian Training, Doctor of Divine Literature, Doctor of Pedagogy, Doctor of Family Life and Doctor of Secretarial Studies.

Summarized by fields, the number of degrees reported by Eells and Haswell in 1960 were:

FIELD	CURRENTLY CONFERRED	ONCE CONFERRED BUT NOT CURRENTLY CONFERRED	HONORARY DEGREES
Liberal Arts, General	55	34	10
Humanities	101	111	28
Natural Sciences	208	134	19
Social Sciences	93	21	8
Agriculture	75	18	7
Architecture	49	36	4

FIELD	CURRENTLY CONFERRED	ONCE CONFERRED BUT NOT CURRENTLY CONFERRED	HONORARY DEGREES
Art	59	23	4
Business	176	50	19
Dentistry	18	17	4
Education	256	62	17
Engineering	348	128	33
Fine Arts	64	5	3
Forestry	34	17	5
Home Economics	44	19	4
Journalism	12	2	3
Law	53	66	20
Library Science	16	5	1
Medical Sciences	146	152	17
Music	90	13	5
Nursing	25	13	3
Pharmacy	13	15	3
Public Administration	51	17	18
Social Work	17	3	1
Speech	37	19	2
Theology	82	89	18
Miscellaneous	2	19	—

This table confirms the proliferation of degrees, with Business, the Natural Sciences, Education, Engineering and the Medical Sciences being the chief offenders. Only the State of New York limits institutions within its borders to certain specified degrees with a single authorized abbreviation for each. As Dean W. Gordon Whaley of the Graduate School of the University of Texas recently noted in *The Educational Record* (Vol. 47, p. 537), it would appear that those responsible for learning and the advancement of knowledge could title academic degrees in a logical and simple manner.

If the titles and numbers of degrees appear confused, the situation becomes more chaotic in view of the multiplicity of abbreviations used. A glance at the appendix listing degrees and their abbreviations shows that a dozen or more abbreviations are used for a single degree. Two or more abbreviations may represent 200 to 300 degrees, and in numerous cases a single abbreviation stands for several degrees. There is great need for uniformity and simplification in the terminology and letters used. The situation is also confusing in other countries around the world, and various international groups have been working with only moderate success on the problem of determining the equivalence of degrees in various countries.

Academic degrees and titles have been in use in the modern sense for more than eight centuries, the first recorded degree being a Doctor of Civil Law conferred by the University of Bologna in the middle of the twelfth century. This was followed by degrees in canon law, divinity, medicine, grammar, logic and philosophy. The use of degrees spread from Italy to other European countries and from Spain, France and England to the colonies in the Americas.

The baccalaureate, the ancestor of our own degree of that name, originated at the University of Paris about 1231. It was set up as a preliminary degree to the *licentia docendi*. It was conferred during a student initiation ceremony in which university officials had no part. When the titles of master and doctor came to be distinguished, and especially when the first stage in the candidacy was designated "bachelor," the successive steps were called steps (*gradus*) or degrees. In Europe the baccalaureate gradually became synonymous with matriculation. In England, however, it came to mean the completion of a certain degree of study and this usage was followed by Harvard and other American colleges.

Originally in medieval times the titles of master, doctor and professor were synonymous, the doctorate common to all being a license to teach. Over a period of years the master's degree became common in faculties of arts, while the doctor's degree was generally used by the professional faculties of law, theology and medicine. The concept of degrees was borrowed from the medieval guilds in which an apprentice, after a period of satisfactory service, was given a license to practice his craft or trade.

At Oxford and Cambridge the bachelor's degree was the first earned degree. It was followed by the master's degree, usually granted after a period of residence and the payment of prescribed fees. The doctorate was generally an honorary degree until after World War I, when the Ph.D. was established primarily for American students. Today British universities confer a wide variety of degrees.

In the German universities the doctorate gradually replaced the earlier title of *magister* and became the only recognized degree for the successful completion of a course of study in the faculty of arts or, as it was later called, the faculty of philosophy. The German doctorate in philosophy, Ph.D., has been the highest earned degree in the United States since the 1860's.

It was a bold step when Harvard College conferred degrees on nine young men in 1642. Heretofore, the conferring of academic titles was a prerogative of sovereignty exercised by authority of the Pope or Emperor. The action of President Henry Dunster and the Board of Overseers has since been followed by American colleges and universities in conferring degrees on qualified students.

Privately controlled institutions in the United States receive authority to grant degrees from their charters. Most of these documents have been granted by the state legislatures, and they vary in the power authorized. Publicly controlled colleges and universities receive authority to confer degrees from special charters or more usually from the legislative acts creating them. Sometimes teachers colleges and junior colleges have received group authorization. Universities and colleges in the District of Columbia and a few special institutions such as the service academies have been chartered by the Congress. Most laws and charters are broad, giving the institution authority to grant such degrees as may be "appropriate" or as are "usually conferred by other universities."

State legislatures have on occasion conferred degrees, and this is quite legal since an agency empowered to authorize others created by it to confer degrees has the power to award degrees itself. Rhode Island and Maryland have conferred medical titles in this manner. The Department of Education of New York, which is officially the University of the State of New York, not to be confused with the State University of New York and its 60-odd divisions, has conferred honorary doctorates for more than a century. Not all institutions of higher learning confer degrees. Several, chiefly by board policy, do not award honorary degrees. Until recent years the five federal service academies and the two service graduate schools did not grant degrees. In some states, the awarding of the doctorate in public institutions is reserved to the state university, other public institutions being limited to the bachelor's, master's and associate's degrees.

American institutions of higher learning confer four principal types of earned academic degrees representing different levels of achievement: associate, bachelor, master and doctor. A few institutions confer additional types representing other levels of accomplishment such as *Licentiate,* Civil Engineer, Architect, Forester, Dental Hygienist, Graduate, Specialist in Education, and Advanced Master of Education. The degree of Specialist in Education or Education Specialist, first offered by the University of Kansas in 1950, represents at least a year of work beyond the master's level and it is growing in popularity. It is often described as a sixth-year graduate degree. Of the 1,600 degrees studied by Eells and Haswell, approximately 6 percent were associates' degrees, 37 percent bachelors', 33 percent masters', 15 percent doctors' and 9 percent other types of degrees.

Many degrees differ only slightly in terminology, such as Bachelor of Arts in Civil Engineering and Bachelor of Civil Engineering. Requirements may vary somewhat, but one wonders about the distinction between Master of Public Health and Master of Science in Public Health. It is also questionable whether separate degrees are needed to indicate method as well as content. Adjunct in Arts and Bachelor of Liberal Studies degrees, involving extension and correspondence courses, should be Bachelor of Arts degrees if the work completed by adult and off-campus students is really the equivalent of the B.A. degree. Rigid standards are imperative, but the time has long since passed when distinctions in degree titles should be based on age, sex or the place and method of study.

The associate's degree represents the successful completion of two years of collegiate work above the level of high school. Although the youngest in the family of major degrees, its origin goes back a century to England. It was first authorized by the University of Durham in 1865. It was first conferred in the United States at the University of Chicago in 1900 by President William Rainey Harper. This degree is thought of as a junior or community college degree, but it is by no means limited to these schools. Numerous colleges, universities and technical institutes also confer this title. The usual associate degrees are Associate in Arts and Associate in Science, but degrees are also given in applied science, business, education, engineering, music, home economics, secretarial service and other fields. The popularity and increase of two-year institutions means a vast growth in the number of associate degrees.

The bachelor's degree usually represents the satisfactory completion of a four-year course of study of college level work. It is the oldest and best known academic degree in the United States, particularly under the designation Bachelor of Arts or B.A. For many years this title was referred to as A.B. from the Latin *artium baccalaureus*. The relatively recent Bachelor of Science degree is almost always represented by B.S., very few institutions using the form S.B., derived from *scientiae baccalaureus*.

Following the lead of Harvard, other colonial colleges awarded the Bachelor of Arts degree and for 125 years the A.B. was the only earned degree used in American colleges. The next bachelor's degree was Bachelor of Medicine or Bachelor of Physic as it was more commonly known. It was awarded to ten students by the

College of Medicine in Philadelphia in 1768. The College of William and Mary conferred the first Bachelor of Law degree in 1793. No other types of baccalaureates were conferred by American institutions before the nineteenth century, although honorary titles were bestowed.

The B.A. degree is conferred by the largest number of colleges and universities. Next in frequency is the B.S. degree. This degree appears in some 400 forms, the most frequent being Bachelor of Science in Education. Other four-year degrees used by over 100 colleges and universities are Bachelor of Business Administration, Bachelor of Divinity, Bachelor of Education, Bachelor of Home Economics and Bachelor of Music. Most institutions of higher education offer a variety of undergraduate degrees, but 115 use the B.A. only, regardless of the curriculum completed. During the last quarter of the nineteenth century and through the period of World War I, the Bachelor of Philosophy degree, B.Ph., was popular with students who did not relish Greek and Latin.

The Master of Arts or M.A. degree generally represents one year of work beyond the baccalaureate but in some colleges and universities or in a few fields it requires two years of graduate work. Until the 1870's, however, there were few masters' degrees in course. A master's was usually conferred automatically three years after graduation on holders of the A.B. who were engaged in professional or literary pursuits and who paid the prescribed fee. Before the establishment of regular graduate schools, this type of degree was conferred on hundreds of graduates of numerous colleges. The M.A. has also been conferred as an honorary degree.

The modern master's degree with a prescribed course of study, thesis and final examination was initiated by Harvard in 1869. Yale, Pennsylvania, Michigan and other institutions soon started a trend. After 1880, few schools awarded the degree automatically, and today it is rarely granted *honoris causa*.

The M.A. degree is currently conferred by about 400 institutions and the M.S. is awarded by approximately 300. There are

120 varieties of M.A.'s and 270 types of M.S. degrees. Master of Education, Master of Business Administration, Master of Music and Master of Fine Arts degrees are conferred by more than fifty colleges and universities. It is estimated that approximately 1,500,000 masters' degrees were conferred from 1875 to 1965.

The doctor's degree is the most advanced degree conferred by colleges and universities in the United States or other countries. It is of two types, the professional or practitioner's degree, as in medicine or dentistry, and the research degree usually leading to the Ph.D. The latter no longer carries any implication of a knowledge of philosophy, but may represent advanced research in various fields of knowledge.

The American Ph.D. was modeled on the German doctorate, and it was first conferred by Yale University in 1861. Had the German faculties of liberal arts not been called philosophy to distinguish them from the professional faculties of law, medicine and theology, the Ph.D. degree would probably be known as the Doctor of Liberal Arts degree.

The Ph.D. requires a minimum of three years between the baccalaureate and the doctorate, the median being approximately six years and the average age of graduates slightly past thirty. In addition to the usual required courses and a reading knowledge of two foreign languages, the candidate must pass a comprehensive examination, generally written and oral, and write and defend a dissertation that is intended to make an original contribution to knowledge. Although many poorly prepared colleges offered the Ph.D. as an earned degree and some well-known institutions conferred it as an honorary degree, standards were stabilized under the leadership of the Association of American Universities, and today this degree is a badge of excellence in scholarship.

Much more recent as an advanced degree is the Doctor of Education or Ed.D degree. This was first offered by Harvard in 1920, and today it is conferred by some seventy institutions. The Ed.D. degree is equivalent to the Doctor of Pedagogy degree, first conferred by New York University in 1891. The greatest differences in requirements for the Ed.D. and the Ph.D. in Education exist in the foreign language requirements, but even here there are wide variations among leading universities.

Other earned doctorates of the research type are Doctor of Business Administration, Doctor of Engineering, Doctor of Jurisprudence, Doctor of Library Science, Doctor of Medical Sciences, Doctor of Public Health, Doctor of Religious Education, Doctor of Science, Doctor of Social Work and Doctor of Theology. Today more than 200 institutions in the United States offer programs leading to research and professional doctorates. These institutions and their hood colors appear in Appendix II. Since the Ph.D. was first awarded in the United States, it is estimated that 265,000 individuals have received this degree, of which approximately 12 percent have been women.

In 1920, four of the five leading universities awarding the largest number of doctorates were under private control. Today, however, the top three are public, University of California at Berkeley, University of Illinois and the University of Wisconsin. Five other Big Ten universities are among the first twelve today in the number of doctorates awarded, Michigan, Ohio State, Minnesota, Purdue and Indiana. The older private universities of the East are still to be reckoned with, but since World War II the large state universities have come to dominate much of American higher education.

Mention was made earlier of specialized degrees, particularly the sixth-year degree of Education Specialist. This, however, has not solved the Ph.D. drop-out problem of "A.B.D." students, those who have completed academic requirements "all but the dissertation." These students are receiving increased attention from deans, study committees, and slow-moving graduate faculties. Dean Stephen H. Spurr of the University of Michigan urges a Candidate in Philosophy degree intermediate between the M.A. or M.S. and the Ph.D. He believes this would assist a substantial group of scholars in a positive manner, protect the integrity of the Ph.D., and provide needed teachers and scholars for society. The Candidate in Philosophy degree would be philosophical and not professional, and it should be "a mark of affirmation and not one of negation."

Various approaches are being considered and taken to provide respectable intermediate credentials by graduate schools. Some universities have strengthened the master's degree by requiring a minimum of two years of study with thesis and more rigid examinations. The award of a teaching D. Phil. parallel to the research Ph.D. has been advocated. Yale has followed the lead of the University of Toronto in offering a new Master of Philosophy degree. Professor Fredson Bowers of the University of Virginia has suggested a Doctor of Liberal Arts degree to require preparation equal to that required for advancement to Ph.D. candidacy but without a dissertation. Pending a generally acceptable intermediate degree, the University of Michigan awards a certificate stating that the student has completed all requirements for the doctorate up to a dissertation. In 1968, Northwestern and the universities of Indiana and Minnesota announced that they also would grant Candidate in Philosophy "certificates" to qualified students.

Dr. Everett Walters, Vice-President for Academic Affairs at Boston University, is generally sympathetic to the idea of an intermediate degree to help eliminate the A.B.D. situation, but he wonders if the nation's ranking graduate schools will be willing to move. He notes that a few graduate schools have indicated acceptance of a Candidate's Certificate rather than a Candidate's Degree, and he urges that those concerned with graduate education seriously consider the establishment of a recognized degree for college teachers, a well-defined, first-quality degree and "not just a tinkering with the Ph.D." In addition to the Master of Philosophy at Yale, the University of Tennessee has established a two-year Master of Arts in College Teaching degree, and the Carnegie Institute of Technology, with the assistance of the Carnegie Corporation, has launched a Doctor of Arts program. Perhaps these and plans at California for a new degree will solve the A.B.D. bottleneck and provide a quality degree for college teachers.

Professional doctorates, as distinguished from the research type, are largely limited to the medical and legal fields. The earliest medical schools conferred the degree of Bachelor of Medicine. Then, after a period of practice and study of advanced courses, the bachelor was expected to return and receive the M.D. degree. This system, then in use in England, was short-lived in the United States. The practicing physicians were generally known as doctors, and they were too busy to return to college. The B.M. degree was generally abandoned by 1812, graduates in medicine receiving the Doctor of Medicine degree.

The Baltimore College of Dental Surgery (1840), now a part of the University of Maryland, was the first dental school in the United States. In 1841, it conferred the degree of Doctor of Dental Surgery. The New York College of Veterinary Surgeons awarded the degree of Veterinary Surgeon to two students in 1867. In 1872, this college granted the degree of Bachelor of Veterinary Science to Daniel E. Salmon. After a period of study and clinical experience in Europe, his *alma mater* conferred on him the degree of Doctor of Veterinary Medicine, the first degree of this type in the United States.

Most schools of pharmacy offer the Bachelor of Science in Pharmacy. A few, however, offer the Doctor of Pharmacy as the first professional degree. There are other professional doctorates such as Doctor of Surgical Chiropody, Doctor of Chiropractic, Doctor of Optometry, Doctor of Osteopathy and Doctor of Podiatry.

Graduates in law generally receive the Bachelor of Laws or LL.B. degree as their first professional degree. For many years a few schools have conferred the Doctor of Jurisprudence or J.D. degree as well as the LL.B. In recent years there has been a trend toward the J.D. degree to indicate clearly that the work is beyond baccalaureate level. The first law degree, be it LL.B. or J.D., may be followed by the graduate degrees of Master of Law, LL.M., and Doctor of Juridical Science, S.J.D. The Doctor of Laws degree, LL.D. is generally recognized as an honorary degree.

Among the colleges of law offering the J.D. degree are those of Chicago, Florida, Georgetown, Kansas, Michigan, New York University, Ohio State, Toledo and Southern California. Several law schools have conferred the J.D. retroactively on alumni holding LL.B. degrees.

The first professional doctor's degree earned by a woman was conferred on Elizabeth Blackwell, a native of England. In 1849, the Geneva College Medical School of Geneva, New York, awarded her the degree of Doctor of Medicine. The first research doctor's degree awarded to a woman was the Ph.D. conferred on Helen Magill in 1877 by Boston University. This lady subsequently took honors at Cambridge University, and in 1890 she married President Andrew D. White, first president of Cornell University. The first Doctor of Science degree conferred on a woman was received by Caroline W. Baldwin in 1895 from Cornell University. Today women receive approximately 35 percent of all bachelors' degrees, 33 percent of all masters' and 12 percent of all doctors' degrees conferred in the United States.

The Doctor of Philosophy degree is always abbreviated Ph.D. from the Latin form *philosophiae doctor*. In a similar manner M.D. is used for Doctor of Medicine and LL.D. for Doctor of Laws, but the degree of Doctor of Music is generally abbreviated as D. Mus. The degree of Doctor of Fine Arts is always D.F.A. and never F.A.D., and the degree of Doctor of Engineering is usually abbreviated as D. Eng. A list of the several hundred most frequently used earned and honorary degrees and their abbreviations appears as Appendix I.

Honorary degrees have long been awarded and they are often controversial, but most American colleges and universities have conferred them since 1692 when Harvard awarded the Doctor of Sacred Theology degree to its president, Increase Mather. At its best, an honorary degree is merited recognition of scholarly or

*President Nicholas Murray Butler of Columbia and Al Smith, then
governor of New York, at Columbia commencement when Smith
received an honorary degree.*

creative attainments or distinguished public service. At its worst, such a degree is awarded for the satisfaction of personal vanity, disguised commercial or political considerations or for publicity purposes. Generally, the recipients of honorary degrees are carefully selected, and such awards encourage endeavor, brighten commencements and add to the total of human happiness.

The Constitution of the United States may bar titles of nobility, but it has no effect on the number and variety of honorary degrees. Currently some 120 different honorary degrees are bestowed annually on more than 2,500 individuals by American institutions of higher learning.

Harvard and Yale conferred honorary M.A.'s on Benjamin Franklin in 1753, and Harvard conferred the LL.D. degree on George Washington and the youthful Marquis de Lafayette during the Revolution. Washington's degree was really more than a LL.D. Actually it was probably the most comprehensive degree ever awarded by an American college or university since it made him a "Doctor of Laws, the Law of Nature and of Nations, and of Civil Law." The first honorary Doctor of Medicine was conferred *in absentia* by Yale in 1723 on the distinguished physician and author Daniel Turner. King's College, now Columbia, conferred the first honorary Doctor of Laws degree on its president, the Reverend Myles Cooper, in 1768. The first honorary Doctor of Music degree was awarded to Henry Dielman by Georgetown University in 1849, President Zachary Taylor attending the commencement exercises and assisting with the awards.

During the 1870's the number of honorary Ph.D.'s exceeded the number of earned ones. Eminent colleges and universities, such as Amherst, Dartmouth, Dickinson, Lafayette, Michigan, Princeton, Union, Western Reserve and Wisconsin, were guilty of the practice, not to mention lesser known colleges. Several institutions and organizations denounced the custom, and the number gradually dwindled until apparently the last Ph.D. *honoris causa* was conferred in 1959. College and university organizations strive to protect earned degrees, particularly the Ph.D., from being used as honorary titles. The most important honorary doctorates in order of frequency are: Doctor of Laws, Doctor of Humane Letters, Doctor of Divinity, Doctor of Science, Doctor of Literature, Doctor of Letters and Doctor of Music.

Yale University confers the honorary *privatim* or *ex officio* master's degree upon members of the corporation or faculty who have not already received the university's master's or doctor's degree. Although followed in some European universities, this custom in the United States is apparently restricted to New Haven. Between 1900 and 1960, Yale awarded some 457 *privatim* degrees, the diplomas being sent through the mail or bestowed in private ceremonies in the Corporation Room. One can but wonder what would happen to the diploma market if all accredited colleges and universities conferred *privatim* degrees.

During the eighteenth and part of the nineteenth century Harvard and Yale awarded *ad eundem* degrees. Under this practice, graduates of other colleges, particularly bachelors and masters, were admitted upon application to the same degree. In 1702, when Yale conferred its sole baccalaureate degree, it awarded A.B. degrees *ad eundem* to four Harvard graduates. Harvard abandoned this agreeable academic reciprocity about 1830, but Yale retained the practice until 1874. Wesleyan University awarded masters' degrees *ad eundem* prior to the Civil War. The custom was resumed in 1894 and appears to follow closely the *privatim* degrees conferred at Yale. Recipients of *ad eundem* degrees from Harvard, Yale and Wesleyan are listed under the heading of honorary degrees although the degree may be an early form of institutional courtesy and accreditation.

Early in the nineteenth century, the M.D., even more than the A.B., was awarded as an honorary degree. Harvard had conferred this title *honoris causa* on three professors of its new medical school in 1786, and in 1811 this institution conferred four M.D.'s in course and bestowed six *honoris causa*. Harvard's last honorary M.D. degree was awarded in 1909 to its retiring president, Charles W. Eliot. The most frequently conferred honorary degree at Yale

Notre Dame's President Theodore M. Hesburgh awarded an honorary degree to the Cardinal Bishop of Milan, Giovanni Battista Montini, who became Pope Paul VI. The hood is old gold and royal blue, for Notre Dame, given to all honorary degree recipients. Father Hesburgh wears the doctoral robe; his hood is scarlet, for the degree in sacred theology. His doctorate is from The Pontifical University (The Catholic University of America), which requires a black biretta with scarlet pompom and scarlet trimming instead of the traditional mortarboard.

between 1820 and 1840 was the M.D. In 1828, eight of the nine honorary doctorates granted were Doctor of Medicine. Columbia followed the example of Harvard and other universities in giving honorary M.D.'s to faculty members of its struggling medical school.

Notwithstanding the fact that clergymen generally disparage worldly honors, this professional group has received a liberal share of all honorary degrees. From colonial days until well into the 1920's, more Doctor of Divinity degrees were conferred than any other honorary title. Church-related colleges have recognized untold bishops, ministers and lay leaders, and in the nineteenth century they were ably assisted by state institutions. The University of North Carolina, for instance, conferred 36 Doctor of Divinity degrees before 1860 as contrasted with 21 Doctor of Laws degrees. Church journals occasionally decried the "inferior quality of literary gingerbread passed around indiscriminately by our colleges," but pleas and pressures for honorary titles persist to this day. For many years it has been possible for serious students of Bible, theology and religious education to earn doctorates at leading universities and professional theological seminaries.

Educators, trustees and particularly college presidents have long been the recipients of honorary degrees. In fact, an informal system of reciprocity obtains among some of the older universities of the East. A new president is installed and within a very few years sometimes months, his merits are usually recognized by sister institutions in the region. In like manner, he comes to appreciate the contributions of leaders and friends of institutions that have honored him and his university. There is no fixed pattern, and all is done with decorum, but a glance through the pages of *Who's Who in America* or the *Dictionary of American Biography* indicates that college and university administrators and scholars are diligent in the care of their colleagues.

In recent times captains of industry, generals and admirals, scientists and government officials have crowded commencement platforms. Presidents of the United States and governors of the several states along with leaders of the judiciary are hardy perennials. Recognition has also been given to authors, artists and leaders in the mass communications media. Farm and labor groups seem to have been neglected. Over-all, however, members of the four ancient learned professions now widely share their scholarly honors with men and women from most walks of life.

The late President Herbert Hoover was distinguished in several fields—engineering, relief administration, government service and letters. A graduate of Stanford, he held honorary degrees from 85 institutions in the United States and abroad. This is probably an all-time record. He also received an additional 468 medals, awards and special citations, the number being much too great to list in *Who's Who*.

In addition to academic degree titles there are royal, religious, diplomatic, military, political, fraternal, and association titles. Degree titles sometimes occasion confusion and embarrassment because the layman is not schooled in this field. Most handbooks of etiquette give guidance on proper forms of address and the use of titles on social and business cards, stationery, and formal invitations. Certainly, the term doctor should be used with discretion to avoid the extremes of braggadocio and undue modesty. In cases of doubt, one is always safe in using "Mr.," "Miss," or "Mrs."

It is often wise to identify the field because a Doctor of Medicine (M.D.) is a doctor but the term physician is more precise. A college teacher may be "Mister," "Professor," "Doctor," or all three. Generally, doctoral titles are used by ministers, physicians, dentists, professors, and research scientists, but not by those engaged in business. Honorary titles may be used according to the preference of the holder. Spurious titles should be ignored. There is no single or final authority on the use of academic titles and usage may vary at different institutions, but, as with manners, good taste and custom generally prevail.

There are no accurate figures on the total number of earned and

Alma Mater, *statuary group at the University of Illinois, by Illinois alumnus Lorado Taft. Alma Mater, with outstretched arms, welcomes youth; the two figures represent the liberal arts and the applied arts, symbolizing the university's motto, "Learning and Labor."*

COURTESY UNIVERSITY OF ILLINOIS.

honorary degrees conferred since 1642. The late Walter C. Eells estimated that 10,500,000 baccalaureate degrees were conferred up to 1961. College and university enrollments were very small until the twentieth century. Today, with some 6,900,000 students enrolled in institutions of higher learning, college degrees are almost taken for granted.

The ease with which college and university charters may be obtained in some states and the lack of direct federal legal control over academic degrees has led to abuses in many quarters. So-called diploma mills have sprung up at different times and places offering degrees for a price that require little or no serious study. Some have been closed by the Federal Trade Commission for false advertising and others have been closed by states or the Post Office Department under fraud statutes, but often they reappear under new names in different locations under the same management. These institutions should not be confused with legitimate and reputable correspondence schools.

Some of the fraudulent colleges offer courses in residence but most operate by mail. Some of the degrees sold duplicate legitimate titles, but others are coined titles not current in the academic world, such as Diplomat of Metaphysics, Doctor of Electro-Therapy, Doctor of Scientology and Doctor of Divinity in Bio-Psycho-Dynamic Religions. The evil of spurious degrees has been with us for more than a century, and numerous Americans and foreign nationals are fleeced each year. From time to time federal and state agencies and educational associations bemoan the fraudulent institutions and warn the public but little concerted action has ever been taken to eradicate them.

Colleges and universities and educational groups have a special responsibility for the integrity of the academic degree. They have labored assiduously through accrediting agencies and professional associations with great success to raise and maintain standards. They are properly alarmed when proposals are advanced in any quarter that government agencies other than the seven military service institutions offer academic degrees. But these institutions and associations have not really organized and given a first priority to the elimination of diploma mills. Perhaps other problems are closer home, but this is an important item of unfinished business confronting educators and law enforcement agencies.

Academic degrees are of increasing importance in modern society, but only a minority of the students matriculating ever qualify for them. Many drop out of college for various reasons; some fail and others only desire special subjects or non-degree programs. Sometimes it is contended that there is too much emphasis on credits, degrees and activities and not enough on education. Undergraduate and graduate scholarship, however, are generally at a high level and adult and continuing education are being emphasized as never before.

All too often academic degrees mean little more than the completion of minimum course requirements. Little effort is made, or possibly can be made, in the larger institutions to know students as individuals and to evaluate them in subjective terms after four years of campus exposure. Most institutions make idealistic statements concerning their purposes and they stress effective citizenship, but degrees do not really identify the graduates as human beings. This may be asking too much but the matter is of vital importance. It is related to character, conduct, alienation, citizenship, and philosophy of life. In some way the education of the "whole man" needs greater emphasis in higher education. Stated in the form of a question: Is higher education sufficiently liberal and is our "liberal education" liberal?

All types of education and methods of instruction will play increasingly important roles as institutions redefine their purposes and adjust to meet some of the many demands made upon them. Through flexible approaches rather than vested curricula, methods and standards, ways will be found by institutions and professional societies to allow for individual differences and special situations. Degrees will be enhanced, and the "credentialling myopia," justly denounced by Harold Howe II, U.S. Commissioner of Education, will be corrected so that admissions and certifying procedures will permit meritorious exceptions and open-door examinations that are fair to individuals, institutions and the public. As Commissioner Howe observed, colleges and universities must maintain high standards and also find better ways to measure potential ability and serve those ". . . who missed their footing on some step of the social, economic and educational escalator. . . ."

Teachers within and citizens without colleges and universities will come to view them as a whole and as related to sister institutions and to society. An understanding of ideals as related to practices, and of strengths to weaknesses, is essential in planning and establishing priorities. Faculties must be involved along with the administrations and trustees and share fully in accountability. Students and alumni must participate in meaningful ways, and the total enterprise will have to be related to the institution's various sources of financial support. A new creativeness will be required to protect values of the past and to resist the forces opposed to tradition.

If all or a substantial part of the above is accomplished, the contemplative scholar will become, at least at times, a man of action. He and his students will utilize technology and new instructional methods to free themselves for more meaningful relationships on the campus and with the work-a-day world. As technology brings the best teachers into contact with larger numbers of students, the students must be conditioned to use self-teaching devices and methods. Rather than being mass processed, they must be motivated for independent study. Degrees will be earned, their integrity protected, and new scholars in ever greater numbers will join the on-going parade.

Despite occasional overemphasis, academic degrees have many tangible and intangible values. They represent achievement and open doors to employment and professional service that would otherwise be closed. They are badges of distinction in a democratic society that is struggling to assist individuals to develop to their greatest potential free from arbitrary restrictions including race, class, creed and national origin. But most important, college and university degrees, and all that they signify, encourage and bring about self-fulfillment. They help individuals to know and live with themselves and to make a maximum contribution to the welfare of society.

"... and now, as you leave these ivied halls, rest assured you'll be hearing from us from time to time."

COURTESY *Changing Times, The Kiplinger Magazine.*

Appendix I

❦

SELECTED LIST OF MORE COMMON DEGREES AND
THEIR ABBREVIATIONS*

A.A.   Associate of Arts *or* Associate in Arts *or* Associate in Accounting
A.A.S.   Associate in Applied Science
A.A.Tech.   Associate in Automotive Technology
A.Ae.E.   Associate in Aeronautical Engineering
A.Agr.   Associate in Agriculture
A.Av.Tech.   Associate in Aviation Technology
A.B.   Bachelor of Arts
A.B.A.   Associate in Business Administration
A.B.Ed.   Bachelor of Arts in Education
A.B. in J.   Bachelor of Arts in Journalism
A.B. in Sec.Ed.   Bachelor of Arts in Secondary Education
A.B.L.S.   Bachelor of Arts in Library Science
A.Bus.   Associate in Business
A.C.   Associate in Commerce
A.C.S.   Associate in Commercial Science
A.E.   Aeronautical Engineer *or* Agricultural Engineer *or* Associate in Education *or* Associate in Engineering
A.E.T.   Associate in Electrical Technology

* *Collier's Encyclopedia* (1967), Vol. I, pp. 48–52. Courtesy of the publisher, Crowell Collier and Macmillan, Inc., New York.

230

A.Ed.   Associate in Education
A.Eng.   Associate in Engineering
A.F.A.   Associate in Fine Arts
A.G.E.   Associate in General Education
A.G.S.   Associate in General Studies
A.H.E.   Associate in Home Economics
A.I.Ed.   Associate in Industrial Education
A.L.A.   Associate in Liberal Arts
A.M.   Master of Arts
A.M.E.   Advanced Master of Education
A.M. in Ed.   Master of Arts in Education
A.M.L.S.   Master of Arts in Library Science
A.M.S.W.   Master of Arts in Social Work
A.M.T.   Associate in Mechanical Technology *or* Associate in Medical
 Technology *or* Master of Arts in Teaching
A.Mus.   Associate in Music
A.Mus.D.   Doctor of Musical Arts
A.N.   Associate in Nursing
A.P.A.   Associate in Public Administration
A.R.E.   Associate in Religious Education
A.Rel.   Associate in Religion
A.S.   Associate in Science
A.S.S.   Associate in Secretarial Science *or* Associate in Secretarial
 Studies
A.T.A.   Associate Technical Aide
A.Tech.   Associate in Technology
Adj.A.   Adjunct in Arts
Ae.E.   Aeronautical Engineer
Ag.E.   Agricultural Engineer
Arch.E.   Architectural Engineer
Arts D.   Doctor of Arts (usually honorary)

B.A.   Bachelor of Arts
B.A.A.   Bachelor of Applied Arts
B.A.Arch.   Bachelor of Arts in Architecture
B.A.E.   Bachelor of Arts in Education *or* Bachelor of Arts Educa-
 tion *or* Bachelor of Aeronautical Engineering *or* Bachelor of Agri-
 cultural Engineering *or* Bachelor of Architectural Engineering
B.A.Ed.   Bachelor of Arts in Education
B.A. in Ed.   Bachelor of Arts in Education
B.A. in J.   Bachelor of Arts in Journalism

B.A. in L.S.   Bachelor of Arts in Library Science

B.A. in Nurs.   Bachelor of Arts in Nursing

B.A. in Rel.Ed.   Bachelor of Arts in Religious Education

B.A. (Jour.)   Bachelor of Arts in Journalism

B.A.M.   Bachelor of Arts in Music *or* Bachelor of Applied Mathematics

B.A.Mus.Ed.   Bachelor of Arts in Music Education

B.A.O.   Bachelor of Arts in Oratory

B.A.P.C.T.   Bachelor of Arts in Practical Christian Training

B.A.S.   Bachelor of Applied Science *or* Bachelor of Arts in Speech

B.Acc.   Bachelor of Accountancy

B.Adm.Eng.   Bachelor of Administrative Engineering

B.Ae.E.   Bachelor of Aeronautical Engineering

B.Ag.   Bachelor of Agriculture

B.Ag.E.   Bachelor of Agricultural Engineering

B.App.Arts   Bachelor of Applied Arts

B.Arch.   Bachelor of Architecture

B.Arch.E.   Bachelor of Architectural Engineering

B.B.A.   Bachelor of Business Administration

B.C.E.   Bachelor of Civil Engineering *or* Bachelor of Christian Education

B.C.L.   Bachelor of Civil Law

B.C.M.   Bachelor of Church Music

B.C.P.   Bachelor of City Planning

B.C.S.   Bachelor of Commercial Science

B.Cer.E.   Bachelor of Ceramic Engineering

B.Ch.   Bachelor of Chemistry

B.Ch.E.   Bachelor of Chemical Engineering

B.Com.Sc.   Bachelor of Commercial Science

B.D.   Bachelor of Divinity

B.Des.   Bachelor of Design

B.E.   Bachelor of Education *or* Bachelor of Engineering

B.E.E.   Bachelor of Electrical Engineering

B.E.M.   Bachelor of Engineering of Mines

B.E.P.   Bachelor of Engineering Physics

B.E.S.   Bachelor of Engineering Science

B.Ed.   Bachelor of Education

B.F.   Bachelor of Forestry

B.F.A.   Bachelor of Fine Arts

B.F.A.Mus.   Bachelor of Fine Arts in Music

B.F.S.   Bachelor of Foreign Service

B.F.T.   Bachelor of Foreign Trade
B.G.E.   Bachelor of Geological Engineering
B.Gen.Ed.   Bachelor of General Education
B.H.L.   Bachelor of Hebrew Literature *or* Bachelor of Hebrew Letters
B.I.D.   Bachelor of Industrial Design
B.I.E.   Bachelor of Industrial Engineering
B.I.T.   Bachelor of Industrial Technology
B.Ind.Ed.   Bachelor of Industrial Education
B.J.   Bachelor of Journalism
B.L.A.   Bachelor of Landscape Architecture
B.L.I.   Bachelor of Literary Interpretation
B.L.S.   Bachelor of Library Science
B.Land.Arch.   Bachelor of Landscape Architecture
Bldg.E.   Building Engineering
B.Litt.   Bachelor of Literature
B.M.   Bachelor of Music *or* Bachelor of Medicine
B.M.E.   Bachelor of Mechanical Engineering *or* Bachelor of Music Education
B.M.Ed.   Bachelor of Music Education
B.M.S.   Bachelor of Marine Science
B.M.T.   Bachelor of Medical Technology
B.Mar.E.   Bachelor of Marine Engineering
B.Met.E.   Bachelor of Metallurgical Engineering
B.Mgt.E.   Bachelor of Management Engineering
B.Min.E.   Bachelor of Mining Engineering
B.Mus.   Bachelor of Music
B.N.   Bachelor of Nursing
B.N.S.   Bachelor of Naval Science
B.P.A.   Bachelor of Professional Arts
B.P.E.   Bachelor of Physical Education
B.Pet.E.   Bachelor of Petroleum Engineering
B.Ph.   Bachelor of Philosophy
B.Pharm.   Bachelor of Pharmacy
B.R.E.   Bachelor of Religious Education
B.S.   Bachelor of Science
B.S.A.   Bachelor of Science in Agriculture
B.S.A.A.   Bachelor of Science in Applied Arts
B.S.A.E.   Bachelor of Science in Agricultural Engineering *or* Bachelor of Science in Aeronautical Engineering *or* Bachelor of Science in Architectural Engineering

B.S.Adv.   Bachelor of Science in Advertising
B.S.Ae.E.   Bachelor of Science in Aeronautical Engineering
B.S.Ag.E.   Bachelor of Science in Agricultural Engineering
B.S.Agr.   Bachelor of Science in Agriculture
B.S.Arch.   Bachelor of Science in Architecture
B.S.Arch.E.   Bachelor of Science in Architectural Engineering
B.S.Arch.Eng.   Bachelor of Science in Architectural Engineering
B.S.Art. Ed.   Bachelor of Science in Art Education
B.S.B.A.   Bachelor of Science in Business Administration
B.S.Bus.   Bachelor of Science in Business
B.S.Bus.Mgt.   Bachelor of Science in Business Management
B.S.C.   Bachelor of Science in Commerce
B.S.C.E.   Bachelor of Science in Civil Engineering
B.S.Ch.   Bachelor of Science in Chemistry
B.S.Ch.E.   Bachelor of Science in Chemical Engineering
B.S.Com.   Bachelor of Science in Communications
B.S.D.   Bachelor of Science in Design
B.S.D.Hyg.   Bachelor of Science in Dental Hygiene
B.S.Des.   Bachelor of Science in Design
B.S.E.   Bachelor of Science in Engineering *or* Bachelor of Science in Education
B.S.E.E.   Bachelor of Science in Electrical Engineering *or* Bachelor of Science in Elementary Education
B.S.E.Engr.   Bachelor of Science in Electrical Engineering
B.S.E.M.   Bachelor of Science in Engineering of Mines
B.S.E.P.   Bachelor of Science in Engineering Physics
B.S.E.S.   Bachelor of Science in Engineering Sciences
B.S.Ec.   Bachelor of Science in Economics
B.S.Ed.   Bachelor of Science in Education
B.S.El.E.   Bachelor of Science in Electronic Engineering
B.S.Eng.   Bachelor of Science in Engineering
B.S.F.   Bachelor of Science in Forestry
B.S.F.M.   Bachelor of Science in Forest Management
B.S.F.Mgt.   Bachelor of Science in Fisheries Management
B.S.F.S.   Bachelor of Science in Foreign Service
B.S.F.T.   Bachelor of Science in Fuel Technology
B.S.For.   Bachelor of Science in Forestry
B.S.G.E.   Bachelor of Science in General Engineering
B.S.G.Mgt.   Bachelor of Science in Game Management
B.S.Gen.Ed.   Bachelor of Science in General Education
B.S.Geol.E.   Bachelor of Science in Geological Engineering

B.S.Gph.   Bachelor of Science in Geophysics
B.S.H.A.   Bachelor of Science in Hospital Administration
B.S.H.E.   Bachelor of Science in Home Economics
B.S.H.Ec.   Bachelor of Science in Home Economics
B.S.H.Ed.   Bachelor of Science in Health Education
B.S.Hyg.   Bachelor of Science in Hygiene
B.S.I.E.   Bachelor of Science in Industrial Engineering *or* Bachelor of Science in Industrial Education
B.S.I.R.   Bachelor of Science in Industrial Relations
B.S.I.T.   Bachelor of Science in Industrial Technology
B.S. in A.E.   Bachelor of Science in Aeronautical Engineering
B.S. in Acc.   Bachelor of Science in Accountancy
B.S. In Ae.   Bachelor of Science in Aeronautics
B.S. in Agr.   Bachelor of Science in Agriculture
B.S. in Agr. Ed.   Bachelor of Science in Agricultural Education
B.S. in Agric.   Bachelor of Science in Agriculture
B.S. in App. Arts   Bachelor of Science in Applied Arts
B.S. in Arch.   Bachelor of Science in Architecture
B.S. in Arch. Engr.   Bachelor of Science in Architectural Engineering
B.S. in Art Ed.   Bachelor of Science in Art Education
B.S. in B.A.   Bachelor of Science in Business Administration
B.S. in B.M.S.   Bachelor of Science in Basic Medical Sciences
B.S. in Bus.Ed.   Bachelor of Science in Business Education
B.S. in C.   Bachelor of Science in Commerce
B.S. in C. and B.A.   Bachelor of Science in Commercial and Business Administration
B.S. in C. and E.   Bachelor of Science in Commerce and Economics
B.S. in C.E.   Bachelor of Science in Civil Engineering
B.S. in Cart.   Bachelor of Science in Cartography
B.S. in Cer.Engr.   Bachelor of Science in Ceramic Engineering
B.S. in Cer.Tech.   Bachelor of Science in Ceramic Technology
B.S. in Ch.E.   Bachelor of Science in Chemical Engineering
B.S. in Chem.Tech.   Bachelor of Science in Chemical Technology
B.S. in Com.   Bachelor of Science in Commerce
B.S. in Com.Ed.   Bachelor of Science in Commercial Education
B.S. in Comm.Rec.   Bachelor of Science in Community Recreation
B.S. in D.H.   Bachelor of Science in Dental Hygiene
B.S. in Dent.   Bachelor of Science in Dentistry
B.S. in Diet.   Bachelor of Science in Dietetics
B.S. in E.   Bachelor of Science in Engineering
B.S. in E.E.   Bachelor of Science in Electrical Engineering

B.S. in E.Law   Bachelor of Science in Engineering Law
B.S. in E.M.   Bachelor of Science in Engineering of Mines
B.S. in E.Math.   Bachelor of Science in Engineering Mathematics
B.S. in E.P.   Bachelor of Science in Engineering Physics
B.S. in Elem. Ed.   Bachelor of Science in Elementary Education
B.S. in Engr.Phys.   Bachelor of Science in Engineering Physics
B.S. in Fin.   Bachelor of Science in Finance
B.S. in G.S.   Bachelor of Science in General Studies
B.S. in G.W.E.   Bachelor of Science in Group Work Education
B.S. in Gen.Bus.   Bachelor of Science in General Business
B.S. in Gen.Eng.   Bachelor of Science in General Engineering
B.S. in Glass Tech.   Bachelor of Science in Glass Technology
B.S. in Gph.E.   Bachelor of Science in Geophysical Engineering
B.S. in H. and P.E.   Bachelor of Science in Health and Physical Education
B.S. in H. and R.A.   Bachelor of Science in Hotel and Restaurant Administration
B.S. in Home Ec.   Bachelor of Science in Home Economics
B.S. in Home Ec.Ed.   Bachelor of Science in Home Economics Education
B.S. in I.A.   Bachelor of Science in Industrial Arts
B.S. in Ind.Chem.   Bachelor of Science in Industrial Chemistry
B.S. in J.   Bachelor of Science in Journalism
B.S. in L.S.   Bachelor of Science in Library Science
B.S. in Lab.Tech.   Bachelor of Science in Laboratory Technology
B.S. in M.A.   Bachelor of Science in Mechanical Arts
B.S. in M.E.   Bachelor of Science in Mechanical Engineering
B.S. in M.S.   Bachelor of Science in Military Science
B.S. in M.T.   Bachelor of Science in Medical Technology
B.S. in Mech.Arts   Bachelor of Science in Mechanical Arts
B.S. in Med.   Bachelor of Science in Medicine
B.S. in Med.Rec.   Bachelor of Science in Medical Records
B.S. in Med.Rec.Lib.   Bachelor of Science in Medical Records Librarianship
B.S. in Med.Sc.   Bachelor of Science in Medical Science
B.S. in Med.Tech.   Bachelor of Science in Medical Technology
B.S. in Mgt.Engr.   Bachelor of Science in Management Engineering
B.S. in Mktg.   Bachelor of Science in Marketing
B.S. in Mus.   Bachelor of Science in Music
B.S. in N.   Bachelor of Science in Nursing
B.S. in N.E.   Bachelor of Science in Nursing Education

B.S. in N.Ed.   Bachelor of Science in Nursing Education
B.S. in N.S.   Bachelor of Science in Natural Science
B.S. in Nurs.   Bachelor of Science in Nursing
B.S. in Occ.Ther.   Bachelor of Science in Occupational Therapy
B.S. in Opt.   Bachelor of Science in Optics *or* Bachelor of Science in Optometry
B.S. in P.A.   Bachelor of Science in Public Administration
B.S. in P.E.   Bachelor of Science in Petroleum Engineering *or* Bachelor of Science in Physical Education
B.S. in P.H.N.   Bachelor of Science in Public Health Nursing
B.S. in P.S.M.   Bachelor of Science in Public School Music
B.S. in Pet.E.   Bachelor of Science in Petroleum Engineering
B.S. in Ph.   Bachelor of Science in Pharmacy
B.S. in Pharm.   Bachelor of Science in Pharmacy
B.S. in Pr.Ge.   Bachelor of Science in Professional Geology
B.S. in Pr.Met.   Bachelor of Science in Professional Meteorology
B.S. in R.T.   Bachelor of Science in Radiological Technology
B.S. in S.E.   Bachelor of Science in Sanitary Engineering
B.S. in S.S.   Bachelor of Science in Social Service *or* Bachelor of Science in Social Science
B.S. in S.Sc.   Bachelor of Science in Social Science
B.S. in S.W.   Bachelor of Science in Social Work
B.S. in Sec.Sci.   Bachelor of Science in Secretarial Science
B.S. in Sp.   Bachelor of Science in Speech
B.S. in T.E.   Bachelor of Science in Textile Engineering
B.S. in Textile Eng.   Bachelor of Science in Textile Engineering
B.S. in Voc.Ag.   Bachelor of Science in Vocational Agriculture
B.S. in Voc.Ed.   Bachelor of Science in Vocational Education
B.S.Ind.Ed.   Bachelor of Science in Industrial Education
B.S.Ind.Engr.   Bachelor of Science in Industrial Engineering
B.S.Ind.Mgt.   Bachelor of Science in Industrial Management
B.S.J.   Bachelor of Science in Journalism
B.S.L.   Bachelor of Sacred Literature *or* Bachelor of Science in Law *or* Bachelor of Science in Linguistics
B.S.L.A. and Nurs.   Bachelor of Science in Liberal Arts and Nursing
B.S.L.Arch.   Bachelor of Science in Landscape Architecture
B.S.L.M.   Bachelor of Science in Landscape Management
B.S.L.S.   Bachelor of Science in Library Science
B.S.Lab.Rel.   Bachelor of Science in Labor Relations
B.S.M.   Bachelor of Science in Medicine *or* Bachelor of Science in Music *or* Bachelor of Sacred Music

B.S.M.E.   Bachelor of Science in Mechanical Engineering *or* Bachelor of Science in Mining Engineering *or* Bachelor of Science in Music Education

B.S.M.T.   Bachelor of Science in Medical Technology

B.S.Med.Tech.   Bachelor of Science in Medical Technology

B.S.Met.   Bachelor of Science in Metallurgy

B.S.Met.E.   Bachelor of Science in Metallurgical Engineering

B.S.Min.   Bachelor of Science in Mineralogy

B.S.Mus.Ed.   Bachelor of Science in Music Education

B.S.N.   Bachelor of Science in Nursing

B.S.N.A.   Bachelor of Science in Nursing Administration

B.S.O.T.   Bachelor of Science in Occupational Therapy

B.S.Orn.Hort.   Bachelor of Science in Ornamental Horticulture

B.S.P.   Bachelor of Science in Pharmacy

B.S.P.A.   Bachelor of Science in Public Administration

B.S.P.E.   Bachelor of Science in Physical Education

B.S.P.H.   Bachelor of Science in Public Health

B.S.P.H.N.   Bachelor of Science in Public Health Nursing

B.S.P.T.   Bachelor of Science in Physical Therapy

B.S.Phar.   Bachelor of Science in Pharmacy

B.S.Pharm.   Bachelor of Science in Pharmacy

B.S.R.T.   Bachelor of Science in Radiological Technology

B.S.Radio-TV.   Bachelor of Science in Radio and Television

B.S.Rec.   Bachelor of Science in Recreation

B.S.Ret.   Bachelor of Science in Retailing

B.S.S.   Bachelor of Secretarial Science *or* Bachelor of Social Science

B.S.S.A.   Bachelor of Science in Secretarial Administration

B.S.S.E.   Bachelor of Science in Secondary Education

B.S.S.S.   Bachelor of Science in Secretarial Studies *or* Bachelor of Science in Social Science

B.S.T.&I.E.   Bachelor of Science in Trade and Industrial Education

B.S.Trans.   Bachelor of Science in Transportation

B.Sc.   Bachelor of Science

B.Sc. in Agr.   Bachelor of Science in Agriculture

B.Sc. in C.E.   Bachelor of Science in Civil Engineering

B.Sc. in Dent.   Bachelor of Science in Dentistry

B.Sc. in M.E.   Bachelor of Science in Mechanical Engineering

B.Sc. in Med.   Bachelor of Science in Medicine

B.Sc. in Nurs.   Bachelor of Science in Nursing

B.Sc. in Opt.   Bachelor of Science in Optometry

B.Sc. in Phar.   Bachelor of Science in Pharmacy

B.Sc. in Rest.Mgt.   Bachelor of Science in Restaurant Management
B.Sch.Music   Bachelor of School Music
B.T.Ch.   Bachelor of Textile Chemistry
B.T.E.   Bachelor of Textile Engineering
B.Th.   Bachelor of Theology
B.V.A.   Bachelor of Vocational Agriculture
B.V.E.   Bachelor of Vocational Education
B.W.E.   Bachelor of Welding Engineering

C.A.S.   Certificate of Advanced Studies
C.E.   Civil Engineer
Cer.E.   Ceramic Engineer
Ch.E.   Chemical Engineer
Chem.E.   Chemical Engineer

D.Agr.   Doctor of Agriculture
D.Arch.   Doctor of Architecture
D.B.   Bachelor of Divinity
D.B.A.   Doctor of Business Administration (earned and honorary)
D.C.   Doctor of Chiropractic
D.C.L.   Doctor of Civil Law (usually honorary)
D.C.S.   Doctor of Commercial Science (usually honorary)
D.Ch.E.   Doctor of Chemical Engineering
D.Comp.L.   Doctor of Comparative Law
D.D.   Doctor of Divinity (honorary)
D.D.S.   Doctor of Dental Science *or* Doctor of Dental Surgery
D.D.Sc.   Doctor of Dental Science
D.Ed.   Doctor of Education (both earned and honorary)
D.Eng.   Doctor of Engineering (often honorary)
D.Eng.S.   Doctor of Engineering Science (both earned and honorary)
D.F.   Doctor of Forestry
D.F.A.   Doctor of Fine Arts (usually honorary)
D.H.   Doctor of Humanities (usually honorary) *or* Doctor of Humanics (honorary)
D.H.L.   Doctor of Hebrew Literature *or* Doctor of Hebrew Letters (both earned and honorary)
D.J.T.   Doctor of Jewish Theology (usually honorary)
D.Journ.   Doctor of Journalism (both earned and honorary)
D.L.S.   Doctor of Library Science
D.M.D.   Doctor of Dental Medicine
D.M.L.   Doctor of Modern Languages

D.M.S.   Doctor of Medical Science
D.Mus.   Doctor of Music (usually honorary)
D.O.   Doctor of Osteopathy
D.P.A.   Doctor of Public Administration (both earned and honorary)
D.P.E.   Doctor of Physical Education
D.P.H.   Doctor of Public Health
D.P.S.   Doctor of Public Service (usually honorary)
D.Ped.   Doctor of Pedagogy (now usually honorary)
D.R.E.   Doctor of Religious Education (both earned and honorary)
D.S.   Doctor of Science (usually honorary)
D.S.C.   Doctor of Surgical Chiropody
D.S.M.   Doctor of Sacred Music
D.S.S.   Doctor of Social Science
D.S.W.   Doctor of Social Welfare *or* Doctor of Social Work
D.Sc.   Doctor of Science (usually honorary)
D.V.M.   Doctor of Veterinary Medicine

E.A.A.   Engineer in Aeronautics and Astronautics
E.E.   Electrical Engineer
E. in E.E.   Engineer in Electrical Engineering
E. in M.E.   Engineer in Mechanical Engineering
E.M.   Engineer of Mines *or* Mining Engineer
E.Met.   Engineer of Metallurgy
E.S.   Education Specialist
Ed.B.   Bachelor of Education
Ed.D.   Doctor of Education (both earned and honorary)
Ed.M.   Master of Education
Ed.R.D.   Doctor of Religious Education
Ed.S.   Education Specialist *or* Specialist in Education
Eng.D.   Doctor of Engineering (often honorary)
Engr.   Engineer

For.   Forester

G.N.   Graduate Nurse
Geol.E.   Geological Engineer
Gp.E.   Geophysical Engineer

HH.D.   Doctor of Humanities (usually honorary)

I.E.   Industrial Engineer

Ind.E.   Industrial Engineer

J.C.B.   Bachelor of Canon Law
J.C.D.   Doctor of Canon Law (both earned and honorary)
J.C.L.   Licentiate in Canon Law
J.D.   Doctor of Jurisprudence (both earned and honorary)
J.S.D.   Doctor of the Science of Law
Jur.M.   Master of Jurisprudence

L.H.D.   Doctor of Humane Letters (usually honorary)
L.Th.   Licentiate in Theology
Litt.B.   Bachelor of Literature
Litt.D.   Doctor of Letters *or* Doctor of Literature (usually honorary)
Litt.M.   Master of Letters (sometimes honorary)
LL.B.   Bachelor of Laws
LL.D.   Doctor of Laws (usually honorary)
LL.M.   Master of Laws

M.A.   Master of Arts
M.A.Arch.   Master of Arts in Architecture
M.A.E.   Master of Aeronautical Engineering *or* Master of Art Education *or* Master of Arts in Education
M.A.Ed.   Master of Arts in Education
M.A. in L.S.   Master of Arts in Library Science
M.A.L.D.   Master of Arts in Law and Diplomacy
M.A.L.S.   Master of Arts in Library Science *or* Master of Arts in Liberal Studies
M.A.R.   Master of Arts in Religion
M.A.T.   Master of Arts for Teachers *or* Master of Arts in Teaching
M.Ac.   Master of Accountancy
M.Aero.E.   Master of Aeronautical Engineering
M.Ag.Ec.   Master of Agricultural Economics
M.Ag.Ed.   Master of Agricultural Education
M.Agr.   Master of Agriculture
M.Arch.   Master of Agriculture
M.Arch.E.   Master of Architectural Engineering
M.B.   Bachelor of Medicine
M.B.A.   Master in Business Administration
M.C.E.   Master of Civil Engineering
M.C.J.   Master of Comparative Jurisprudence
M.C.I.   Master of Comparative Law *or* Master of Civil Law

M.C.P. Master of City Planning *or* Master in City Planning
M.C.R. Master of Comparative Religion
M.C.S. Master of Commercial Science
M.Ch.E. Master of Chemical Engineering
M.Crim. Master of Criminology
M.D. Doctor of Medicine
M.D.S. Master of Dental Surgery
M.Des. Master of Design
M.E. Mechanical Engineer *or* Master of Education *or* Master of Engineering
M.E.A. Master of Engineering Administration
M.E.P. Master of Engineering Physics
M.E.P.A. Master of Engineering and Public Administration
M.Ed. Master of Education
M.El.Eng. Master of Electrical Engineering
M.Eng. Master of Engineering
M.F. Master of Forestry
M.F.A. Master of Fine Arts
M.F.S. Master of Food Science *or* Master of Foreign Service *or* Master of Foreign Study
M.F.T. Master of Foreign Trade
M.For. Master of Forestry
M.Geol.E. Master of Geological Engineering
M.H.A. Master in Hospital Administration *or* Master of Hospital Administration
M.H.E. Master of Home Economics
M.H.E.Ed. Master of Home Economics Education
M.H.L. Master of Hebrew Literature
M.I.A. Master of International Affairs
M.I.D. Master of Industrial Design
M.I.E. Master of Industrial Engineering *or* Master of Irrigation Engineering
M.I.L.R. Master of Industrial and Labor Relations
M.I.S. Master of International Service
M. in Psych.Nurs. Master in Psychiatric Nursing
M.Ind.E. Master of Industrial Engineering
M.J. Master of Journalism
M.L.A. Master of Landscape Architecture
M.L.Arch. Master of Landscape Architecture
M.L.S. Master of Library Science
M.M. Master of Music

M.M.E. Master of Mechanical Engineering *or* Master of Music Education

M.M.Sc. Master of Medical Science

M.Met.E. Master of Metallurgical Engineering

M.Mgt.E. Master of Management Engineering

M.Mus. Master of Music

M.Mus.Ed. Master of Music Education

M.N.A. Master of Nursing Administration

M.N.E. Master of Nuclear Engineering

M.N.S. Master of Nutritional Science

M.Nurs. Master of Nursing

M.O.I.G. Master of Occupational Information and Guidance

M.Opt. Master of Optometry

M.P.A. Master of Public Administration *or* Master of Professional Accounting *or* Master of Public Affairs

M.P.E. Master of Physical Education

M.P.H. Master of Public Health

M.P.L. Master of Patent Law

M.P.S. Master of Personnel Service

M.Ph. Master of Philosophy

M.Pharm. Master of Pharmacy

M.R.E. Master of Religious Education

M.R.P. Master in Regional Planning *or* Master of Regional Planning

M.S. Master of Science

M.S.A. Master of Science in Agriculture

M.S.A.E. Master of Science in Aeronautical Engineering

M.S.A.M. Master of Science in Applied Mechanics

M.S.Arch. Master of Science in Architecture

M.S.B.A. Master of Science in Business Administration

M.S.B.C. Master of Science in Building Construction

M.S.Bus. Master of Science in Business

M.S.C.E. Master of Science in Civil Engineering

M.S.C.P. Master of Science in Community Planning

M.S.Ch.E. Master of Science in Chemical Engineering

M.S.Cons. Master of Science in Conservation

M.S.D. Doctor of Medical Science *or* Master of Science in Dentistry

M.S.Dent. Master of Science in Dentistry

M.S.E. Master of Science in Engineering *or* Master of Science in Education

M.S.E.E. Master of Science in Electrical Engineering

M.S.E.M. Master of Science in Engineering Mechanics *or* Master of Science in Engineering of Mines

M.S.Ed.   Master of Science in Education
M.S.Ent.   Master of Science in Entomology
M.S.F.   Master of Science in Forestry
M.S.F.M.   Master of Science in Forest Management
M.S.For.   Master of Science in Forestry
M.S.G.M.   Master of Science in Government Management
M.S.G.Mgt.   Master of Science in Game Management
M.S.Geol.E.   Master of Science in Geological Engineering
M.S.H.A.   Master of Science in Hospital Administration
M.S.H.E.   Master of Science in Home Economics
M.S.H.Ec.   Master of Science in Home Economics
M.S.Hort.   Master of Science in Horticulture
M.S.Hyg.   Master of Science in Hygiene
M.S.I.E.   Master of Science in Industrial Engineering
M.S. in A.E.   Master of Science in Aeronautical Engineering
M.S. in Ag.Ec.   Master of Science in Agricultural Economics
M.S. in Agr.Ed.   Master of Science in Agricultural Education
M.S. in Cer.E.   Master of Science in Ceramic Engineering
M.S. in Com.   Master of Science in Communications
M.S. in E.E.   Master of Science in Electrical Engineering
M.S. in G.E.   Master of Science in General Engineering
M.S. in Gp.Engr.   Master of Science in Geophysical Engineering
M.S. in H.R.   Master of Science in Human Relations
M.S. in Home Ec.   Master of Science in Home Economics
M.S. in I.M.   Master of Science in Industrial Management
M.S. in Ind.Ed.   Master of Science in Industrial Education
M.S. in L.S.   Master of Science in Library Science
M.S. in M.E.   Master of Science in Mechanical Engineering
M.S. in Min.E.   Master of Science in Mining Engineering
M.S. in Mus.   Master of Science in Music
M.S. in Mus.Ed.   Master of Science in Music Education
M.S. in N.Ed.   Master of Science in Nursing Education
M.S. in N.T.   Master of Science in Nuclear Technology
M.S. in Nucl.E.   Master of Science in Nuclear Engineering
M.S. in Nurs.   Master of Science in Nursing
M.S. in Nutr.   Master of Science in Nutrition
M.S. in P.A.   Master of Science in Public Administration
M.S. in P.H.   Master of Science in Public Health
M.S. in Path.   Master of Science in Pathology
M.S. in Pet.E.   Master of Science in Petroleum Engineering
M.S. in Rec.   Master of Science in Recreation
M.S. in Ret.   Master of Science in Retailing

M.S. in S.E. Master of Science in Sanitary Engineering
M.S. in S.S. Master of Science in Social Service
M.S. in S.W. Master of Science in Social Work
M.S. in Text.Eng. Master of Science in Textile Engineering
M.S. in Trans. Master of Science in Transportation
M.S.J. Master of Science in Journalism
M.S.L. Master of Science in Linguistics
M.S.M. Master of Sacred Music *or* Master of Science in Music
M.S.M.E. Master of Science in Mechanical Engineering
M.S.Met.E. Master of Science in Metallurgical Engineering
M.S.Mgt.E. Master of Science in Management Engineering
M.S.N. Master of Science in Nursing
M.S.Orn.Hort. Master of Science in Ornamental Horticulture
M.S.P.E. Master of Science in Physical Education
M.S.P.H. Master of Science in Public Health
M.S.P.H.E. Master of Science in Public Health Engineering
M.S.P.H.Ed. Master of Science in Public Health Education
M.S.Phar. Master of Science in Pharmacy
M.S.Pharm. Master of Science in Pharmacy
M.S.S. Master of Social Service *or* Master of Social Science
M.S.S.E. Master of Science in Sanitary Engineering
M.S.Sc. Master of Social Science
M.S.T. Master of Science in Teaching
M.S.W. Master of Social Work *or* Master of Social Welfare *or* Master in Social Work
M.Sc. Master of Science
M.Sc.D. Doctor of Medical Science
M.Sc. in Agr.Eng. Master of Science in Agricultural Engineering
M.Sc. in E.E. Master of Science in Electrical Engineering
M.Sc. in M.E. Master of Science in Mechanical Engineering
M.Sc. in Phar. Master of Science in Pharmacy
M.Sc.Med. Master of Medical Science
M.TV. Master of Television
M.Th. Master of Theology
M.U.P. Master of Urban Planning
M.V.Ed. Master of Vocational Education
M.W.T. Master of Wood Technology
Mar.E. Marine Engineer
Mar.Mech.E. Marine Mechanical Engineer
Mat.E. Materials Engineer
Med.Sc.D. Doctor of Medical Science

Met.E.   Metallurgical Engineer
Min.E.   Mineral Engineer
Mining Eng.   Mining Engineer
Mus.B.   Bachelor of Music
Mus.D.   Doctor of Music (usually honorary)
Mus.M.   Master of Music

Nav.Arch.   Naval Architect
Nav.E.   Naval Engineer
Nuc.E.   Nuclear Engineer

O.D.   Doctor of Optometry

P.E.   Petroleum Engineer
P.E.Dir.   Director of Physical Education
P.H.E.   Public Health Engineer
P.R.E.   Petroleum Refining Engineer
Ped.D.   Doctor of Pedagogy (usually honorary)
Pet.E.   Petroleum Engineer
Ph.B.   Bachelor of Philosophy
Ph.C.   Pharmaceutical Chemist
Ph.D.   Doctor of Philosophy
Ph.L.   Licentiate in Philosophy
Ph.M.   Master of Philosophy
Pharm.D.   Doctor of Pharmacy (both earned and honorary)
Prof.Eng.   Professional Engineer

S.B.   Bachelor of Science
S.D.   Doctor of Science (usually honorary)
S.J.D.   Doctor of Juridical Science *or* Doctor of the Science of Law
S.M.   Master of Science
S.M.B.   Bachelor of Sacred Music
S.M.D.   Doctor of Sacred Music (both earned and honorary)
S.M.M.   Master of Sacred Music
S.Sc.D.   Doctor of Social Science
S.T.B.   Bachelor of Sacred Theology or Bachelor of Theology
S.T.D.   Doctor of Sacred Theology (both earned and honorary)
S.T.L.   Licentiate in Sacred Theology
S.T.M.   Master of Sacred Theology
San.E.   Sanitary Engineer
Sc.B.   Bachelor of Science

Sc.B.C. Bachelor of Science in Chemistry
Sc.B.E. Bachelor of Science in Engineering
Sc.D. Doctor of Science (usually honorary)
Sc.D.Hyg. Doctor of Science in Hygiene
Sc.D.Med. Doctor of Medical Science
Sc.M. Master of Science
Sc.M.Hyg. Master of Science in Hygiene
Sch.Mus.B. Bachelor of School Music
Sp.Ed. Specialist in Education

Th.B. Bachelor of Theology
Th.D. Doctor of Theology
Th.M. Master of Theology

Wood Tech. Wood Technologist

Appendix II

❧⚜❧

COLORS AND DESIGNS OF HOODS OF SELECTED
INSTITUTIONS CONFERRING THE DOCTOR'S DEGREE*

Adelphi University (New York)	gold, brown chevron
Akron, University of (Ohio)	navy blue, old gold chevron
Alabama, University of	crimson, white chevron
Alaska, University of	gold, royal blue chevron
Alfred University (New York)	purple, 2 old gold chevrons
American University (Washington, D.C.)	red, white chevron, blue
Arizona State University	maroon, gold chevron
Arizona, University of	red, blue chevron
Arkansas, University of	cardinal, white chevron
Auburn University (Alabama)	orange, royal blue chevron
Ball State University (Indiana)	red, white chevron
Baylor University (Texas)	emerald green, gold chevron
Berkeley Baptist Divinity School (California)	royal purple, gold chevron
Boston College (Massachusetts)	maroon, old gold chevron
Boston University (Massachusetts)	scarlet, white chevron
Bowling Green State University (Ohio)	burnt orange, dark brown chevron
Brandeis University (Massachusetts)	Wedgwood blue

* Courtesy of Cotrell and Leonard, Inc., Albany, New York

248

Brigham Young University (Utah)	white above azure blue, per chevron
Brown University (Rhode Island)	seal brown, cardinal chevron
Bryn Mawr College (Pennsylvania)	old gold, white chevron
Buffalo, State University of (New York)	Yale blue, white chevron
California Institute of Technology (California)	orange, white chevron
California Medical College (California)	gold, purple chevron
California, University of	gold, Yale blue chevron
Carnegie-Mellon University (Pennsylvania)	Carnegie tartan
Case Western Reserve University (Ohio)	navy blue, steel gray chevron
Catholic University of America (Washington, D.C.)	lemon yellow, white bar
Chicago Medical School (Illinois)	purple, gold chevron
Chicago, University of (Illinois)	maroon
Cincinnati, University of (Ohio)	bright red, 2 black chevrons
Clark University (Massachusetts)	white, emerald green chevron
Clemson University (South Carolina)	purple, gold orange chevron
Colorado School of Mines	navy blue, silver gray, per chevron
Colorado State College	gold, purple chevron
Colorado State University	golden yellow, emerald green chevron
Colorado, University of	gold, silver gray chevron
Columbia University (New York)	light blue, white chevron
Connecticut, University of	navy blue, white chevron
Cornell University (New York)	carnelian red, 2 white chevrons
Creighton University (Nebraska)	light blue above white, per chevron
Dartmouth College (New Hampshire)	dark green
Delaware, University of	blue, gold chevron
Denver, University of (Colorado)	crimson, gold chevron
Detroit, University of (Michigan)	cardinal above white, per chevron
Drew University (New Jersey)	blue, emerald green chevron

Dropsie College (Pennsylvania)	Yale blue, gold chevron
Duke University (North Carolina)	Yale blue, white chevron
Duquesne University (Pennsylvania)	scarlet, navy blue
East Texas State University	royal blue, gold chevron
Emory University (Georgia)	blue, gold chevron
Farleigh–Dickinson University (New Jersey)	maroon, white chevron
Florida State University	garnet, gold chevron
Florida, University of	orange, navy blue chevron
Fordham University (New York)	maroon
Garrett Biblical Institute (Illinois)	purple, white chevron
George Peabody College for Teachers (Tennessee)	garnet, light blue chevron
George Washington University (Washington, D.C.)	navy blue, buff chevron
Georgetown University (Washington, D.C.)	gray, navy blue chevron
Georgia Institute of Technology (Georgia)	old gold, white chevron
Georgia, University of	red, black, per chevron
Hahnemann Medical College (Pennsylvania)	Yale blue, gold chevron
Hartford Seminary Foundation (Connecticut)	old gold
Harvard University (Massachusetts)	black hood crimson lined
Hawaii, University of	emerald green, 2 white chevrons
Hebrew Union College (Ohio)	old gold
Houston, University of (Texas)	scarlet, white chevron
Howard University (Washington, D.C.)	blue, white chevron
Idaho, University of	silver, two gold chevrons
Iliff School of Theology (Colorado)	light blue, white chevron
Illinois Institute of Technology (Illinois)	scarlet, gray chevron
Illinois, University of	navy blue, 2 orange chevrons
Indiana University	crimson, cream chevron
Iowa State University	gold, cardinal, per chevron
Iowa, University of	old gold

Jefferson Medical College (Pennsylvania)   black, light blue chevron

Jewish Theological Seminary (New York)   light blue, white chevron

Johns Hopkins University (Maryland)   black, gold chevron

Kansas State University   purple, 2 white chevrons

Kansas, University of   cardinal, Yale blue chevron

Kent State University (Ohio)   orange, navy blue chevron

Kentucky, University of   azure blue, white chevron

Lawrence University (Wisconsin)   Yale blue, 2 white chevrons

Lehigh University (Pennsylvania)   dark brown, white chevron

Loma Linda University (California)   gold, purple chevron

Louisiana State University   purple, old gold per chevron

Louisville, University of (Kentucky)   black, cardinal, party per chevron

Lowell Technological Institute (Massachusetts)   scarlet, black chevron

Loyola University (Illinois)   maroon, gold chevron

Maine, University of   light blue

Marquette University (Wisconsin)   Yale blue, gold chevron

Maryland, University of   black, old gold chevron

Massachusetts College of Pharmacy   cherry, cream chevron

Massachusetts Institute of Technology   bright red, silver gray chevron

Medical College of South Carolina   gold, black chevron

Medical College of Virginia   myrtle green, white chevron

Miami, University of (Florida)   orange above, white chevron green below

Michigan State University   dark green, white chevron

Michigan, University of   deep gold, Michigan blue chevron

Middlebury College (Vermont)   Yale blue, white chevron

Minnesota, University of   old gold, maroon chevron

Mississippi State University   white, maroon chevron

Mississippi, University of   bright red, royal blue chevron

Missouri, University of   old gold, 2 black chevrons

Montana State University   royal blue, goldenrod chevron reversed

Montana, University of   copper, double bar, one silver one gold

Nebraska, University of — scarlet above cream per chevron

Nevada, University of — royal blue, silver chevron

New Hampshire, University of — blue, white per chevron

New Mexico Institute of Mining and Technology — silver, gold chevron

New Mexico State University — crimson, white chevron

New Mexico, University of — silver gray, bright red chevron

New York Medical College — gold, crimson chevron reversed

New York University — violet

New Orleans Baptist Theological Seminary (Louisiana) — purple, gold chevron

New School for Social Research (New York) — emerald green, white chevron

North Carolina College at Durham — maroon, gray chevron

North Carolina State University — cardinal, white chevron

North Carolina, University of — light blue, 2 white chevrons

North Dakota State University — lemon yellow, grass green chevron

North Dakota, University of — rose pink, apple green chevron

Northeastern University (Massachusetts) — cardinal, black chevron

North Texas State University — emerald green, white chevron

Northwestern University (Illinois) — purple, gold chevron

Notre Dame, University of (Indiana) — gold, royal blue per chevron

Occidental College (California) — burnt orange, black chevron

Ohio State University — scarlet, silver gray chevron

Ohio University — olive green, white chevron reversed

Oklahoma State University — orange, black chevron

Oklahoma, University of — crimson, cream chevron

Oregon State University — orange

Oregon, University of — lemon yellow, emerald green chevron

Pacific School of Religion (California) — emerald green, gold chevron

Pacific, University of the (California) — orange, black chevron

Pennsylvania State University — navy blue, white chevron

Pennsylvania, University of — cardinal, navy blue chevron

Philadelphia College of Osteopathy (Pennsylvania) — maroon, silver gray chevron

Philadelphia College of Pharmacy (Pennsylvania)	blue, white chevron
Pittsburgh, University of (Pennsylvania)	navy blue, gold chevron
Portland, University of (Oregon)	purple, white chevron
Princeton Theological Seminary (New Jersey)	Yale blue, scarlet velvet chevron
Princeton University (New Jersey	orange, black chevron
Puerto Rico, University of	scarlet, white chevron
Purdue University (Indiana)	black, 2 old gold chevrons
Radcliffe College (Massachusetts)	crimson, white chevron
Rensselaer Polytechnic Institute (New York)	white, cherry red chevron
Rhode Island, University of	white, blue chevron
Rice University (Texas)	Yale blue, silver gray chevron
Rochester, University of (New York)	dandelion yellow
Rockefeller University (New York)	gold, 2 royal blue chevrons
Rutgers–The State University (New Jersey)	scarlet
St. John's University (New York)	bright red, white chevron
St. Louis University (Missouri)	white, azure blue chevron
St. Mary's College (Indiana)	blue, white chevron
St. Mary's Seminary and University (Maryland)	light blue, tri chevrons of gold, white, black
Seton Hall University (New Jersey)	Yale blue, white chevron
Smith College (Massachusetts)	white, gold chevron
South Carolina, University of	garnet, black chevron
South Dakota State University	light blue, 2 yellow chevrons
South Dakota, University of	bright red
Southern California, University of	gold, cardinal chevron
Southern Illinois University	maroon, white chevron
Southern Methodist University (Texas)	Yale blue, crimson chevron
Southern Mississippi, University of	black, gold chevron
Southwestern Baptist Theological Seminary (Texas)	blue, white chevron
Springfield College (Massachusetts)	maroon, white chevron

Stanford University (California)	cardinal
Syracuse University (New York)	orange
Temple University (Pennsylvania)	white, cardinal chevron
Tennessee, University of	white, orange chevron
Texas A & M University	maroon, white chevron
Texas, University of	orange, white chevron
Texas Woman's University	maroon, white chevron
Toledo, University of (Ohio)	midnight blue, old gold chevron
Tufts University (Massachusetts)	dark brown, blue chevron
Tulane University of Louisiana	olive green, light blue chevron
Tuskegee Institute (Alabama)	crimson, gold chevron
Union College and University (New York)	garnet
Union Theological Seminary (New York)	scarlet
Union Theological Seminary (Virginia)	azure blue, white chevron
Utah State University	navy blue, white per chevron
Utah, University of	bright red, white chevron
Vanderbilt University (Tennessee)	gold, black chevron
Vermont, University of	dark green, gold chevron
Virginia Polytechnic Institute	orange, maroon chevron
Virginia, University of	navy blue, orange chevron
Wake Forest College (North Carolina)	old gold, 3 black chevrons
Washington State University	bright red, silver gray per chevron
Washington, University of	purple, gold per chevron
Washington University (Missouri)	green, red chevron
Wayne State University (Michigan)	green, old gold chevron
West Virginia University	navy blue, old gold chevron
Wisconsin, University of	cardinal
Woman's Medical College of Pennsylvania	maroon, silver gray chevron
Woodstock College (Maryland)	gold, white chevron
Worcester Polytechnic Institute (Massachusetts)	light gray, crimson chevron
Wyoming, University of	brown, yellow chevron
Yale University (Connecticut)	Yale blue
Yeshiva University (New York)	sky blue

Appendix III

SUBJECT GUIDE TO DOCTORAL GOWN TRIM, HOOD
TRIM AND TASSEL COLORS*

Field	Subject	Robe Trim	Hood Trim**
Agriculture	Agriculture	black or maize	maize
Anatomy	Science	black or golden yellow	golden yellow
Anthropology	Philosophy	black or dark blue	dark blue
Architecture	Fine Arts	black or brown	brown
Art	Fine Arts	black or brown	brown
Astronomy	Science	black or golden yellow	golden yellow
Bacteriology	Science	black or golden yellow	golden yellow
Biochemistry	Science	black or golden yellow	golden yellow
Biology	Science	black or golden yellow	golden yellow
Botany	Science	black or golden yellow	golden yellow
Business Administration	Commerce	black or drab	drab
Chemistry	Science	black or golden yellow	golden yellow
Dentistry	Dentistry	black or lilac	lilac
Divinity	Theology	black or scarlet	scarlet

* From George K. Schweitzer, *The Doctorate, A Handbook,* 1965.
Courtesy of the publisher, George C. Thomas, Springfield, Ill.
** Tassel may be black or gold thread or the same color as hood trim.

Economics	Economics	black or copper	copper
Education	Education	black or light blue	light blue
Engineering	Engineering	black or orange	orange
Forestry	Forestry	black or russet	russet
Geography	Science	black or golden yellow	golden yellow
Geology	Science	black or golden yellow	golden yellow
History	Philosophy	black or dark blue	dark blue
Home Economics	Economics	black or copper	copper
Journalism	Journalism	black or crimson	crimson
Languages	Philosophy	black or dark blue	dark blue
Law	Law	black or purple	purple
Letters	Arts	black or white	white
Library Science	Library Science	black or lemon	lemon
Literature	Philosophy	black or dark blue	dark blue
Mathematics	Science	black or golden yellow	golden yellow
Medicine	Medicine	black or pink	green
Music	Music	black or apricot	pink
Nursing	Nursing	black or green	apricot
Optometry	Optometry	black or seafoam green	seafoam green
Osteopathy	Osteopathy	black or green	green
Pharmacy	Pharmacy	black or olive green	olive green
Philosophy	Philosophy	black or dark blue	dark blue
Physical Education	Physical Education	black or sage green	sage green
Physics	Science	black or golden yellow	golden yellow
Physiology	Science	black or golden yellow	golden yellow
Podiatry	Podiatry	black or nile green	nile green
Political Science	Philosophy	black or dark blue	dark blue
Psychology	Philosophy	black or dark blue	dark blue
Public Administration	Public Administration	black or peacock blue	peacock blue
Public Health	Public Administration	black or salmon pink	salmon pink
Religion	Theology	black or scarlet	scarlet
Science	Science	black or golden yellow	golden yellow
Social Work	Social Work	black or citron	citron
Sociology	Philosophy	black or dark blue	dark blue
Speech	Oratory	black or silver gray	silver gray

Theatre	Oratory	black or silver gray	silver gray
Theology	Theology	black or scarlet	scarlet
Veterinary Medicine	Veterinary Science	black or gray	gray
Zoology	Science	black or golden yellow	golden yellow

Appendix IV

❦

AN ACADEMIC COSTUME CODE AND AN ACADEMIC
CEREMONY GUIDE*

THE HISTORY OF ACADEMIC DRESS reaches far back into the early days of the oldest universities. A statute of 1321 required that all "Doctors, Licentiates and Bachelors" of the University of Coimbra wear gowns. In England, in the second half of the fourteenth century, the statutes of certain colleges forbade "excess in apparel" and prescribed the wearing of a long gown. It is still a vexed question whether academic dress finds its sources chiefly in ecclesiastical or in civilian dress. Gowns may have been counted necessary for warmth in the unheated buildings frequented by medieval scholars. Hoods seem to have served to cover the tonsured head until superseded for that purpose by the skullcap. This was itself displaced by a headdress more or less like one or another of those now recognized as "academic." Both Cambridge and Oxford have made academic dress a matter of university control to the extent of even its minor details and have repeatedly issued revised regulations governing it. In the Laudian days in Oxford it was prescribed that any tailor who departed from the authorized design "even by a nail's breadth" in the making of any article of collegiate costume was to be punished by the vice-chancellor of the university.

* From Allan M. Cartter, ed., *American Universities and Colleges*, 9th ed., pp. 1250–1253. Courtesy of the publisher, American Council on Education.

European institutions continue to show great diversity in their specifications of academic dress. When American colleges and universities desired to adopt some suitable system of academic apparel a half-century ago, it seemed to them best to agree on some definite system which all might follow. Accordingly, there was held on May 16, 1895, at Columbia University, a conference of representatives of the governing boards of various interested institutions. From that meeting came the suggestion of "a By-Law, Regulation, or Statute" for the establishment of a suitable code of academic dress for the colleges and universities of the United States. It followed in 1902 that the Regents of the University of the State of New York gave a charter to an organization named the Intercollegiate Bureau of Academic Costume to serve as a source of information and guidance in such matters. The firm of Cotrell and Leonard of Albany, New York, was designated by the Regents to act as repository. In that capacity the firm still continues to serve. In nearly every instance of the many hundreds of colleges and universities of the United States which have adopted academic dress, the standards thus prescribed have been adopted and followed, either wholly or at least in the main.

In 1932 the American Council on Education authorized the appointment of a committee "to determine whether revision and completion of the academic code adopted by the conference of the colleges and universities in 1895 is desirable at this time, and, if so, to draft a revised code and present a plan for submitting the code to the consideration of the institutional members of the Council."

The committee thus authorized reviewed the situation through correspondence and conference and approved a code for academic costumes that has been in effect since that year.

A Committee on Academic Costumes and Ceremonies, appointed by the American Council on Education in 1959, again reviewed the costume code and made several significant changes. The president of Cotrell and Leonard, representing the Intercollegiate Bureau of Academic Costume, was a member of the committee and officially endorsed the new code, presented below. The committee voted unanimously that *the approved changes in academic costume should apply only to articles manufactured after publication of the revised code in the spring of 1960, and that all articles in existence at that time which meet the requirements of the 1932 code may appropriately be used as long as they are in good condition.*

In response to numerous requests from educational institutions, the committee also prepared an Academic Ceremony Guide, which appears on pp. 265–267.

THE ACADEMIC COSTUME CODE

GOWNS

Pattern. Gowns recommended for use in the colleges and universities of this country have the following characteristics. The gown for the bachelor's degree has pointed sleeves. It is designed to be worn closed. The gown for the master's degree has an oblong sleeve, open at the wrist, like the others. The sleeve base hangs down in the traditional manner. The rear part of its oblong shape is square cut and the front part has an arc cut away. The gown is so designed and supplied with fasteners that it may be worn open or closed. The gown for the doctor's degree has bell-shaped sleeves. It is so designed and supplied with fasteners that it may be worn open or closed.

Material. Cotton poplin or similar material for the bachelor's and master's degree, and rayon or silk ribbed material for the doctor's degree. As a means of adaptation to climate, the material of the gowns may vary from light to very heavy, provided that the material, color, and pattern follow the prescribed rules.

Color. Black is recommended. (For permissible exceptions, see below.)

Trimmings. None for the bachelor's or master's degrees. For the doctor's degree, the gown to be faced down the front with black velvet with three bars of the same across the sleeves; or these facings and crossbars may be of velvet of the color distinctive of the subject to which the degree pertains, thus agreeing in color with the binding or edging of the hood appropriate to the particular doctor's degree in every instance.

For all academic purposes, including trimmings of doctors' gowns, edging of hoods and tassels of caps, the colors associated with the different subjects are as follows:

Agriculture	maize
Arts, Letters, Humanities	white
Commerce, Accountancy, Business	drab
Dentistry	lilac
Economics	copper
Education	light blue
Engineering	orange
Fine Arts, including Architecture	brown
Forestry	russet
Journalism	crimson

Law	purple
Library Science	lemon
Medicine	green
Music	pink
Nursing	apricot
Oratory (Speech)	silver gray
Pharmacy	olive green
Philosophy	dark blue
Physical Education	sage green
Public Administration, including Foreign Service	peacock blue
Public Health	salmon pink
Science	golden yellow
Social Work	citron
Theology	scarlet
Veterinary Science	gray

In some instances American makers of academic costumes have divided the velvet trimming of the doctor's gown in such a fashion as to suggest in the same garment two or more doctor's degrees. Good precedent directs that only a single degree from a single institution should ever be indicated by a single garment.

HOODS

Pattern. As usually followed by the colleges and universities of this country, but with observation of the following specifications:

Material. The same as that of the gown in all cases.

Color. Black in all cases.

Length. The length of the hood worn for the bachelor's degree to be three feet, for the master's degree three and one-half feet, and for the doctor's degree, four feet; while that worn for the doctor's degree only shall have panels at the sides.

Linings. The hoods to be lined with the official color or colors of the college or university conferring the degree; more than one color is shown by division of the field color in a variety of ways, such as chevron or chevrons, equal division, etc. The various academic costume companies have in their files complete data on the approved colors for various institutions.

Trimmings. The binding or edging of the hood to be of velvet or velveteen, in width two inches, three inches, and five inches for the bachelor's, master's and doctor's degrees, respectively; while the color should be distinctive of the subject to which the degree pertains (see above). For example, the trimming for the degree of Master of Science in Agriculture should be maize, representing agriculture, rather than golden yellow, representing science. No academic hood should ever have its border divided to represent more than a single degree.

CAPS

Material. Cotton poplin, broadcloth, rayon, or silk, to match gown, or, for the doctor's degree only, velvet.

Form. Mortarboards are generally recommended, although soft square-topped caps are permissible for women.

Color. Black.

Tassel. A long tassel to be fastened to the middle point of the top of the cap only and to lie as it will thereon; to be black or the color appropriate to the subject, except that the doctor's cap may have its tassel of gold thread.

OTHER APPAREL

It is recommended that institutions require that graduates wear shoes and other articles of visible apparel of dark colors that harmonize with the academic costume. Flowers and decorative jewelry should not be worn on the academic gown.

SOME PERMISSIBLE EXCEPTIONS

Members of the governing body of a college or university, and they only, whatever their degrees may be, are counted entitled to wear doctors' gowns (with black velvet), but their hoods may be only those of degrees actually held by the wearers or those especially prescribed for them by the institution.

In some colleges and universities, it is customary for the president, chancellor, or chief officer to wear a costume similar to that used by the head of a foreign university. This practice should be strictly limited.

The chief marshal may wear a specially designed costume approved by his institution.

It is customary in many large institutions for the hood to be dispensed with by those receiving bachelor's degrees.

Persons who hold degrees from foreign universities may wear the entire appropriate academic costume, including cap, gown and hood.

Members of religious orders and similar societies may suitably wear their customary habits. The same principle applies to persons wearing military uniforms or clad in special attire required by a civil office.

It is recommended that collegiate institutions that award degrees, diplomas or certificates below the baccalaureate level use caps and gowns of a light color, e.g., light blue for teacher-training and light gray for other types of institutions.

ADDENDUM TO THE COSTUME CODE

ASSOCIATE, SPECIALIST AND
PHYSICAL THERAPY DEGREES

In November, 1967, the Commission on Academic Affairs of the American Council on Education distributed a memorandum to member institutions on regulations affecting academic costumes. It advised that it is impossible to lay down enforceable rules, that the governing force is tradition from the Middle Ages, and that the latter should be departed from as sparingly as possible. It noted that changes must keep pace with academic growth and it made recommendations concerning dress for graduates of two-year community colleges, six-year specialist programs, and for the recipients of bachelor's and master's degrees in physical therapy and comparable fields.

The Commission urged that those receiving associate degrees wear (1) a bachelor's type gown, (2) that it be gray for all except those in teacher education where light blue is suitable, and (3) that the hood be of the same shape as the one worn by bachelors except that it have no velvet border and that the institutional colors be on the lining and that the outside be black. The flat shield hood was mentioned as a permissible option but it was not recommended.

For specialist degrees such as the Master of Arts in Teaching it was noted that these are master's degrees and that master's costumes should be worn. For institutions desiring hoods, the Commission stated that hoods may be specially designed (1) intermediate in length between the master's and doctor's hoods, (2) with a four-inch velvet border intermediate between the borders of master's and doctor's hoods, and (3) with black cap tassels, and colors distributed according to the usual custom. Standard academic dress appropriate to the baccalaureate or master's degree was recommended for graduates in physical therapy and comparable fields. If the degree conferred is in arts, the hood border should be white, and if in science, golden yellow. It was also recommended that institutions provide suitable costumes for guests participating in academic ceremonies.

AN ACADEMIC CEREMONY GUIDE

Many factors, such as the nature of the institution, the size of the graduating class, the weather and the place of the ceremony (indoors or outdoors), affect the details of the various kinds of academic ceremonies. Institutions have wide latitude in meeting these conditions. It is therefore recognized that the following suggestions do not answer all pertinent questions concerning any specific ceremony.

WEARING THE COSTUME

Caps. Those wearing academic costumes always wear their caps in academic processions and during the ceremony of conferring degrees. Men may remove their caps during prayer, the playing of the National Anthem and the *Alma Mater,* and at other specified times, e.g., during the baccalaureate sermon or the commencement address. It is traditional that all such actions be done in unison. Hence the plan for each ceremony should be carefully drawn in advance. The participants should be notified in advance and someone (usually the presiding officer) should be designated to give the cues for removing and replacing the caps.

There is no general rule for the position of the tassel on a mortarboard. However, numerous institutions have adopted the practice, during commencement exercises, of requiring candidates for degrees to wear the tassels on the right front side before degrees are conferred and to shift them to the left at the moment when degrees are awarded to them. This custom is in some respects a substitute for individual hooding.

Gowns. At ceremonies where degrees are conferred, it is proper for a candidate to wear the gown in keeping with the degree to be received. (Permissible exception: Some medical schools permit candidates to wear doctors' gowns, although the first degree conferred is a bachelor's degree.)

Hoods. If a person holds more than one academic degree, he may wear only one hood at a time. The hood worn should be appropriate to the gown.

The traditional rule is that a candidate for a degree should not wear the hood of that degree until it is actually conferred. This rule still applies to those who are to be individually hooded during the commencement ceremony; they should not wear the hoods in the preliminary academic procession. However, when degrees are to be conferred en masse, without individual hooding, the groups involved, e.g., masters' degree candidates at large universities, may wear their hoods in the preliminary procession and throughout the ceremony.

Many institutions have dispensed entirely with bachelors' hoods. It is quite appropriate for the bachelor's gown to be worn without a hood.

ACADEMIC PROCESSIONS IN GENERAL

There is wide variation in customs concerning academic processions. In some institutions, the procession is led by a mace-bearer, in others by the chief marshal. Either may be followed by a color guard. (On some occasions the colors are displayed on the stage and are not moved during the ceremony.) At some institutions there are more divisions in the procession than are indicated below, e.g., church dignitaries. Such groups have traditional places in the procession, determined by the individual institution.

COMMENCEMENT EXERCISES

The preliminary procession. The commencement procession is usually composed of the following divisions: (1) the speakers, trustees, administrative officers and other members of the platform party; (2) the faculty; and (3) candidates for degrees, with candidates for advanced degrees in the lead and others in groups according to the degrees for which they are candidates. The divisions may march in the above order, or in reverse order. If the latter procedure is chosen, the candidates for degrees, after reaching their seats, face toward the center aisle as a mark of respect while the faculty and trustees proceed to their places.

The commencement ceremony. The essential elements of the ceremony are the conferring of degrees and the commencement address. Earned degrees are usually conferred in ascending order, with baccalaureate degrees first and doctorates last. Honorary degrees are conferred, with individual citations, after the earned degrees. (At some institutions, this order is reversed, with baccalaureate degrees conferred last.)

The subsequent procession. Divisions 1 and 2 leave the hall in that order. Recipients of degrees may be required to join the procession or may be permitted to disperse from their seats when the first two divisions have left the hall.

BACCALAUREATE SERVICE

The preliminary procession for the baccalaureate service differs from that for commencement exercises in the following chief respects: (a) divisions 1, 2, and 3 most frequently march in that order; and (b) candidates for degrees are not required to march in a special order determined by degrees to be conferred.

INAUGURATION EXERCISES

The preliminary procession. When a president or chancellor of a college or university is to be inaugurated, it is traditional for the academic procession to include at least the following divisions in this order: (1) delegates of colleges and universities, arranged according to the dates when the respective institutions were founded; (2) delegates of learned societies and associations; (3) the faculty; (4) the trustees; and (5) the speakers and other dignitaries in the president's party; with the person to be inaugurated marching alone at the very end of the procession.

The ceremony. The essential components of the ceremony are the installation, usually by the chairman of the board of trustees, and the inaugural address by the new head of the institution. Additional addresses preceding the inaugural address may be made by representatives of governments, churches, other institutions, alumni, etc., as appropriate.

The subsequent procession. The newly inaugurated president or chancellor leads the procession from the hall, followed by the five divisions listed above, in reverse order.

Selected Bibliography

Ackerman, R. *A History of the University of Oxford, its Colleges, Halls, and Public Buildings.* 2 vols. London, 1814.

Adams, Herbert B. *Thomas Jefferson and the University of Virginia.* Washington, 1888.

Alma Mater: University of Helsinki. Helsinki, 1952.

American Association of University Professors Bulletin. 1915—.

American Universities and Colleges. American Council on Education. Washington, 1964.

American Scholar, The. 1932–.

Arnold, Matthew. *Higher Schools and Universities in Germany.* London, 1874.

Ashby, Eric. *Universities: British, Indian, and African.* Cambridge, Mass., 1966.

Association of American Universities, Proceedings. 1901–1948.

Backman, E. Louis. *Doktorsdiputationens Tredje Opponent.* Uppsala, 1964.

———. *Jubeldoktoratet vid Universiteten i Uppsala och Lund.* Uppsala, 1962.

Baird, William R. *Baird's Manual of American College Fraternities.* Menasha, Wis., 1940.

Barzun, Jacques. *Teacher in America.* New York, 1945.

———. *The American University: How It Runs, Where It is Going.* New York, 1968.

Battle, Kemp P. *History of the University of North Carolina.* 2 vols. Raleigh, 1907–1912.

Baty, T. *Academic Colours.* Tokyo, 1934.

Baxter, Frank C., and Walters, Helen. *Caps, Gowns and Commencements.* Chicago, 1966.

Bishop, Morris. *A History of Cornell.* Ithaca, 1962.

Blauch, Lloyd E. *Accreditation in Higher Education.* Washington, 1959.

————, ed. *Education for the Professions.* Washington, 1955.

Blocker, Clyde E., Plummer, Robert H., and Richardson, Richard C., Jr. *The Two-Year College: A Social Synthesis.* Englewood Cliffs, N.J., 1965.

Bochnak, Adam. *Les insignes de l'université Jagellonne.* Cracow, 1962.

Bonnerot, J. *L'Université de Paris du moyen age à nos jours.* Paris, 1933.

Bowman, Claude C. *The College Professor in America.* Philadelphia, 1938.

Brickman, William W., and Lehrer, Stanley (editors). *A Century of Higher Education: Classical Citadel to Collegiate Colossus.* New York, 1962.

Brooks, Robert P. *The University of Georgia Under Sixteen Administrators, 1785–1955.* 1956.

Brown, David G. *The Mobile Professor.* Washington, 1967.

Brown, Hugh S., and Mayhew, Lewis B. *American Higher Education.* New York, 1965.

Brownell, Baker. *The College and the Community.* New York, 1952.

Brubacher, John S., and Rudy, Willis. *Higher Education in Transition —A History of American Colleges and Universities, 1636–1956.* New York, 1958.

Bryson, Lyman, ed. *An Outline of Man's Knowledge of the Modern World.* New York, 1960.

Bullock, Henry M. *A History of Emory University, 1836–1936.* Nashville, 1936.

Butler, Nicholas Murray. *Across the Busy Years.* New York, 1939.

Butts, R. Freeman. *The College Charts its Course, Historical Conceptions and Current Proposals.* New York, 1939.

Buxton, L. H. D., and Gibson, S. *Oxford University Ceremonies.* Oxford, 1935.

Caplow, Theodore, and McGee, Reece J. *The Academic Marketplace.* Garden City, N.Y., 1958.

269 SELECTED BIBLIOGRAPHY

Carmichael, Oliver C. *Graduate Education: A Critique and a Program.* New York, 1961.
Carter, Harold J. (editor). *Intellectual Foundations of American Education.* New York, 1965.
Cassidy, F. P. *Catholic College Foundations and Developments in the United States, 1677–1850.* Washington, 1924.
Cheyney, Edward P. *History of the University of Pennsylvania, 1740–1940.* Philadelphia, 1940.
Cohen, Mitchell, and Hale, Dennis. *The New Student Left: An Anthology.* Boston, 1966.
Coleman, Helen Turnbull Waite. *Banners in the Wilderness: Early Years of Washington and Jefferson College.* Pittsburgh, 1956.
Collier's Encyclopedia. 24 vols. New York, 1967
Commager, Henry S. *Freedom, Loyalty, Dissent.* New York, 1954.
Commonwealth Universities Yearbook, 1966. London, 1966.
Coon, Horace. *Columbia: Colossus on the Hudson.* New York, 1947.
Cooper, Russell M. ed. *The Two Ends of the Log.* Minneapolis, 1958.
Coulter, E. Merton. *College Life in the Old South.* Athens, Ga., 1951.
Curti, Merle, and Nash, Roderick. *Philanthropy in the Shaping of American Higher Education.* New Brunswick, N.J., 1965.
Cussans, John E. *The Handbook of Heraldry.* London, 1869.
Daley, S. J., and Lowrie, J. *The Medieval University, 1200–1400.* New York, 1961.
Demarest, William H. S. *A History of Rutgers College, 1766–1924.* New Brunswick, N.J., 1924.
Demerath, Nicholas J., Stephens, Richard W., and Taylor, R. Robb. *Power, Presidents, and Professors.* New York, 1967.
Dennis, Lawrence E., and Kauffman, Joseph F. *The College and the Student.* Washington, 1966.
Dennis, Lawrence E. ed. *Education and a Woman's Life.* Washington, 1963.
DeVane, William C. *Higher Education in Twentieth-Century America.* Cambridge, Mass., 1965.
Dewey, John. *Democracy and Education.* New York, 1916.
Dexter, Franklin B. *Founding of Yale College.* New Haven, 1916.
Dodds, Harold W. *The Academic President, Educator or Caretaker?* New York, 1962.
Durant, Will. *The Reformation.* New York, 1957.
———. *The Renaissance.* New York, 1953.
Dyer, John P. *Tulane: The Biography of a University, 1834–1965.* New York, 1966.

Earnest, Ernest. *Academic Procession, An Informal History of the American College, 1636–1953*. Indianapolis, 1953.

Eddy, Edward D., Jr. *Colleges for Our Land and Time: The Land-Grant Idea in American Education*. New York, 1957.

Education Directory, Part 3, Higher Education, 1964–1965. Washington, 1965.

Educational Record. 1920–.

Eells, Walter C. *Degrees in Higher Education*. Washington, 1963.

———. *Associate's Degree and Graduation Practices in Junior Colleges*. Washington, 1942.

———. *The Junior College*. Boston, 1931.

Eells, Walter C., and Haswell, Harold A. *Academic Degrees: Earned and Honorary Degrees Conferred by Institutions of Higher Education in the United States*. Washington, 1960.

Eells, Walter C., and Hollis, Ernest V. *The College Presidency, 1900–1960, An Annotated Bibliography*. Washington, 1961.

Elliott, Edward C., and Chambers, M. M. *Charters and Basic Laws of Selected American Universities and Colleges*. 1934.

Epler, Stephen E. *Honorary Degrees, A Survey of Their Use and Abuse*. Washington, 1943.

Erskine, John. *My Life as a Teacher*. Philadelphia, 1948.

Eurich, Alvin C., ed. *Campus 1980*. New York, 1968.

Evans, Joan, ed. *The Flowering of the Middle Ages*. London, 1966.

Ferrier, William W. *Origin and Development of the University of California*. Berkeley, 1930.

Fitzgerald, F. Scott. *This Side of Paradise*. New York, 1920.

Fitzpatrick, Edward A. *Great Books, Panacea or What?* Milwaukee, 1952.

———. *How to Educate Human Beings*. Milwaukee, 1950.

Fletcher, Robert S. *A History of Oberlin College from Its Foundation Through the Civil War*. 2 vols. Oberlin, 1943.

Flexner, Abraham. *Universities: American, English, and German*. New York, 1930.

Foerster, Norman. *The American State University, Its Relation to Democracy*. Chapel Hill, 1937.

Fowlkes, John Guy, ed. *Higher Education for American Society*. Madison, 1949.

Franklyn, Julian. *Shield and Crest*. New York, 1960.

Free, A. R. *Social Usage*. New York, 1960.

French, John Calvin. *A History of the University Founded by Johns Hopkins*. Baltimore, 1946.

Gall, Franz. *Die Insignien der Universität Wien.* Graz, 1965.

Gardner, John W. *Self-Renewal, The Individual and the Innovative Society.* New York, 1963.

General Education in a Free Society, The Report of the Harvard Committee. Cambridge, Mass., 1945.

Gleazer, Edmund J., Jr. *American Junior Colleges.* Washington, 1967.

Govan, Gilbert E., and Livingood, James W. *The University of Chattanooga: Sixty Years.* Chattanooga, 1947.

Hargreaves-Mawdsley, W. N. *A History of Academic Dress in Europe Until the End of the Eighteenth Century.* London, 1963.

Harper, William A., ed. *1968 Junior College Directory.* Washington, 1968.

Harris, Seymour E., Deitch, Kenneth, and Levensohn, Alan, eds. *Challenge and Change in American Education.* Berkeley, Calif., 1965.

Hassenger, Robert, ed. *The Shape of Catholic Higher Education.* Chicago, 1967.

Hay, Dennis. *Europe in the Fourteenth and Fifteenth Centuries.* New York, 1966.

Haycraft, F. W. *Degrees and Hoods of the World's Universities and Colleges.* Cheshunt, Herts., 1948.

Higher Education for American Democracy: The Report of the President's Commission on Higher Education. New York, 1947.

Hill, Alfred T. *The Small College Meets the Challenge.* New York, 1959.

Hoffman, Nicholas von. *The Multiversity.* New York, 1966.

Hofstadter, Richard, and Smith, Wilson. *American Higher Education: A Documentary History.* 2 vols. Chicago, 1961.

Holmes, D. O. W. *The Evolution of the Negro College.* New York, 1934.

Hook, Sidney. *Heresy, Yes, Conspiracy, No.* New York, 1953.

Hope, Arthur J. *Notre Dame, One Hundred Years.* Notre Dame, Ind., 1943.

Hoppner, O. J. *Academic Costume in America.* Albany, 1965.

Howes, Raymond F., ed. *Vision and Purpose in Higher Education: Twenty College Presidents Examine Developments During the Past Decade.* Washington, 1962.

Hubbart, Henry Clyde. *Ohio Wesleyan's First Hundred Years.* Delaware, Ohio, 1943.

Hutchins, Robert M. *Some Observations on American Education.* Cambridge, Mass., 1956.

————. *The Higher Learning in America.* New Haven, 1936.

International Handbook of Universities and Other Institutions of Higher Education. Paris, 1966.

Irsay, S. d'. *L'Histoire des universités françaises et étrangères à nos jours.* 2 vols. Paris, 1933–35.

James, Henry. *Charles W. Eliot, President of Harvard University. 1869–1909.* 2 vols. Cambridge, Mass., 1930.

Jones, Howard Mumford. *One Great Society: Humane Learning in the United States.* New York, 1959.

Jones, Thomas E., Sanford, Edward V., and White, Goodrich C. *Letters to College Presidents.* Englewood Cliffs, N.J., 1964.

Jordan, David S. *The Voice of the Scholar.* San Francisco, 1903.

Journal of Higher Education. 1930——.

Junior College Journal. 1930——.

Kerr, Clark. *The Uses of the University.* Cambridge, Mass., 1963.

Kirk, Russell. *Academic Freedom.* Chicago, 1955.

Knight, Douglas M. *The Federal Government and Higher Education.* Englewood Cliffs, N.J., 1960.

Knight, Edgar W. *What College Presidents Say.* Chapel Hill, N.C., 1940.

Liberal Education, The Bulletin of the Association of American Colleges. 1914–.

Lipset, Seymour Martin and Wolin, Sheldon S., eds. *The Berkeley Student Revolt.* Garden City, N.Y., 1965.

Livingstone, Sir R. W. *Education and the Spirit of the Age.* Oxford, 1952.

Lockmiller, David A. *History of the North Carolina State College of Agriculture and Engineering, 1899–1939.* Raleigh, N.C., 1939.

————. *The Consolidation of the University of North Carolina.* Raleigh, N.C., 1942.

Lynn, Kenneth S., ed. *The Professions in America.* Cambridge, Mass., 1965.

McConnell, T. R. *A General Pattern for American Public Higher Education.* New York, 1962.

McCormack, Richard P. *Rutgers: A Bicentennial History.* New Brunswick, N.J., 1966.

McGrath, Earl J., ed. *Universal Higher Education.* New York, 1966.

MacKinney, Loren C. *The Medieval World.* New York, 1938.

Madan, Falconer. *Oxford Outside the Guide Books.* Oxford, 1923.

Malagola, C. *Statuti della Università e dei Collegi dello Studio Bolognese.* 1888.

273   SELECTED BIBLIOGRAPHY

Malden, H. *On the Origins of Universities and Academical Degrees.* London, 1835.

Mallet, Sir C. E. *A History of the University of Oxford.* 3 vols. London, 1924–27.

Mayhew, Louis B., ed. *Higher Education in the Revolutionary Decades.* Berkeley, Calif., 1967.

Menashe, Louis and Radosh, Ronald, eds. *Teach-Ins: U.S.A.* New York, 1967.

Millet, Fred B. *Professor: Problems and Rewards in College Teaching.* New York, 1961.

Millett, John D. *Financing Higher Education in the United States.* New York, 1952.

Milton, Ohmer, and Shoben, E. J. eds. *Learning and the Professors.* Athens, Ohio, 1968.

Mims, Edwin. *History of Vanderbilt University.* Nashville, Tenn., 1946.

Morison, Robert S., ed. *The Contemporary University: U.S.A.* Boston, 1966.

Morison, Samuel Eliot. *The Founding of Harvard College.* Cambridge, Mass., 1936.

———. *Three Centuries of Harvard, 1636–1936.* Cambridge, Mass., 1936.

Mullinger, J. B. *The University of Cambridge from the Earliest Times to the Decline of the Platonist Movement.* 3 vols. Cambridge, 1873–1911.

Ness, Frederic W. (editor). *A Guide to Graduate Study: Programs Leading to the Ph.D. Degree.* Washington, 1960.

Nevins, Allan. *The State Universities and Democracy.* Urbana, Ill., 1962.

Newcomer, Mabel. *A Century of Higher Education for American Women.* New York, 1959.

O'Connell, Thomas E. *Community Colleges: A President's View.* Urbana, Ill., 1968.

Osgood, Charles G. *Lights in Nassau Hall, A Book of the Bicentennial, Princeton 1746–1946.* Princeton, 1951.

Pangburn, Jesse M. *The Evolution of the American Teachers College.* 1932.

Patillo, Manning M., Jr., and Mackenzie, Donald M. *Eight Hundred Colleges Face the Future.* St. Louis, 1965.

Phelps, William Lyon. *Autobiography.* New York, 1939.

Pierson, George W. *Yale: College and University, 1871–1937.* 2 vols. 1952–55.

Power, Edward J. *A History of Catholic Higher Education in the United States.* Milwaukee, 1958.

President's Committee on Education Beyond the High School. Washington, 1957.

Rashdall, Hastings. *The Universities of Europe in the Middle Ages,* ed. F. M. Powicke and A. B. Emden. 3 vols. London, 1936.

Reid, Robert H. *American Degree Mills.* Washington, 1959.

Ridgeway, James. *The Closed Corporation, American Universities in Crisis.* New York, 1968.

Riesman, David, and Jenks, Christopher. *The Academic Revolution.* New York, 1968.

Roberts, S. C. *British Universities.* London, 1947.

Robertson, Sir Charles G. *The British Universities.* London, 1944.

Roszak, Theodore. *The Dissenting Academy.* New York, 1968.

Rudolph, Frederick. *The American College and University.* New York, 1962.

Ruprecht-Karl Universtät, 1386–1961. Heidelberg, 1961.

Sack, Saul. *A History of Higher Education in Pennsylvania.* Harrisburg, 1962.

Sagendorph, Kent. *Michigan: The Story of the University.* 1948.

Schachner, Nathan. *The Medieval Universities.* London, 1938.

Schmidt, George P. *The Liberal Arts College: A Chapter in American Cultural History.* New Brunswick, N.J., 1957.

Schweitzer, George K. *The Doctorate: A Handbook.* Springfield, Ill., 1965.

Selden, William K. *Accreditation, A Struggle Over Standards in Higher Education.* New York, 1960.

Shaw, Charles G. *Trends of Civilization and Culture.* New York, 1932.

Sheard, Kevin. *Academic Heraldry in America.* Marquette, Mich., 1962.

Shiver, Elizabeth N., ed. *Higher Education and Public International Service.* Washington, 1967.

Shuster, George N. *Catholic Education in a Changing World.* New York, 1968.

Smith, G. Kerry, ed. *Current Issues in Higher Education, 1965: Pressures and Priorities in Higher Education.* Washington, 1965.

Snavely, Guy E. *A Search for Excellence.* New York, 1964.

———. *The Church and the Four-Year College.* New York, 1955.

Snyder, Henry Nelson. *An Educational Odyssey*. Nashville., Tenn., 1947.

Spectorsky, A. C., ed. *The College Years*. New York, 1958.

Sweet, William Warren. *Religion on the American Frontier, 1773–1840*. New York, 1936.

Taylor, Harold. *On Education and Freedom*. New York, 1954.

Tewksbury, Donald G. *The Founding of American Colleges and Universities Before the Civil War*. New York, 1965.

Thomas, F. S. *University Degrees, What They Mean, What They Indicate, and How to Use Them*. New York, 1887.

Thomas, Russell. *The Search for a Common Learning: General Education, 1800–1960*. New York, 1962.

Thorndike, L. *University Records and Life in the Middle Ages*. New York, 1944.

Thwing, Charles F. *The American College in American Life*. New York, 1897.

Trueblood, Elton. *The Idea of a College*. New York, 1959.

Veblen, Thorstein. *The Higher Learning in America*. New York, 1918.

Venables, R., and Clifford, R. E. *Academic Dress of the University of Oxford*. Oxford, 1966.

Venn, John. *Early Collegiate Life*. Cambridge, 1913.

Voorhees, Oscar M. *The History of Phi Beta Kappa*. New York, 1945.

Walters, Everett. *Graduate Education Today*. Washington, 1965.

Weidner, Edward D. *The World Role of Universities*. New York, 1962.

Wertenbaker, Thomas Jefferson. *Princeton, 1746–1896*. Princeton, 1946.

Whelan, James F. *Catholic Colleges of the United States of America at the Middle of the Twentieth Century*. New Orleans, 1954.

Whitehead, Alfred N. *The Aims of Education and Other Essays*. New York, 1929.

Whose Goals for American Higher Education. American Council on Education. Washington, 1967.

Wieruszowski, Helene. *The Medieval University*. New York, 1966.

Willis, Elbert, V. *The Growth of American Higher Education*. Philadelphia, 1936.

Wilson, Logan (editor). *Emerging Patterns in American Higher Education*. Washington, 1965.

Wilson, Logan. *The Academic Man*. New York, 1942.

Wilson, Woodrow. *College and State*. 2 vols. New York, 1925.

Woodring, Paul. *The Higher Learning in America: A Reassessment.* New York, 1968.

Woody, Robert H. *The Papers and Addresses of William Preston Few, Late President of Duke University.* Durham, 1951.

Woody, Thomas. *A History of Women's Education in the United States.* 2 vols. New York, 1966.

————. *Liberal Education for Free Men.* Philadelphia, 1951.

Wriston, Henry M. *Academic Procession; Reflections of a College President.* New York, 1959.

Yeomans, Henry, A. *Abbott Lawrence Lowell.* Cambridge, Mass., 1948.

INDEX

Abélard, Peter, 33–34
Aberdeen, University of, 51, 55, 58, 76
Academic Ceremony Guide, 184, 185
Academic Costume Code and An Academic Ceremony Guide, An, 3
Academic Costume Code, 43, 184, 185, 189–91, 194
Adams, Samuel, 67
Adams, John, 67
Adult Education Association of the United States of America, 150
Air Force Institute of Technology, 153
Air University, 153
Aix-Marseilles, 33
Agency for International Development, 169
Agnes Scott College, 132
Agriculture, U.S. Department of, 139, 169
Akron, University of, 102–3, 140
Alabama, 94, 130
Alabama College, 132
Alaska, University of, 173
Alexander, William, 145
Alexander VI, Pope, 51
Allen, Ethan, 89
Allen, Ira, 89
Alma Mater, 119
American Academy of Arts and Sciences, 159
American Academy of Political and Social Science, 159
American Alumni Council, 160
American Association for the Advancement of Science, 159
American Association of Junior Colleges, 160
American Association of Universities, 138, 139
American Association of University Professors, 143, 159, 161
American Association of University Women, 159, 165
American Baptist Convention, 97

American Chemical Society, 159
American College of Surgeons, 197
American Council on Education, 3, 23, 160, 162, 184
American Council of Learned Societies, 162, 163
American Economic Association, 159
American Federation of Teachers, 159
American Historical Association, 159
American Library Association, 159
American Mathematical Society, 159
American Philosophical Society, 159
American Physical Society, 159
American Psychological Association, 159
"American Scholar, The," 12
American University, 156, 193
American Woman's Educational Association, 131
Amherst College, 112, 117, 118, 220
Andrea, Novella d', 26
Anglican Church, 46, 49, 67–68, 71, 74, 76, 77, 78, 101
Annapolis, U.S. Naval Academy at, 88
Antioch College, 94, 172, 190
Aquinas, Thomas, 20, 34
Aristotle, 20, 28, 35–36, 178
Arkansas, University of, 128, 146
Armed Forces Staff College, 153
Army War College, 153
Associated Colleges of the Midwest, 18
Association for Higher Education, 160
Association of American Colleges, 160, 162
Association of American Universities, 160, 215
Association of Governing Boards of Universities and Colleges, 160
Association of State Colleges and Universities, 160
Association of Urban Universities, 160
Athens College, 94
Atlanta University, 129
Atomic Energy Commission, 169

277

Pierce, George F., 93
Pisa, University of, 31
Pitt, William, 77
Pittsburgh, University of, 174
Poitiers, University of, 33
Poland, 37
Polytechnic Institute of Brooklyn, 112
Portland State College, 173
Portugal, 6, 32, 33
Post Office Department, 226
Prague, University of, 37, 41
Prairie View A and M College, 129
Pratt Institute, 140
Presbyterian Church, 52, 62, 71–72, 78,
  102, 103, 120; post-revolutionary col-
  leges founded by, 99–100
Princeton University, 13, 62, 78, 79, 87,
  89, 100, 107, 112, 132, 144, 146, 165,
  184, 220; curricula, 72; early leaders
  of, 72; founding of, 71–72
Principia College, 132
Processions, academic, 2, 3–4, 5, 30, 36–
  37, 180, 181, 205
Professor, title of, 19–20, 209
Protestant Churches, colleges founded
  by in 20th century, 173
Protestant Episcopal Church, 101, 103
Public Broadcasting Act (1967), 173
Puerto Rico, 1
Puerto Rico, University of, 172–73, 194
Puget Sound, College of, 140
Puritanism, 46, 63–64, 69
Purdue University, 128, 146, 216

Queen's College of New Jersey, see Rutgers University
Quincy, Josiah, 67

Radcliffe College, 132
Ramus, Petrus, 84
Randolph, Peyton, 68
Randolph-Macon Woman's College,
  110, 132
Reeve, Judge Tapping, 113
Reformation, Protestant, 21, 31, 38, 39,
  44, 46, 48, 52; universities founded
  due to, 38
Renaissance, 20, 30, 44
Rensselaer Polytechnic Institute, 112,
  114
Reserve Officers Training Program, 148,
  154, 176, 201
Retired Professors Registry, 160
Revolution, American, 8, 69, 71, 77, 80,
  81, 82, 84, 85, 86, 87, 88, 97, 101, 108,
  111, 138, 189, 220
Revolution, French, 35–36, 39

Rhode Island, 211
Rhode Island College, see Brown Uni-
  versity
Rice, Luther, 97
Rice, William M., 166
Rice University, 165
Richard I (of England), 204
Richmond College (New York), 172
Rittenhouse, David, 78
Roanoke College, 193
Rochester, University of, 165, 192
Rockefeller, John D., 137, 166
Rockefeller Brothers Fund, 168
Rockefeller Foundation, 151, 167
Rockefeller University, The, 165
Rockford College, 95
Rockne, Knute, 145
Rollins College, 172
Roman Catholic Church, 35–36, 38;
  colleges founded by in 20th century,
  173, 174; post-revolutionary colleges
  founded by, 100–1; see also Papacy
Rome, University of, 31, 58
Roosevelt, Franklin D., 177
Roosevelt, Theodore, 158
Roosevelt University, 173
Rostock, University of, 37
Rudolph IV, Duke, 37
Rush, Benjamin, 78
Rust, Dr. James D., 162
Rust College, 129
Rutgers, Colonel Henry, 81
Rutgers–the State University, 62, 103,
  144, 190, 192; charter of, 81; early
  curricula, 81; first conferral of de-
  grees, 81; founding of, 80–81; during
  Revolutionary period, 81–82; see also
  Colleges, colonial

St. Andrew, University of, 50, 55, 58
St. Augustine's College, 129, 190
St. Bernard, 34
St. Elizabeth, College of, 132
St. John's College (Maryland), 87, 172,
  189–90
St. Louis University, 113
St. Thomas, College of, 140
Salamanca, University of, 32, 33
Salerno, medical school at (9th cen-
  tury), 20, 25
San Francisco State College, 172
San Marcos, National University of, 32,
  63
Sarah Lawrence College, 172
Savonarola, Girolamo, 26–27
Scholars, in government, 177
Scholasticism, 20, 48

Virginia, University of, 10, 11, 87, 112, 113, 114, 136, 165, 216; early liberal curricula in, 90–91; founding of, 90, 91
Virginia Military Institute, 124, 156
Virginia State College, 129
Vocational Education Act (1963), 150
Vocational Rehabilitation Administration, 169

Wade, Benjamin, 127
Walter, Dr. Everett, 216
Wardlaw, Bishop Henry, 50
Warner, Glenn, 145
Washburn College, 102
Washburn University of Topeka, 102
Washington, George, 68, 75, 76, 78, 84, 117, 220
Washington, University of, 146
Washington and Jefferson College, 90, 194
Washington College, 77–78
Washington State University, 128
Washington Technical Institute, 173
Watt, James, 50
Webster, Daniel, 109, 119
Webster, Noah, 71
Weld, Theodore, D., 110, 119
Wellesley College, 131
Wells College, 96, 131
Wesley, John, 47, 48
Wesleyan College, 93–94
Wesleyan University, 132, 221
Western College, 132
Western Reserve University, 113, 132, 220
Western Washington State College, 172
West Indies, 83
Westminster College, 155
West Point, U. S. Military Academy at, 88, 111, 114
West Virginia, 92, 103
West Virginia University, 128
Whaley, Gordon, 208
Wharton, Thomas, 78
Wheelock, Eleazer, 71, 82
Wheelock, John, 82
White, Andrew D., 91–92, 137, 218
Whitefield, Reverend George, 76, 77, 82
Whitehead, Alfred North, 13
Whitney, Eli, 71
Whittier College, 194
Who's Who in America, 223, 224
Wichita, Municipal University of, 102
Wilberforce University, 29, 103
Wiley College, 129

Wilhelm, Friedrich, 38
Wilkinson, Bud, 145
Willard, Emma, 130
William and Mary, College of, 62, 87, 103, 113, 114, 213; change of curriculum by Jefferson, 90; charter of, 68; early curricula of, 68–69; early discipline at, 69; founding of, 67–68; as pioneer of common law study, 68–69; see also Colleges, colonial
William of Champeaux, 33
William of Ockham, 20, 47
William the Silent, 38
William of Orange, 68
Williams, Roger, 78
Williams College, 118, 183
William Smith College, 132
William Woods College, 131
Wilson, James, 78
Wilson, Woodrow, 13–14, 146, 177
Wilson College, 131
Winthrop College, 132
Wisconsin, 150
Wisconsin, University of, 13, 112, 138, 150, 172, 192, 216, 220
Witherspoon, Reverend Dr. John, 72
Wittenberg, University of, 37
Wolsey, Thomas, 47
Woman's Medical College of Pennsylvania, 96
Worcester Polytechnic Institute, 194
World War I, 124, 149, 151, 154, 155, 156, 157, 177, 210, 213
World War II, 124, 149, 150, 152, 154, 155, 156, 177
Wren, Christopher, 48, 68
Wycliffe John, 47, 50
Wythe, George, 68, 69

Yale, Elihu, 69
Yale Report (1828), 87–88
Yale University (College), 13, 62, 71, 72, 73, 80, 82, 84, 87, 88, 89, 91, 112, 113, 114, 117, 125, 132, 135, 144, 146, 165, 184, 190, 192, 213, 214, 216, 220, 221, 223; academic costume, 70; charter, 69; early discipline at, 71; first conferral of degrees, 70; founding of, 69–70; see also Colleges, colonial
Yost, Fielding, 145
Young Men's Christian Association, 102, 108, 157
Young Women's Christian Association, 108, 157

Zaragosa, University of, 32

DATE LOANED	BORROWER'S NAME	DATE RETURNED
